The Secret Life of Humans

Stan Gooch

J. M. Dent & Sons Ltd
London Melbourne Toronto

First published 1981
© 1981 Stan Gooch

Printed in Britain by Billing & Sons Ltd,
Guildford, London, Oxford & Worcester

for J. M. Dent & Sons Ltd
Aldine House   33 Welbeck Street   London   W1M 8 LX

This book is set in 11 on 13 Quadritek Times
by Altonprint, 49 Normandy Street, Alton, Hants.

Gooch, Stan
The Secret Life of Humans
1. Psychical research
1. Title
133   BF1031
ISBN 0-460-04527-X

Contents

Into the future   189

For
Oliver Caldecott

Herman Gombiner had long ago arrived at the conclusion that modern man was as fanatic in his non-belief as ancient man had been in his faith.

Isaac Bashevis Singer

Introduction

There is a condition, fully acknowledged by the medical profession, known as phantom pregnancy. In this condition a woman exhibits all the physiological signs of being pregnant – the stopping of monthly periods, the gradual swelling of the stomach, the presence of appropriate chemicals in the urine, and so on. Standard medical tests cannot distinguish between phantom pregnancy and real pregnancy. But in the former the woman is not literally pregnant and does not give birth to a child.

In one case I came across in my own work as a professional psychologist, a woman nursed such a phantom pregnancy. She carried her fully swollen stomach and distended breasts through a summer and a winter and a summer. At the end of eighteen months she gave birth to a son. This particular case again emphasizes the total similarity between the phantom pregnancy and real pregnancy. During those eighteen months the woman had become genuinely pregnant, yet no difference was detected in her symptoms.

The question I want to put firstly to doctors and psychologists in this book is the following: if this complex phenomenon is possible, then what is not possible?

A police sergeant in Britain had a slight accident while cycling on his rounds. A litte shaken, he returned home. When he stepped across the threshold his dog Tim, a wire-haired terrier, began running wildly about the house, staring fixedly at nothing. But he did not bark, and in fact never barked again. The sergeant went up to bed to rest. At first his few grazes gave no cause for concern, but steadily his condition grew worse. The dog lay permanently under the bed and refused to eat or drink. As the sergeant's illness progressed, the dog developed identical symptoms – blindness and paralysis of the limbs. These symptoms were officially confirmed by a vet who examined the dog. The police sergeant died at home one morning a few days later. The dog died at the same moment.

There are many similar cases on record and they are confirmed by the doctors and vets involved in the incidents. Sadly, on these particular matters, the medical profession as a whole remains silent. But if such happenings are possible, then the reasonable person must ask: what is not possible?

An American television producer had an unusually vivid dream, in colour. In the dream he was watching a horse race. He could hear the commentary. Three horses were neck and neck at the finish. The final result went to an outsider, a horse not expected to win.

The name of the winning horse stayed in the producer's mind for several days, although he was not a betting man and not interested in horse racing. Finally he recalled that a former acquaintance of his had once had a part share in a horse of that name. He rang his acquaintance, who said he had sold his share of the horse some time before, because it had never looked like doing well. But he did happen to know that the horse was to run in a race in the near future.

With some effort, the producer located the race in which the horse was due to run. To his astonishment he found the other two horses named in his dream were also in the race. Now he told the story to his studio colleagues, and himself placed a sizeable sum of money on the horse. He proposed that the studio staff sit together and watch the race on television, and they did. The race came out exactly as the dream predicted – all three horses involved in a tight neck-and-neck finish, with the outsider as the final winner.

This remarkable story, as with many others like it, involves a large number of reputable, independent witnesses, all of whom testify to the events involved. Mainstream academic psychology, I regret to say, has no comment to make on these matters. It does not even report them. The reasonable person, however, must again ask the same question: since such events are possible, then what is not possible? And how are we to describe not just a universe, but also the human brain in which such events occur?

The three incidents described take us through three expanding stages of complexity, each one more marvellous than the one before. The first involves a body or a mind somehow separate from our normal consciousness and somehow in charge of its own destiny. The second involves a deep and total communion between two minds physically separated by the outer shells not just of two persons, but of two totally different organisms. And the third involves us in a universe where the apparently unshakable laws of mortal time and space cease even to exist.

This book is one of an increasing number which are at last giving the lie to the shameful and unforgivable silence of the majority of scientists, doctors and priests on these subjects.

The secret life of humans is finally being made public.

Out of the past

1 Bearers of the message

Dr Stephen Arnold is a researcher into developmental psychology who likes to involve himself directly in the phenomena he is studying. He takes an active part in the often esoteric exercises which his subjects and students practise to develop their powers of mind, including powers of mind over body. In the course of these exercises he found that his forehead was changing, forming what he jokingly calls 'a simian ridge'. He has ended up with a pronounced and easily visible projecting growth of bone over his eyes. Photographs of himself as a young adult show no such ridge. The case of Dr Arnold is no isolated incident, and we shall look at many other instances.

The following study was carried out at the Human Dimensions Institute in New York by Carol Liaros, assisted by another psychologist and a physicist. Dr Liaros had for some time been running classes designed to develop extrasensory abilities in normal people. It now occurred to her to attempt the same work with the blind. Twenty blind volunteers were obtained from several organizations for the blind in New York. Each volunteer had a long and detailed medical history of blindness. As an added experimental precaution preliminary tests were performed on all subjects, to see for instance how well they negotiated a chair maze unaided, and to see whether they could sense colour differences by holding their hands near, but not touching, coloured paper. Now the subjects took the seven week ESP course.

During and at the end of the course numerous further tests were run, including scanning sheets of coloured paper by hand for instance, as before. In addition subjects were also asked to identify photographs as being pictures of either males or females by similarly holding the hands two or three inches away from the photographs. One subject, for example, said of one photograph: 'This is a woman with her hair pulled tightly back from her face. But what is that round ball on the top of her head?' It was a photograph of a woman who wore her hair severely back from her face in an old fashioned 'bun' on the top of her head. Subjects were also able to detect body scars and bodily illness in fully clothed people by passing their hands close to the person's body. In a fourth kind of test the blind subjects were asked to identify objects held one or two feet away from their foreheads – they had all received

ESP training in the faculty of 'seeing through their foreheads'. Their ability to distinguish successfully between such varied objects as marbles, dice and electric light bulbs increased as the course progressed.

But more impressive still than the results of all these formal tests were those reported from more informal sessions, and from outside the course entirely. Some subjects were now able to give spontaneous and detailed descriptions of objects and colours across a totally dark room. They also said that they could now 'see' light in their own heads where before there had been total darkness. They had a far greater sense generally of precisely where objects were, a claim borne out by their increased mobility. One man now walks in the street without a cane because he can 'see' lamp posts and plate glass windows 'out of the side of his forehead'. Another woman can select clothing on the basis of colour, not just from her own wardrobe but when out shopping, by holding her hand a few inches from the articles. Yet another woman reported waking in the middle of the night and 'seeing' her apartment lit up in 'golden glows', so bright that she could see the outlines of the furniture. Her immediate reaction was that the apartment was on fire, but intellectually she realized that this was an absurd idea, because she could not see fire anyway. Finally convinced that there was nothing wrong with the apartment, she just sat down and enjoyed seeing for the first time for years.

Experimental work such as this is being conducted in research institutes and hospitals in America, Britain and Europe, in China, the Soviet Union, South Africa and South America. It is part of a revolution which is breaking up the monolithic, unbelieving academic establishment from within. Meanwhile events outside scientific institutions are also rapidly gathering pace. Just as today the so-called fringe theatre bursts with life while the established theatre steadily loses custom, so the ideas of the emerging future are frequently developing away from the traditional seats of learning.

The time is now overdue for a genuine charter of that emerging future, both within and without the establishment. And we very much want something more than a confusion of amazing anecdotes and miracles, or reports of isolated research breakthroughs which, shattering enough as they are in their own right, are then successfully smothered by the establishment. Such 'lost' breakthroughs, incidentally, occurred among a group of French doctors in Paris in the early part of this century, and in America in a psychiatric hospital in the nineteen twenties – and we shall look at those in great detail.

What is now needed is an attempt to see all the related, and apparently unrelated, aspects of our 'secret life' in one unifying context and perspective – as a first step, in its *own* perspective. And then we also

5

need to see how that whole context relates to the context of scientific orthodoxy. We want both a proper long-term view of our subject matter and equally a projection of its future. So we need too a biological framework, one which can give us the explanation of these wonders in an evolutionary sense.

In brief, we face two questions. Are the events described in the Introduction to this book and in the first pages of this chapter part of some strange universe with laws of its own? Or are they, after all, just a rather unexpected extension of what we call normality? We may find that the two questions are applicable to different aspects of the secret life.

The ideas we are centrally concerned with in this book have in one sense been around for a long time. Our oldest spoken legends, let alone the written ones, speak quite clearly of 'miracles'. And though we have to make allowances for the very different frame of reference – usually a religious one, of course – we can see that at least some of these miracles describe the same events now occurring in laboratories around the world. Legend also informs us that these events were once more commonplace than now and there are hints, too, that at least some people (priests, adepts and whatever) once understood their manner of working rather well, and could produce them to order.

So our first step in writing the charter of the secret life needs to be a historical one. We first need to examine and sift the accumulated wisdom, or perhaps only the 'wisdom', of the ages to see exactly what it was that was being said and claimed. We can then align and compare that information with the explosion of information on the same subjects that our own culture (sometimes in back streets, sometimes in front streets) is also currently generating. This first research may well throw light in both directions.

The old ways

Anyone wanting chapter and verse on old religion, mythology and mysticism, even in those forms which have survived into our own times, faces a mass of material large enough to sink the bravest heart. That is true even if the researcher decides to concentrate on the evolution of just one people or just one culture. Is there any kind of short cut, then, that can bring us immediately to the central aspects of the old occultisms, the mystery religions, the secret rites – and equally, of course, to the miracle and mystery aspects of religion today? The answer is yes.

Two steps which are of enormous help in such research are distilling and sampling. What we do in distilling is, so to speak, boil away the detailed aspects of each ancient or modern religion or cult and keep only the general aspects in which each resembles all others. This productive exercise occupies the rest of this chapter.

In sampling, on the other hand, we take one particular form of ancient religion, and study it in depth and detail. We discard nothing, and instead examine all aspects of the practices and beliefs concerned in their own terms, as well as forming also a more detached estimate. It is clear, I hope, that this is no mere intellectual exercise. Religions, whatever objective values they may have, centre on what are usually called spiritual values and subjective attitudes. These last are absolutely essential to religious and magical experience. In no way can we ignore or belittle them – although, certainly, we may want to re-define or re-describe them. The people selected for depth sampling are the Australian Aborigines.

Now to the distilling. First a word on the sheer magnitude of what we are undertaking. Consider, for instance, 'Ancient Egypt'. This is a phrase many toss around as if it represented some kind of obvious unit, but the term covers three thousand years of recorded history, preceded by several thousand years of pre-history. Even the recorded history of Egypt is one thousand years longer than the whole of our present Christian era, which is just coming up to its two-thousandth birthday. And in the Christian era, in Britain alone, we have seen such variations as the Dark Ages (with King Arthur and his knights), the Norman conquest, the Middle Ages, the Renaissance, the Reformation, and the Industrial Revolution. Is it at all surprising that of Ancient Egypt one commentator can say helplessly 'no religion was ever so complex, so contradictory, so baffling'?

During the three thousand years of its history, Egyptian religion and mythology swirled and changed and flowed ever onward like the Nile itself. Helpfully from one point of view, bewilderingly from another, the Egyptians never abandoned old ways and ideas, but accommodated them alongside the new. The many fundamental contradictions and anomalies this habit produced never seemed to bother them.

Or what of the North American Indians? Here we are talking about a total of twenty thousand years in time, and some four hundred major tribal groups involving something like one hundred and eighty distinct language families, and therefore many more individual languages. In a masterpiece of understatement one anthropologist comments that 'these multitudinous peoples show a great variety of religious practices and beliefs'. Similar forms of American Indian religion are found in different areas, while totally different forms can exist side by side in one locality. Some tribes had a single shaman or medicine man in charge of religious affairs. Others had a large

7

hierarchy of priests administering a complex calendrical religion, where the tribe devoted almost the whole year to the staging of religious ceremonies. Such comments apply equally to the religious backgrounds of the Chinese, Japanese, Melanesians, Polynesians, Malaysians, Hindus, South American Indians, Greeks, Norsemen – and so on. It is this diversity and complexity of material which we attempt to summarize and distil.

Yet the at first sight perhaps improbable undertaking gains a good deal in credibility from two circumstances. One is that we are, after all, members all of one species. And religion, whatever else it may be, is a behaviour of the species (which is why Sir Alister Hardy can give his books titles like *The Biology of God)*. The behaviours of different varieties of man – sleeping, eating, learning, making love – always in the last analysis have much in common.

A second more remarkable circumstance is that modern research is steadily uncovering evidence that all human religions and mythologies, despite their current diversity, once shared a common origin. This apparently improbable idea is supported by a growing body of hard evidence.

Figure 1, for example, shows some maze designs recovered from four widely separated parts of the world – Cornwall (England), Knossos (Crete), Mysore (India), and from the Hopi Indians (Arizona, USA). The similarity of these designs is obvious at a glance. Later we shall be hazarding a guess at the exact meaning of this pattern. But the real headache as far as orthodoxy is concerned lies not in explaining the significance of these designs, it lies in their age. And the problem is not the age of each representation but the age of their common origin.

To determine the precise age of a rock carving is never easy. Ages of buildings are usually easier, though we are often talking about plus or minus a few hundred years. A cultural artefact – say, a design used in weaving or religious ceremony – may again be impossible to date. At any rate, no one disputes that each of the four maze diagrams of Figure 1 is several thousand years old, whether two, three or four thousand. But the real problem (for orthodoxy) is that the ancestors of the Hopi Indians entered North America from China about twenty thousand years ago. Must they not have had the design with them then? If so, this must make the design at least twenty thousand years old. Nor is the problem here an isolated case.

The ancient Greeks attached legendary stories to what they considered to be the main star groups of the sky. One of the two stories concerning the origin of the star group we call the Pleiades, a group of six stars and a fainter seventh, involves six sisters and their mother. (The second version, incidentally, also involves seven women – the

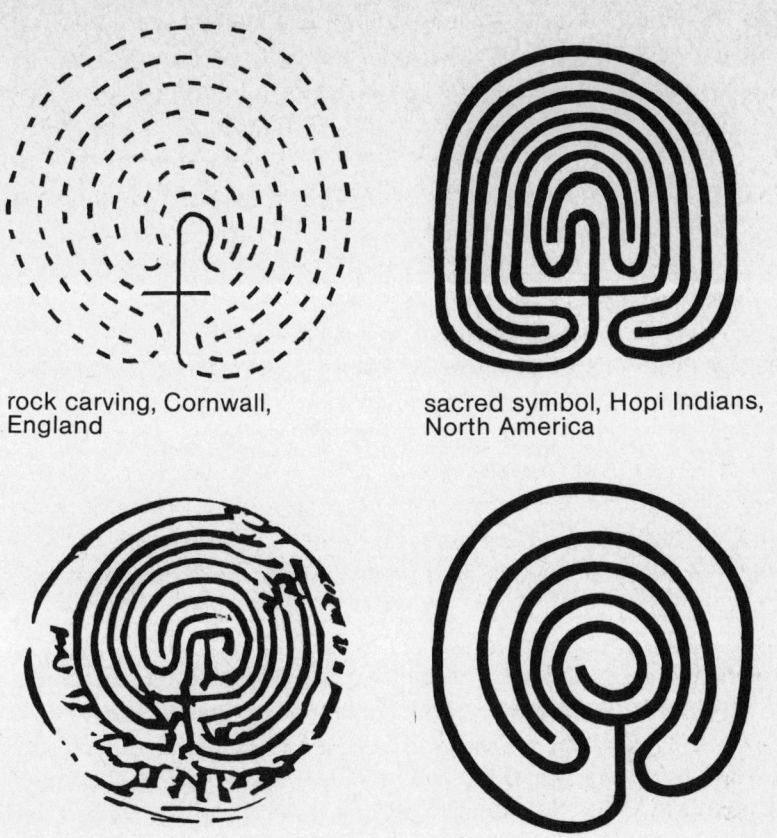

rock carving, Cornwall,
England

sacred symbol, Hopi Indians,
North America

coin design, Crete

Halebid temple, Mysore, India

Figure 1　Maze designs from different parts of the ancient world.

seven daughters of Atlas and Pleione.) The version we are looking at
tells how amorous Orion the hunter came upon the six girls and their
mother in a wood. Seized with passion, he pursued them through the
forest for five years. At this point Zeus took pity on the women, and
turned both parties into stars. So in the heavens we see the seven
Pleiades eternally pursued by Orion the hunter with his hunting dog.

Here is now the story of the Pleiades (which they call Maya-
Mayi) as told by the Australian Aborigines.

Wurrunna the hunter was out in search of game in a strange
district. Here he came upon a camp, in which he found only seven young
girls. He asked the girls where the rest of the tribe were, but the girls
answered that they lived in a far country. The seven maidens had only
made this journey to see what matters were like here.

Wurrunna decided this was a good chance to get himself a wife. By

9

a ruse he separated two of the girls from the other five and seized them about the waist. He told them they must now go with him as his wives, which reluctantly they did. But they pointed out that their sisters would only take them back again.

Now Wurrunna told the girls to cut him some pine-bark to feed the fire. As the girls struck each a different tree, the trees suddenly began to grow rapidly upwards, bearing the two girls with them. At last the tops of the trees touched the sky. Now the other five sisters called out from the sky. The two climbed the rest of the way up the trees and were drawn up by their sisters to live with them in the sky forever.

The parallel elements in the two stories already go beyond the bounds of coincidence (the amorous hunter, chasing seven women, who escape into the sky), though we have by no means finished with the evidence. But the point to emphasize is that the Aborigines have been living in Australia for well over twenty thousand years. Even thirty or forty thousand years are in no way out of the question.

Here now is the legend of the Pleiades as told by one North American Indian tribe.

In north Wyoming is a massive rock formation of volcanic origin. This natural tower of rock is 865 feet high and has an absolutely flat top. The local Indians say this formation originated when seven little girls who were being chased by a bear took inadequate shelter on a low rock. To save them the gods caused the rock to rise up beyond the reach of bears, pushing the girls into the sky, where they are still visible as the seven stars of the Pleiades.

To complete the picture, Peter Lancaster Brown, agreeing first that many elements of the Greek and Australian legends are identical, reports that the Florida Indians also possess what is 'virtually a carbon copy' of the Greek Pleiades story, which those Indians themselves refer to as 'the company of maidens'. The Florida Indians are wholly unconnected with the Wyoming Indians. The two are at opposite ends of America, in the south east corner and north west corner of the continent respectively.

There are many similar astrological and astronomical parallels we could follow up in detail, but shall merely mention in passing. One is that both the Ancient Greeks and all the North American Indians assign bear legends to Ursa Major (the Great Bear). Another is that the constellation Orion is known as 'the Hunter' not just among the ancients of Greece and North America, but throughout Africa, the Middle East, South America and Polynesia – and, if we are willing to agree that Wurrunna is a fragmentary memory of Orion, also in Australia. It is by no means totally unthinkable that Orion and Wurrunna are the selfsame word.

Andrew Tomas further points out that the Maya of Central America applied to the constellation Scorpio the same name as we use, while our name for the constellation Aquarius is again echoed in the Mexican Tlaloc, the Ruler of the Rains. Aries the Ram is the Sheep of China, while Taurus the Bull is the Ox. Parallels between Central America and China are even more striking. The Aztec Calendar had the days of the Alligator, Snake, Rabbit, Dog and Monkey. The Calendar of China-Tibet has the years of the Dragon, Snake, Rabbit, Dog and Monkey. Giorgio de Santillana has also commented on these matters. He writes: 'Yet unknown archaic astronomers are responsible for the naming of the constellations....Someone before history must have blocked them out for reasons known to himself, and with such an authority that the names were repeated without question, substantially the same from Mexico to Africa and Polynesia.'

A quite different indication of the once common origins of the different religions of historical times is found in the worldwide attitudes to, and the uses made of, the material known as red ochre. It is absolutely clear that red ochre was considered to be the blood of the universe, specifically the sacred blood of the mystical All-Mother, who turns out also to be the Moon. For instance, in English and Indo-European 'bless', 'blossom' and 'blood' are all the same word. To bless something was originally to sprinkle it with blood, and such blessing made everything blossom and flourish. Here we are at once at the heart of an old fertility religion. In addition, one of the pillars of the etymological establishment W.W. Skeat, considers that 'moon' and the first syllable of 'mother' are the same word. So all these matters are seen to hang together very coherently. The history of words, incidentally, is another powerful key in unlocking the mysteries of our secret life.

Finally in this brief survey, the history of the number thirteen, and its connection with the most ancient zodiacs of which we have knowledge (and which pre-date the later solar zodiacs of twelve divisions), throws up yet more unifying evidence. This particular material is best evaluated in connection with present-day astrology – and red ochre itself in the crucial context of earth magnetism.

The items touched on here have already brought the proud forward sweep of modern orthodox western thought to a grinding halt, although a majority of western scientists are still carrying on as if nothing had happened. They are behaving like people, on the second floor of a house, ignoring the fact that the basement is on fire.

Back to our distilling. Our intention was to make a list of the features which all religio-mythologies both past and present have in common. These items give us a ground plan of the central 'religious impulse' for use in our exploration of present-day marvels. At the same time we can checklist these phenomena in the light of the new evidence that arises every day, to see how accurate the views of the ancients really were. The items which now follow are in no particular order. Already, however, we shall begin to indicate ways in which these ideas might be translated into a more modern framework.

The belief in the existence of non-physical gods and spirits. To say that every religion believes in beings or spirits that exist on some non-physical plane, but yet are in one way or another connected with ourselves and with life in general, is almost to give a definition of religion. Such gods or spirits can be male or female or androgynous, are very often organized in hierarchies of power or areas of influence, may be actively well-disposed or ill-disposed to humanity, or just indifferent. But there, anyway, they all very much and centrally are.

The belief in life after death. In every religion there is a belief that some part of the human being in one way or another survives the death of the physical body. The Ancient Egyptians, for instance, subscribed basically to a belief in a ka (or astral body) which more or less duplicated the physical body and personality, and a truly immortal soul, the ba. (Just to complicate matters, they also talked for instance of akh, the spiritual power that one attained only after death.)

All religions have an equivalent of the central, immortal soul (the ba), but not every single religion has an equivalent of the ka. Similar to the ka, however, is the etheric double, subtle body or astral body of Hinduism, Buddhism, Yoga and general mysticism. The ka is a very active idea in modern mystical and esoteric thought, often called 'the subtle anatomy' and 'the energy body'. These labels take in such matters as the mystical chakras (centres of bodily influence) of Yoga, and the pressure or stimulation points of acupuncture and esoteric massage.

The etheric double or energy body seems by general agreement to be only semi-immortal. It survives death of the normal body, but perhaps only for a matter of hours or days. In eastern mysticisms, on the other hand, it is the rather longer-lasting vehicle which transports the soul through the series of incarnations (samsara) over hundreds or perhaps thousands of years, until the soul achieves final release from all incarnation. The energy body is then resorbed for re-use into the general fabric of the universe.

This 'energy body' is an important notion. It may, for instance, explain such a remarkable phenomenon as the imprint of Christ's body on the Shroud of Turin. It may also help us to explain the dramatic phenomena of psychic healing.

One last point in this category is that the true soul (unlike the etheric double or astral body, which is of course life-size) is often described as being very small – the 'divine spark', perhaps. The Egyptians said it was like a little bird, and in India it was sometimes described as an insect. This idea is odd enough to be interesting. Would one automatically or logically expect the soul to be small? Were the ancients, perhaps, on to something?

The judgment of the soul. Almost universal among religions is the belief that after death the soul is assessed on actions during life. Some religions punish bad behaviour during life irrevocably, such as by throwing the heart to 'the devourer of hearts', whereas others reincarnate the soul in some wretched existence till the evil is expiated. Good behaviour, on the other hand, admits one sooner or later to the company of the gods, or some other form of bliss or peace. The idea of 'punishment for evil, reward for good' may not seem to a pure rationalist to be an idea of much use in explaining psychic or paranormal phenomena, especially when every religion has widely different views on what is good and what is evil. (Some religions, for instance, say it is good to kill your enemies, others that it is good to forgive them.) Yet we have to be impressed with the circumstance that the polarity of good and evil is universal in all religions, and we can derive real understanding from it. To take just one example, we might translate 'evil' and 'good' into 'stress' and 'relaxation'.

All religions practise the ceremonial disposal of the dead body. This respectful and often complicated ritual is a fairly logical consequence of the belief that some other part of the individual is not dead. Many ceremonies send the body (and/or the soul) on a journey by burning, by sending it off literally on a raft or boat, by burying travel goods with the body and so on. What might that journey really be?

Fulfilling 'divine purpose'. All religions consider there to be a purpose or goal to life. In our individual lives we are helping (or perhaps, misguidedly, not helping) that process to its conclusion. The conclusion may be an ultimate goal, realized once and forever, or merely the end of a cycle, which then repeats.

Primitive religions held this view of an evolving purpose to life and the universe long before there was – apparently – any knowledge of Darwinian evolution or the evolution of stars as we understand these terms today. Religions, it is true, almost always specifically reject the view that man evolved from the animal kingdom and instead treat him as a special one-off act of creation. Even so, the general religious evolutionary view is a subjective version of what we today verify objectively. We can now demonstrate scientifically, for instance, that organisms, including ourselves, progressively develop greater psychological potential and become more self-aware. To take an example, a lower life form never recognizes its reflection in a mirror as being itself, but treats it as another organism. Higher animals, on the other hand, such as chimpanzees, understand the true nature of a reflection and use it, for instance, to examine their teeth and to daub their faces.

An interesting query arises. Did religionists conceive the process of evolution because human beings individually and internally possess by construction some sense of the process of evolution? Or is the religious idea of evolution a twisted and garbled account of a once clearly grasped notion of something like Darwinian evolution? The answer, probably, has to be both. So we find, for instance, the ancient Hindus calling the pineal gland (now buried deep in the human brain) the 'third eye'. We now know that the pineal gland was once, in our reptile ancestors of some hundreds of millions of years ago, a separate pair of eyes placed on top of the head.

The sense of personal purpose. Closely linked to the notion of an overall divine purpose is the conviction among the religious that one's own individual life has a purpose and a point of its own. Most religious and mystical people even feel that they are an essential part of the overall divine plan and that without them it will somehow fail. From such convictions derive all notions of fate, karma and personal destiny. Passive versions of the idea suggest that everything is pre-destined – that what happens is what must happen. Active versions propose that one must work at one's destiny, and that there are choice points.

But are we just talking here about a rationalization of some kind of survival instinct buried deep in the human psyche, a sneaky trick of Nature's to keep us going when things get tough? This may be part of the explanation. On the other hand, when you have been involved (as I and many other psychics have) in a precognitive perception of the future which leads to someone's life being saved – or when (regularly if you are an Australian Aborigine, less often if you are a European) you register the exact moment of death of some relative or loved one thousands of miles away – on such occasions it is impossible to avoid the feeling that things somehow do hang together and also do matter. Even the simple clairvoyant perception of some quite trivial event in the future in some sense establishes the future, before it has happened – before it has become now. These events must stand for what they are, nor can they be swept away or rendered meaningless by the far greater number of trivialities and random horrors so common in human experience.

Immanence. Immanence is the term often used by Christians to describe the presence of God that is everywhere and always in all things. Variant descriptions of the same basic idea are very widespread indeed. Parallel concepts are seen in the Hindu Braham (said to be the supreme reality which holds up the universe, and with which Yoga specifically tries to put us in touch), the Tao of Taoism (the pre-existent and post-existent beingness of everything, as well as every intervening manifestation), the 'dispersion of divine light through everything' of the Jewish kabbala, some aspects of the Dreamtime of Australian Aborigines, and the 'Ultimate Reality' spoken of in all forms of mysticism, sometimes also called Akasha. Akasha is a 'celestial ether' or 'astral light' which fills all space and time. This is thought of as an actual medium in which is stored, for instance, a record of every human being's every action or sentiment or thought. Psychics and visionaries are said to see into this medium and read from it clairvoyantly.

The basically non-religious concept of modern times which most closely parallels such ideas is C. G. Jung's 'collective unconscious'. Jung believed that at some unconscious level all human beings are in touch, or at least potentially in touch, with each other in a telepathic sense. The notion of 'synchronicity' also comes in here. This concept argues for a frame of reference, or a dimension, in which past events, future events, and physically distant events are perceived as if they are, or somehow become, 'here and now'.

Consulting oracles and omens. The practice of consulting natural or induced random phenomena in order to examine and determine the course of future events is, once again, universal in religious practice. Natural phenomena include the wheeling of birds, the shape of clouds, and the cracks or lines in naturally occurring stones and rocks. To summon up a reading, however, you may scatter the entrails of an animal on the ground, bake bones in the fire to induce cracking, or cast pebbles. Latter-day consultants now examine tea-leaves, deal playing cards and scry in crystal balls.

All these practices seem to be ways of bypassing the conscious mind to tap unconscious processes (like synchronicity) and unconscious knowledge (clairvoyance, intuition). Many, though not all, aspects of astrology seem also best understood in this same context.

Priests, intermediaries and psychics. All religions consider that certain individuals have some kind of special relationship to the gods, to spirits or to the magical forces of the universe. These individuals are seen as essential intermediaries of whom ordinary people must at least sometimes avail themselves. The 'priest' of a primitive tribe is likely to be a single 'medicine man' or 'clever man', or the 'wise woman' of a Gypsy group. And from there we range up to complex individuals and offices like the High Priest of Ancient Egypt, the Holy Roman Emperor, or the present-day Pope.

15

It looks as if the office and function of medicine man through to High Priest has its origin in the genuine perception by the population at large that certain people do have genuine 'gifts' which fit them for the task – but that there are actually very few such individuals. As it happens, a great many formal and informal surveys today agree that strongly psychic individuals are a rarity, and that those who can exercise regular or deliberate control over the gift are even rarer. Nonetheless, a good many ordinary people do have an occasional flash of ESP or telepathy or whatever, and this is one circumstance which inclines the general population to accept as genuine the powers of the occasional outstanding individual. Added to that consideration is of course the proof of the pudding, in the sense that prophecies made must at least tend to come true, illnesses improve after psychic treatment, and so on.

Prayers and spells. Orthodox Christians and others may bridle at the suggestion that prayers and the casting of spells are connected, but they are both (along with all kinds of ritual practice) an attempt to persuade or force the secret universe to act favourably towards us. The crucial question is whether these spells work in any literal sense.

Sacred texts and traditions. Every faith has a historical body of knowledge and practice in the form either of sacred writings, or of oral traditions learned by heart by each succeeding generation of priests. To learn the body of Druidic teaching, for instance, is said to have taken a whole lifetime. But are these great masses of material actually of any real or practical use? Again, there seems no simple answer.

Belief that yours is the one true faith. It goes almost without saying that individuals subscribing to a particular religion hold that theirs is the true faith, the best one in some sense. These exclusive claims and counter-claims necessarily look quite unreasonable to the detached observer. A possible though surprising solution to the problem is that all religions are equally valid.

Temples and sacred places. Every religion has its sacred places and shrines. Some places become sacred because, for example, a leading figure of the faith has died or been killed there. Other places are magical or mystical of themselves. Modern attempts to defend mystical thought and practice propose that ancient peoples sensed something objectively important and not just subjectively important about at least some of these sites. Perhaps gifted psychics or diviners felt the presence of underground running water or a local magnetic field of some kind. Other places (alongside overground springs or waterfalls, for instance) may be rich in negative ions, which are known to have soothing effects on the nervous system, and may even influence dreaming and sexual fertility. It is certainly worth emphasizing that for whatever reasons the early Christians built churches on the sites of ancient pagan shrines.

Magical objects. Magical talismans, amulets, stones and so on are rather like portable shrines. Do these objects emit some kind of magnetism or 'good vibrations', can they bring luck or well-being? Have they absorbed 'magical power' from some previous gifted owner, as fragments from the Cross and Jesus's garments are said to have done? There have, as it happens, been some recent very interesting developments in these matters.

Visions and voices. All great religious leaders and priests sometimes see visions and hear voices. These may inspire the leader in a general way, or may give specific instructions. Both happened in the case of Francis of Assisi. A sobering thought, however, is that something rather similar happens to people who starve themselves, or live in conditions of reduced sensory stimulation, or drink too much alcohol too often. Can we make any valid distinction between these two kinds of events? Allied here is prophetic vision, which is like clairvoyance on a grand or filmic scale. The early Christian Church was of course no stranger to prophetic vision, but the modern Church uneasily avoids such matters.

Trance. Many of the more dramatic phenomena of religion and magic are associated with states of rather evident trance. Spiritualist mediums put themselves into trance, North American Indians dance themselves into it, Africans and Orientals drum, drink or drug themselves into it. It seems at least possible that all the phenomena of the secret life are connected with forms of trance – however light. Prayer, meditation, contemplation and dreams can all qualify, and so can vigorous conditions like ecstasy and possession by spirits. The perhaps slightly broader, and perhaps slightly more acceptable, concept of 'altered consciousness' enables us to class together, tentatively at this stage, all the kinds of trance mentioned with other conditions such as 'being in love', 'being under a spell' or the recall of memories from a 'previous incarnation', as well as the phenomena of hypnosis.

Here we seem to find a bridge from the very heart of religion to those miracles of mind, body and matter which orthodox science has repeatedly tried to exorcise, but which have never actually gone away.

Psychic healing and faith healing. Though traditional religion and magic make no distinction at all between these two types of phenomenon, this book will very much need to do so.

Faith healing is best briefly described as the spontaneous remission of hysterical symptoms, using the word hysteria here in the Freudian sense – hysterical blindness, hysterical paralysis, spirit 'possession' and the like. Such spontaneous and instant cure occurs because the individual concerned has faith, or develops faith, in some individual or in some place (like Lourdes) or, again, in some object (like the bones of a saint); or yet again, in some process (the passing of hands, an initiation rite, psychotherapy or whatever).

There is also a counter-side to faith healing which we might call 'faith harming', a process obviously at work in the person suffering from an hysterical illness. As a concept, however, faith harming has wider possibilities than this, for it seems to underlie the very rapid and sometimes instantaneous appearance of religious stigmata and other wounds on the body.

Psychic healing is quite different again. For it works whether or not the person being treated has any belief in it, or in the person administering the treatment. In clear proof of this statement, a number of psychic healers, under the laboratory supervision of doctors and biochemists, healed wounds experimentally made in animals, retarded the growth of experimentally induced tumours, and speeded up the growth of plants. No question of faith can arise in the case of plants and animals, though of course the question of the healer's faith in himself is something we need to examine. Psychic healing, even if more rapid than the normal healing process, is not instantaneous (although it can be in special cases, for obvious reasons – where a blood blockage is removed, for example). In psychic healing we are obliged to speak in terms of an actual energy flowing from one person to another, in faith healing we are not.

Miracles and supernormal physical feats. Great holy men and powerful medicine men have always been said to work miracles. The founder of Christianity was no exception.

Apart from psychic healing, there are reports of holy men changing one physical substance into another, of giving life to inanimate objects and of turning living beings to stone, of levitating, of becoming invisible, of projecting visible thought forms, being able to stay alive while buried in the ground, and much else besides.

While without doubt some (or even many) of these performances involved skilful conjuring, and the hypnosis or even drugging of audiences, there is equally no doubt that at least some of the reports are true. We can be quite sure of this, because there are people alive today who can duplicate these feats. A large majority of these people are professional yogis, fakirs or spiritists, but probably the really interesting point is that a few of the individuals involved are not religious in the slightest.

Initiation or entry rites. Both insiders (those born into a faith) and outsiders (those who enter it from without) are universally required to undergo ceremonies of acceptance or confirmation. These ceremonies may be long, arduous and extremely painful, or relatively simple, as in the Christian practices of Confirmation and Baptism. We need to consider what exactly occurs, as well as what is believed to occur, as a result of such practices.

This completes our survey list.

Today there are still societies in the world which live mainly under the general guidelines of the kinds of matters we have been discussing – the natives of New Guinea, the South American Indians, the Australian Aborigines. These societies are often called 'primitive', and it is true that these peoples do not possess our modern scientific knowledge and cannot handle the physical world with the amazing ease that we do. Yet these same peoples know a good deal more about totally different aspects of life, particularly those matters which the west has unsuccessfully been trying to discard for several hundred years. These aspects of life are our own secret lives. While these 'primitive' peoples still exist we should use the privilege of looking at them – a privilege we shall not have much longer.

2 The eternal Dreamtime

The almost featureless desert stretches to the horizon. An outcropping of chasmed rock glows blood red in the falling sun, its inlets and gullies black streaks on the cliff face. Near a small waterhole, a group of Aborigines sits among the few kurrajong trees. One male is stripping bark from a would-be digging stick with his teeth. The women are rolling chewed vegetable fibre on their thighs to make string. Another male looks up from his bark painting, and gazes into the sunset.

'Garaga is dead.'

Some of the others look up. Here and there are nods of affirmation. The tribe knows for sure that Garaga, away on a hunting trip, is no more. Only those members of the tribe who belong to Garaga's totem group will feel this impulse. His wife will not, for she is not of his totem group. (Otherwise he could not have married her – she would have been taboo.)

Ronald Rose, who has studied the psychic abilities of Australian Aborigines, confirms this ability to sense the death of absent members of the tribe over great distances. Interestingly, he found no ability among them to influence the movement of objects paranormally or to tell the future – at any rate not under test conditions.

It is probably not the great extent and barrenness of Australia, nor the relatively small numbers of Aborigines (perhaps 300,000 at their former peak) which have encouraged the existence of the telepathic faculty. It is rather because their religious rites and kinship structure 'give permission' (just as do differing magical rites all over the world) for telepathy to occur, and the pervasive, ever-present Dreamtime which, for the Aborigine, justifies or explains that faculty.

The Eternal Dreamtime has several meanings and functions. This concept refers firstly to the time far back in the past when the external world and the creatures in it were made. Animistic spirits appeared from the bare ground and moved across it, forming the mountains and trees and animals. Then these spirits ascended to the skies (though some sank back into the ground). Is this aspect of the Dreamtime a faint memory of a zodiac? The close resemblance between the tale of Wurrunna and the seven maidens and the Greek tale of Orion and the seven women gives strong support to such a view.

An extremely important aspect of the Dreamtime is that it also extends into the present. In your dreams, and when it is re-actualized by ritual, you are in direct touch with the Dreamtime. And when you die your spirit wholly rejoins the Dreamtime, from which it originally came. But the Aborigines also say that the spirits of the Dreamtime were very like ourselves, a form of man, and that they did not so much vanish as blend in with ourselves. This aspect of the stories admits of a very literal interpretation. For the Aborigines seem to be saying: there was once a different kind of man from ourselves, who knew all kinds of astonishing things and could perform amazing magic. They were here before we were. They died out, but not before some of them inter-married with us. (A prime candidate as the basis for such a true account would of course be Neanderthal man.)

How long have the Aborigines been in Australia? Virtually no one disputes that we are talking about a minimum of twenty thousand years. One important Australian site has produced a reliable carbon-date of 32,000 years, while an undoubted Australoid skull from Borneo is equally firmly dated 40,000 years Before Present. And one authority (D. J. Mahoney) believes Australia to have been inhabited by Australoids for no less than 150,000 years. As to the former homeland of the Aborigines, almost universal agreement now places this in South East Asia. In physical type the Aborigine is closely related to the Veddas of southern India and Ceylon. Many of these extremely dark individuals could, even today, pass for Aborigines, and experts cannot accurately sort jumbled photographs of these two peoples. Moreover, the Australian language is now known for certain to be related to the Dravidian languages of ancient India.

These objective links are important in that they support yet other links which are just as impressive, but which purely because of their mystical nature, and their implications for the religious history of man, tend to arouse the antagonism of the narrow academic. Here are some of these other links.

Sir Grafton Elliot Smith tells us that the Aborigines of the Torres Straits Islands and elsewhere previously practised a mummification of corpses which closely resembles the mummification practices of one particular Egyptian dynasty. Furthermore, A. A. Abbie tells us, fossil skulls of Australoid type have been found in what is now Israel (at Mount Carmel) with one or both front upper incisor teeth ritually removed, as is common practice among Aborigines today.

The mythological Aborigine 'Rainbow Serpent' has an important function in controlling the weather, especially rain. In Central America, among the Aztec and Maya peoples, the weather is controlled by a plumed serpent, Quetzalcoatl. In considering whether this particular parallel might or might not be pure coincidence, we should not forget the many worldwide astrological parallels we have already noted.

There is a further link. Although Aborigine religion is exclusively male-dominated, with women barred on pain of death (a sentence, incidentally, frequently carried out) from all the more important ceremonies and sites, nevertheless the Aborigines tell how things were once the other way about. Myths tell how at the beginning of time (the Dreamtime again) women had all the sacred things, while men had nothing. These 'Ancestresses' enjoyed unlimited freedom of decision and action, and were much more powerful beings that their male associates. Precisely similar myths are found not just in Melanesia – and that is perhaps geographically not all that surprising – but once again in South America. Moreover, turning to Europe and the Middle East, we also find that the all-powerful gods of modern times were in every case once preceded, in the dim mists of time, by all-powerful goddesses.

Again, the complex kinship structure of Aborigine tribes has rather exact counterparts among many other peoples. A. A. Abbie notes:

> Kinship groups with comparable totemic affiliations were once widespread beyond Australia. They are still found in the less developed people of South East Asia and were common among the North American Indians, who came originally from Asia....They were first explicitly set out in writing for the Jews – who also came from Asia – in the Old Testament. There we discover that a man might not marry his mother, sister, sister-in-law, daughter, daughter-in-law or aunt...that is, every woman who stood in the relationship of 'possible' mother [or] 'possible' sister....The whole system has obvious similarities to the Aboriginal kinship system.... Even the secondary obligations have similarities. If a Jew died childless his brother was expected to lie with the widow until she had a child; if an Aborigine dies his brother takes over the widow.

(In this particular connection, I have myself long argued the general physical similarities between Jews and other groups who seem to carry a more pronounced dash of Neanderthal blood and ways than, for instance, general Europeans. Thus the late Edward G. Robinson, a Rumanian Jew, could easily have passed for an Aborigine, given just a slightly darker skin. The broad, snub nose of the Aborigine is found, incidentally, in no less than twenty per cent of Jews – a statistic which will surprise some.)

On to the question of red ochre, an item whose central significance cannot be overstressed. The anthropologist John Greenway starts us off with this question: 'Why did this material, in almost every religion since Neanderthal man invented that institution, become the most spiritually rich and magical of all substances?...There is no end to the myriad uses of ochre.'

Greenway goes on to remind us that the Red Indians of North America are so called because when the Indians first saw white men, they rubbed themselves all over with magical red ochre as a protection against these alien devils. Alas, this did them no good, for as John Greenway remarks, the white man had even forgotten that this was the substance from which the Easter ashes of Catholicism were originally derived.

Lyall Watson has written a profile of the historical importance of red ochre in his book *Lifetide*. He tells us that the use of the substance has never been casual. Kalahari Bushmen still cross the African desert today to find specularite (another variant) to rub into their hair, while in Australia coastal Aborigines mount major expeditions across hundreds of miles of hostile outback to sacred ochre sites laid down in the Dreamtime. These can be mined only by initiated old men who crawl to the site on all fours. An early burial in our northern hemisphere is that of an old man, a Neanderthal who died forty-six thousand years ago. He was buried in a cave at La Chapelle-aux-Saints, in what is now southern France, his body packed around with red ochre. The oldest known deliberate interment anywhere is in Border Cave, Swaziland. The skeleton of a child who died about eighty thousand years ago was buried there not only with a perforated sea-shell pendant, but with a dusting of ash and ochre. Watson describes the use of red ochre as 'pandemic', a universal craze. The thirty-five thousand year old Red Lady of Paviland in Britain is still to be seen in the University Museum in Oxford encrusted in red ochre which 'coloured the earth for half a yard around'. Solutrean burials in Bavaria twenty thousand years ago were made by surrounding the body with mammoth tusks and submerging the entire structure in a mass of red ochre. Watson concludes: 'The funeral chambers of the Shang dynasty, the cists and sarcophagi of Etruscan and Roman tombs, are all painted red. Homeric dead and even the head of the Catholic Church today are buried in crimson shrouds.'

Raymond Dart, impressed as anyone must be by all this evidence, emphasized that haematite (red ochre) has a quite remarkable cultural history, which begins with Neanderthal ritual burial and extends right through ancient metallurgy and alchemy into the present. It is unique among all minerals, he said, in its formative influence on mankind's cultural and religious practices.

We might already suspect on this evidence alone that red ochre is synonymous with blood, and we come now to some hard evidence for that view, as well as to the question of what precise blood is involved. Here, then, are some of the detailed uses of these two substances among the Aborigines.

In all tribal ceremony (corroborees), whether of the purely sacred (mainly fertility, increase and initiation rites) or the more entertaining variety, red ochre, along with actual blood, is the most important decorative substance. In the private ceremony of the first initiation into manhood and the religious mysteries – these rites actually last almost continuously from the age of fourteen to twenty-five – the young man is painted all over with red ochre. He must stay away from the camp and sleep by himself till the ochre wears of by itself. He can only come to drink at the waterhole at night.

New mothers are decorated with red ochre and must live in the special women's camp, as also must menstruating women and new widows. Some weeks later the new father is also similarly decorated with ochre.

The dead are habitually coated with ochre at burial, and this was the case too with the mummified bodies mentioned earlier.

Actual blood is used in parallel on these occasions. Whole areas of ground may be saturated with blood, and it is also used to stick bird feathers to the body in elaborate patterns. The blood is mainly produced by the older initiated men, who may open their veins in the bend of their elbow, tear off their fingernails, and strike their scalps with pieces of bone. Importantly, blood comes also from the circumcision of the penis with a stone knife in the first initiation ceremony (and certain of the elders then eat pieces of the detached foreskin) and still more from the horrifying subincision of the penis, which is slit open underneath from base to tip. As a result of this operation, the healed penis is much broader.

Of central relevance to these matters, and already mentioned, is the fact that in English as in all Indo-European languages the words 'blood', 'bless' and 'blossom' are at root the same word. To bless means to sprinkle with blood, or with its symbolic equivalent, red ochre. As we have also already seen, the ash mark of Catholics was originally ochre. The Arabs who built Thor Heyerdahl's reed boat *Tigris* slaughtered an animal in order to sprinkle its blood on the prow for good fortune – a tradition reaching back to antiquity. It seems clear that our own breaking of a bottle of champagne on the stern of a ship at launching is likewise descended from this practice.

'Blood-letting' is another very interesting item. Among Aborigines a ceremonial blood-letting is frequently the price exacted for a transgression of a fairly serious kind, particularly where a member of one tribe has acted against another tribe. This custom is found among many other primitive peoples too, but perhaps the most interesting point is that European doctors of only a century or so ago who applied leeches to take blood from the sick – in order to cure them – were certainly following an almost laughably distorted version of this same practice. As we now know, the last thing sick persons need is to have blood taken from them. This procedure, like so much else in our apparently sensible lives, seems once again the misunderstood ancient 'secret life' reaching out to govern us across tens of thousands of years.

But what exactly is this blood in terms of magical ritual, and what precisely does it signify?

It is clear that the substance in question was originally the menstrual blood of woman. Or rather, that the menstrual blood of woman was seen as the local here-and-now copy or re-enactment of the cosmic menstrual bleeding of the great and primal Moon-Mother Goddess. The evidence for this claim is massive, and those interested can find it in Penelope Shuttle and Peter Redgrove's book *The Wise Wound* or in my own *Guardians of the Ancient Wisdom*. But in any case ancient legends report this message in simple direct form. These widespread legends say, with local variations, what Aborigine legend likewise repeats: that the red ochre in the earth is literally the menstrual outflow of the mystical Ancestresses of the Dreamtime.

A number of facts that have till very recently escaped our own attention – and the reason for this lies in the grave distortions brought about in our natural rhythms by our 'civilized' way of life – in no way escaped the attention of 'primitive' man. Our ancestors saw clearly that woman's menstruation (so long as she is exposed naturally to the moon) is directly governed by the moon's action. They observed also that pregnant women and breast-feeding mothers do not menstruate, and do not become pregnant again during breast-feeding. (This cycle or rhythm too has become distorted in ourselves – but it can be observed to work perfectly in chimpanzees and other apes.) They also noted that the new-born child comes into the world bathed in blood. No doubt they also understood that the placenta feeds the baby with blood throughout the pregnancy, via the umbilical cord.

It seems clear that these, and other facts which we shall come to, were very precisely known to early mankind – and probably we are talking here about Neanderthal man. These facts were woven into a complex tapestry of explanation as to how the universe functioned, an explanation which went far beyond the mechanics of 'mere' childbirth and which incorporated knowledge that we ourselves are only just beginning to re-discover. But when we come to what we might call 'modern early man' – that is, to the last twenty thousand years or so – we see what are already only fragmented and often seriously misunderstood versions of the true ancient wisdom. We find only a partial and secretive memory of what was once codified public knowledge. We shall return to those matters shortly, but in the meantime we can understand why both the Aborigine religious initiate and the bodies of the dead are covered with red ochre. It is because both are being re-born. The religious initiate is partially born again into the Dreamtime from which birth into this life has, to an extent and temporarily, separated him. (Christ, who was also in this great tradition, likewise said that a man must die and be born again in order to enter the kingdom of heaven: and all religions and religious initiation everywhere involve just such a death and rebirth.) The dead Aborigine, on the other hand, is totally born again into the Dreamtime. The belief was once universal, and so it is that tombs from one end of Europe to the other end of Asia are coloured red, and popes and babies alike immersed in the menstrual blood of the Goddess. Even so, we have not begun to speak of the real significance of red ochre!

First of all, we need to describe some of the details of Aborigine religious ritual and of religious evolution generally. The broad facts of the matter seem to be these. Large sections of early man (again, almost certainly, we are talking about Neanderthal man) evolved a matriarchal religion and culture ruled by goddesses and priestesses, with the Moon as supreme deity. Menstruation, childbirth and fertility (including the fertility of the countryside itself) were the central pillars of this religion. But another type of early man (and very probably we are talking about the type called Cro-Magnon) instead evolved a patriarchal religion and culture, ruled by gods and priests, with the Sun as supreme god. Hunting, battle and physical prowess were the central preoccupations of this society. From small beginnings numerically (probably also somewhere in Asia), Cro-Magnon overran all Neanderthal peoples, of whom many were simply wiped out. Some were absorbed, perhaps initially kept as slaves or subject peoples. Nevertheless, interbreeding took place.

There are two basic rules for how to behave in respect of the religion of conquered peoples. You retain anything which might be useful (and Cro-Magnon was undoubtedly hugely impressed by the paranormal aspects of Neanderthal religion) as well as anything necessary to prevent the conquered nation engaging in totally suicidal rebellion, that is, as a sop to their feelings. You therefore absorb what you can or must. Just so, the early Christians took over the pagan Saturnalia and called it Christmas. But the second rule is that everything else you stigmatize and ban as unholy.

So it was that the central 'blessing' of the Moon religion, menstruation, became 'the curse' . It is not just European popular speech which describes and mocks that function with abuse. Among Aborigines one of the very strongest swear-word insults is 'kunna nurka tara' – 'bloody vagina!'; or more precisely, 'bloody cunt!'

Circumcision, including among Aborigines subincision of the penis as well, has two meanings. It takes the idea of the powerful menstruating woman and transfers it to the male. He is now the equal of the menstruating female, and so takes over all her magical attributes. It is also a symbolic castration, for there is little doubt that the high point of the major Moon ceremony was the castration of the most excellent male, who had been 'king for a year' (which particular ceremony mimicked the yearly castration of the Sun, by the Moon, at midwinter solstice). Circumcision, among patriarchal peoples, is a nod as it were in the direction of the Moon Goddess, an act of placation for having taken over her kingdom.

We understand these matters from a study of a mass of legendary material, but all we need to do here is quote the Aborigines themselves, when asked why they segregate menstruating women in a special camp. They say it is because the woman's magic at this time is at its most powerful. This is why a menstruating woman who leaves the special camp is literally put to death, as is any woman, menstruating or not, who trespasses on any of the sacred sites even accidentally.

The circumcision of women, practised by Aborigines as well as being widespread throughout Africa, the Middle East and elsewhere, must conversely be understood as an act of punishment or sub-jugation, a reminder (to the Moon Goddess) of who is now boss. The vagina may simply be slashed or, in some Aborigine tribes, the *labia majora* are removed entirely. In Africa and the Middle East the clitoris is also sometimes removed.

The segregation or imprisonment of menstruating women is universal outside modern Europe – among Africans, Red Indians, Eskimoes, Jews, Gypsies and so on. Up until medieval times it was common enough in Europe itself. In some European country districts even today menstruating women are not allowed near the processes of milking, wine-making or seed-planting.

These are, for us, hardly matters of spiritual uplift, but we have to remember that ancient peoples saw them through different eyes from our own. And still there may be more to it. E. Stanton Maxey, whose opinions and research we shall be looking at under the heading of magnetism, believes that menstruating women generate an altered and stronger electromagnetic field, which may affect bioenergetic processes (like wine-making) in their immediate environment. There are in any case rather more appealing aspects to the spiritual life of Aborigines.

The training of the professional 'clever fellow' or medicine man –

the equivalent of a high priest in more evolved societies – is a long and arduous affair involving enormous dedication. This last remark has to be appreciated in a context where the usual religious initiation of a normal male goes on continuously for eleven years. The novitiate stages of priesthood in our modern religions are child's play in comparison.

There are but few of these Aborigine priests, even though there is more than one route to the role. One might, variously, be trained by one's medicine man father, or be chosen as a 'natural' by the community, or respond to the 'call' as a result of deep personal psychic experiences. The gifted, spiritual individual seems to be as rare in Aborigine ranks as in our own. It is worth mentioning also that it is always the whole community which endorses (or not) your spiritual suitability, a practice that the formalized Christian Church might do well to revive.

The Aboriginal novice must endure prolonged isolation, devoted to the quest for spiritual insight. He will sleep upon graves, and must undergo symbolic death and re-birth in extended trance sessions. Trance is sometimes self-induced, sometimes the result of hypnosis, and perhaps sometimes the result of drugs (although officially the Aborigines know of only one plant with drug properties – the pituri). In these trances he visits the spirit world, and has pieces of his viscera (literally?) removed by operation. His tongue, certainly, is literally perforated. He accepts as a permanency restrictions on his diet and behaviour, and his standing with the people rests among other things on his continued strict observance of these limitations. Severity aside, we can recognize that this process of training has elements in common with that of our own priests, but perhaps more specifically with the training of traditional mystics in the East.

Once qualified, the clever man plays a leading part in ceremonies. Aside from this role, his other principle function is to treat illness. This he does through simple plant preparations (which may or may not have medicinal properties), mud-packs and splints for fractures, and by 'operations' where the illness is 'removed' in the form of a stone, a twig, a porcupine quill or whatever. These operations are only skilful conjuring tricks, as clever men have frequently admitted to white men. But in addition the clever fellow performs such more genuinely mystical rituals as 'pointing the bone' at a wrongdoer, which at least sometimes results in the death of the criminal, either through autosuggestion, or perhaps through yet more mysterious processes.

Much religious ceremony is devoted to rites of increase and fertility. They include rain-making, ensuring a good supply of game, and petitioning for women to become pregnant. The greatest such festival is at New Year, paralleling the great solstice ceremonies of all early religion throughout the world. Without such continual religious observance the Aborigines believe 'that the rain would not come, that the animals and trees would die, and men and women become ill – if the sacred rites were not performed and the sacred songs not sung'. In similar words the natives of Central America also endorsed their continual human sacrifices.

In striking parallel with Ancient Egypt, Aborigines believe that man has two souls. The 'real' one is 'the eternal Dreamtime soul which pre-existed and will exist eternally'. The other is the one 'which can appear in dreams, which may take up its abode within another person after its owner's death, or may lie in the bush and play tricks'. This very strongly reminds us not only of the Egyptian ba and ka (see chapter 1) but the two souls of mysticism in general, the semi-immortal subtle body or etheric double as distinct from the truly immortal soul. Again we must ponder on this insistence everywhere on two souls – we would expect one to be enough, or why not seven or eight? – of which one is semi-perishable and the other truly indestructible.

A further detail of Aborigine belief strikingly resembles one found in northern Europe. Aborigines have a myth of a gigantic tree which once stood on a sacred site on the earth and touched the sky, joining the two. The belief that trees connected earth and sky was once widespread in Europe, and in Scandinavia in particular the world tree Yggdrasil was said to be the core of the universe. It is probable that these stories all derive from an original belief that the Earth is the child of the Moon Goddess and her consort the Sun, joined to the Moon by the symbolic umbilical cord of the tree. Hence sacred trees are often depicted as being twined about with one or two serpents, representing the two arteries which actually wind about the human umbilical cord, the Christian Tree of Knowledge with its serpent being one example.

We have already noted the striking similarity between the Greek legend of Orion and the Australian story of Wurrunna. On this same question of precise similarities between legends and legendary names in Australia and Eurasia, another Aborigine legend tells of a creature called the 'Yowie', which means literally 'great hairy man'. It is impossible not to be impressed with the parallel here, both in name and content, to the legend of the Tibetan 'Yeti' or Abominable Snowman, the large hair-covered anthropoid said to roam the Himalayan mountains. The Australian Yowie supposedly inhabits the mountains of eastern Australia, and the naturalist Rex Gilroy has recently collected more than three thousand reports of alleged sightings of the creature, including many by white Australians. There are two implications. One is that the Australian and Tibetan legends have the same origin, which on the face of it seems certain. Two, that such a creature does actually inhabit the Tibetan and/or the Australian mountains. I myself and many other scientists are already convinced of the reality of the Tibetan Yeti (and the evidence is summarized in *Guardians of the Ancient Wisdom*). Perhaps the Australian Yeti also really exists.

A still more topical aspect of Aborigine life concerns the dolphin. Scouts sit on headlands, watching for shoals of fish, which are seen as darker patches moving in the water. As soon as the scouts sight one, they signal the news to base camp by wailing, and then run down to the water's edge and beat the water with pieces of wood. Noise travels well in water. Now groups of dolphins appear from the sea in answer, and round up the fish, driving them into the shallows. Here the fish are speared by the natives and flung ashore. Meanwhile the dolphins dash back and forth further out, preventing the fish heading back into deep water. At the end the Aborigines share the catch with the dolphins. Aborigine legend says that dolphins have 'always' helped men in this way.

Apart from the great interest of this story in itself, dolphins really do seem 'always' to have had a special relationship with man. In Ancient Greece, as is well known, dolphins befriended man to such an extent that young boys rode on dolphins' backs. In modern times reports still come in of native priests and medicine men who can call dolphins from the sea – not by beating it with wood, but purely by telepathy. Lyall Watson has reported such a case in his *Gifts of Unknown Things*.

As already briefly discussed, many features of Aborigine life – the mummified burials of the Torres Straits, for instance – suggest that it has not evolved, but devolved. It looks as if the life of Aborigines was once far more complex and based on far greater knowledge. We come to another important piece of evidence for this view in a moment. Probably it was the harshness of life in Australia which occasioned the fall. It is said that human life is harder in only one place in the world – Tierra del Fuego.

The important new evidence presented here concerns red ochre (red oxide of iron), also known as haematite, a term derived from the Greek work for blood. Chemically it is Fe_2O_3 and is frequently a product of the weathering of magnetite, Fe_3O_4. In other words, when magnetite is exposed to atmosphere at the surface, it turns into haematite. Digging down through the haematite, one comes upon the magnetite, and it is clear that the one turns into the other.

Magnetite, as it happens, is highly magnetic. It is the ancient lodestone (i.e. the leading stone). Thanks to an archaeological discovery in 1967, we now know that the Olmecs of Central America had invented the compass at least one thousand years before the Chinese, who had previously been credited with its discovery (about two thousand years ago). The Olmec method was to make a sliver or bar of polished magnetite (lodestone) and place it on a piece of wood or cork floating in a bowl of water. The bar then veered to point to magnetic north. As further proof, we know that Olmec ceremonial centres were laid out to point a few degrees west of true north – i.e. to magnetic north. Also remarkable in this connection is a large Olmec stone head of a turtle carved in basalt, and rich in naturally magnetized iron. The head is shaped in such a way that the lines of magnetic force run to a point at the snout.

Only since 1975 have we in the modern west come to realize that many, and perhaps all, animals and plants sense and respond to the earth's magnetic field. They variously navigate by it, tell the time of day by it, and the season by it. They do this by means of magnetite. Strings of magnetite molecules have been found in tiny sea bacteria, and a cluster of magnetite in the head of the homing pigeon. Both of these organisms use the earth's magnetic field to determine their position. Will we now also find such clusters in the snout of the turtle, one of the great navigators of this planet? It seems virtually certain, and it seems equally certain that the Olmec, somehow, already knew this independently.

To revert to the Australian Aborigine: did they, then, and all other primitive peoples worship red ochre because they – or someone earlier – knew it to be a form of magnetite, whose magnetic properties they fully appreciated? Did the early people fully understand the magnetic properties also of this whole planet, and the effect of the moon (whose menstrual blood was haematite) not only on the tides but equally on the earth's whole magnetic field? And did they know that water flowing underground produces a magnetic field above it and more besides?

Yet just in case anyone stubbornly thinks the Australian Aborigine and other early peoples incapable of the magnetite-haematite connection, Aborigines today still understand how to smelt yellow hydrated iron oxide to produce the coveted red oxide. It is the oldest evidence of smelting that we possess anywhere in the world.

It is already clear therefore that the 'secret life' of ancient and so-called primitive peoples has a great deal to tell us about our own secret life and its potential. Nevertheless, we must be very much on our guard against the currently fashionable and absurd view that we should accept *all* the ways or the ideas of primitives without any inspection, and as a total package. Here, then, is a glimpse of the distaff or negative side of Aborigine life. Anyone who believes, again, that this picture must be completely exceptional should also read *A Saint Among Savages,*

Rosemary Kingsland's book about South American Indians.

Under natural conditions, some thirteen percent of all Aborigine children died within their first year, and twenty-five percent by the end of the fifth year. The best possible expectation of life was forty years. Among the causes of death were magical beliefs, the desperate business of finding enough to eat, and disease. In bad times (in protracted drought, for instance) every second child was eaten, principally by the preceding child. The babies were roasted before being eaten. Sometimes even children several years old met this fate. This practice existed basically to keep numbers down and to help the rest stay alive, but some tribes made the practice habitual, saying that to the first child would be added the strength of the second. The Central tribes also induced abortions in order to eat the foetus. Sometimes the mother herself procured the abortion to feed the cooked foetus to her starving family, but sometimes the tribal elders performed the operation by pressing down heavily and repeatedly on the woman's abdomen.

All deformed and handicapped babies were automatically smothered at birth (either by putting charcoal or sand in the mouth, or by beating the head with a stick), especially also the first born of twins, and sometimes both twins. The belief in these cases was that an evil spirit had entered the woman, and that at least one of the twins was the evil spirit. What we see here is perhaps a rationalization or justification of the stark fact that no Aborigine woman could carry or breast-feed two children at once, and this is probably the real reason every second normal child was killed anyway. The chances were that the mother would still be breast-feeding the first, probably well beyond the time of normal weaning, when the second came along.

We need not linger over all the, to us, horrific practices of Aborigine life. The abandonment of old women to die on the trail is in comparison a minor one. Worse is the execution of women who, however accidentally, have trespassed on a sacred site. Since the coming of the white man such practice is forbidden, but cases have recently come to light (as a result of burial of the corpse in unconsecrated ground) of considerable cunning in pursuing this rite, including two as follows. The condemned woman was held on the ground and her breasts pushed up. Then one of the elders knelt on her chest under the breasts until the ribs fractured, puncturing the lung cavity. Then the woman was released, to die gradually over the next few weeks. Both the women involved died in silence with 'honour', and in religious fear, atoning for their 'dishonoured' life.

Lastly, a genetically homosexual youth had been debarred from the religious initiation ceremonies which begin at fourteen. The boy was by now well over age, but the father repeatedly pleaded for him to receive the rites. The elders finally agreed. The boy was circumcised and the penis slit underneath from end to end. In these ceremonies the initiate is expected to bear these operations in silence, but the boy screamed all through the ceremony and at the end sobbed uncontrollably. At this point the elders speared him to death for having disgraced the rites.

When it is claimed, as it often is today, that the European has wantonly destroyed the 'fine' life which native peoples led before his coming, only one part of the statement is true. The European *has* destroyed the old way of life, but it was not fine. What we have done is simply replaced their kind of 'madness' with our own. On the other hand, whereas their madness worked for them and enabled them to survive, ours does not work for them. Conversely, in a dreadful kind of way, our own madness does work, or has worked, for us at least in the sense that it has kept us going till now – just. But the native madness certainly will not work for us.

We now have to learn to do much better than either of these kinds of extremes if mankind is to have a future. For we ourselves in the west are now face-to-face with the extinction we have so generously doled out to others – not just to members of our own species, but to the biological environment as a whole. We should also realize, incidentally, that native peoples do not necessarily conserve or guard the environment. The Australian Aborigine frequently sets fire to grassland, scrub and forest to drive out game (such as snakes, marsupial mice and the like, rather than kangaroo). Many plant species not well-adapted to withstand fire have as a result largely disappeared from the Aborigine's main routes, and some have disappeared from Australia altogether. The native inhabitant is therefore also very much a destroyer of species.

But we, thoroughly modern man, do nevertheless very much need some of the practices and beliefs of our ancestors that primitive peoples also still preserve, if we are to solve the problems of our own present and of our future. The great legacy to us of the Australian Aborigine is his stubborn and unquenchable belief in the reality of the Eternal Dreamtime. He insists that it describes and partakes of 'a continuity of life unlimited by space and time'. Though our here-and-now is finite and unlimited, and though we are in a sense separted from it, the Dreamtime can always be contacted and re-actualized by religious ritual. Importantly, the Aborigine maintains that our dreams in particular are an aspect of, and a contact with, the Dreamtime. and a contact with, the Dreamtime.

In these respects the concept of the Aborigine Dreamtime both supports and is supported by such concepts in other communities as Tao (in China), Brahman (in India) and Immanence (in Christianity).

Numerous Christian phrases like 'unchanging', 'from everlasting to everlasting', 'that which was, is now, and ever more shall be' implacably emphasize that this realm or dimension or aspect of divinity is utterly different from the finite, impermanent, always changing, cause-and-effect reality of the physical, here-and-now universe.

This age-old belief – or rather, I think, description – is so clearly, so emphatically, so often, and so universally spelt out that we cannot but take it seriously. It is too persistent and too detailed in our history to be anything other than perceived and proven truth. In any case, there are many ways of contacting it now.

3 But what does it all mean?

Many people involved in the paranormal and the occult believe they have heard everything. There is no unusual event they have not heard about. After all, the unusual is their bag, as we say. But these people do not read the *Journal of Neurology, Neurosurgery and Psychiatry* nor do they as a rule read books written by professional psychiatrists, or psychologists, or neurologists, or neuroanatomists, which do not happen to catch the headlines – or which are in any case not written for the general reader. There is unusual material in these publications that I guarantee will have escaped the attention of every paranormalist. Furthermore, apart from needing an explanation, this unusual material throws unbearable strains on the kinds of interpretation with which paranormalists and occultists are usually content.

If it is true that paranormalists rarely read the professional documents of psychology and neurology, it is equally true that doctors, psychologists and neurologists hardly ever read books written by, or about, psychic healers, mediums and holy men. So for those professions too, there are matters they have never heard of but which nevertheless very much require explanation. And those explanations throw unbearable strains on the kinds of interpretation with which professional doctors, psychologists and other scientists are usually content.

It turns out to be not so much a matter of finding the right answers, but of finding the right questions. It is not so much that the answers which we have at present are wrong. It is the frameworks in which the answers exist that are giving all the trouble. A great deal of ground therefore needs to be cleared, and in this chapter we shall try to gain a better view of the astonishing material that makes up the remainder of this book. It is an attempt to find the framework in which we can look at all the material available instead of only some of it.

Probably the first point which the orthodox scientist needs to get out of the way is the idea that modern science somehow grew out of religion, mysticism and the belief in the paranormal. Scientists often argue that religion and mythology were man's early and fumbling first attempts to explain his universe. Most of these attempts were nonsense, scientifically speaking, although they did enable man somehow to 'hang on' till he gradually began to sort small grains of true wheat from the overwhelming mass of chaff. On this model, the far-fetched and fanciful 'explanations' of religion yielded finally to the 'true' understanding of physical matter and evolution which science has so brilliantly manifested, particularly in the last century or so.

This view of events has a great appeal, especially for the narrow and orthodox scientist. It is a nice, tidy picture, coherent and neatly developmental. It 'solves' the problem of what to do about religion. Religion turns out just to have been an early false start – necessary, perhaps, and in the circumstances quite understandable. It can even be looked upon as a praiseworthy beginning. It did get us where we are today. But now mankind has moved beyond (so goes the explanation) religion, and we must gently but firmly stop its remains from getting in the way and holding up further progress. We need to put those remnants back in the drawer with the main mass of this redundant material, and then close the drawer firmly. The only people who should be allowed to open the drawer are social historians, psychologists perhaps, and a few other such specialists for whom this material has a specific and of course completely self-contained use.

This is a tidy picture in some ways and a rather comforting one. Progress can be seen to have occurred and this progress will go on occurring, more and more so now that the religious stage has finally been left behind. One specific example in miniature which very nicely illustrates what the well-meaning scientist is saying here is given by the biologist J. L. Randall – who, I hasten to add, is himself no narrow or unrestructured scientist. The example is taken from his book *Parapsychology and the Nature of Life*:

> Out of one hundred and three men who sailed with Jacques Cartier on his second voyage to Newfoundland in 1535, all but three soon became desperately ill with scurvy, and twenty-five of them died. In their fear and distress the sailors 'set up an image of Christ upon the shore and prostrated themselves before it in the deep snow, chanting litanies and penitential psalms'. The pestilence continued unabated, however.
>
> There could hardly be a clearer illustration of the power of Matter over Mind than this grim story. Despite the claims of religious propagandists, it is a commonplace experience that, in general, prayers for the healing of physical ailments are *not* answered, at least not in any direct and straightforward manner... countless millions all over the world continue to suffer in spite of the agonized entreaties of patients, relatives and friends. In the vast majority of cases the gods – if such there be – turn a deaf ear. On the other hand, materialistically-based modern science often produces the most dramatic cures....Even Cartier's sailors discovered the

effectiveness of a purely physical treatment, for one of them later learned from the Red Indians how to cure the scurvy with a decoction made from the needles of spruce trees. The effects of the medicine were highly dramatic: the disease disappeared almost immediately. Of course, it all seems so simple to us; for we have known for over half a century that scurvy is caused by a deficiency of vitamin C in the diet. To the sailors of Cartier's day, the contrast between the almost magical effects of the chemical treatment and the apparent futility of the religious rituals must have been striking.

How puzzling it is, then, especially in the face of endless examples of the success of science in so many areas of human problem, that religion not only refuses to lie down and die, but is actually more vigorous after every defeat than ever. So the legendary Hercules found when he wrestled with Antaeus. Every time Hercules dashed his opponent to the ground, Antaeus sprang up with renewed vigour. The more violent Hercules' attacks became, so Antaeus grew proportionately ever more powerful.

And so we find the Moslem religion today, for example, in a ferment of large-scale and determined revival, notably in Iran, Pakistan and some other parts of the Middle East. In Poland, again, despite all attempts by the all-powerful secular authorities to finish off the once apparently moribund local Catholicism, we find now a dramatic resurgence of that faith on a scale and with an intensity not seen since the Middle Ages. The secular authorities, despite the totalitarian nature of Polish government, seem quite helpless against it.

But perhaps the religious revival has occurred in these countries because they are backward and have a low standard of living? What, then, caused spiritualism to run wildfire through the western world of the late nineteenth century? In a Britain, a United States and a Europe triumphantly riding the crest of Darwinian explanations and a strikingly successful Industrial Revolution, when science and technology raced in seven-league boots towards a glowing and limitless materialist future, this most basic of all forms of religious expression – that of human possession by discarnate spirit entities – took off like one of the moon rockets of the following century.

This mention of space travel brings us appropriately to the present day in the west. Once again, we are here witnessing a religious revival of an intensity and dedication that has the scientists and the logical humanists throwing up their hands in despair. Bronowski describes it as 'a terrible loss of nerve, a retreat from knowledge'; and in response to this comment Carl Sagan writes about 'the increasing popularity of various forms of marginal, folk or pseudo-science, mysticism and magic', and adds: 'There is today in the west...a resurgent interest in vague, anecdotal and often demonstrably erroneous doctrines....' The top dressing of 'pseudo-science' in such aspects of the revival as UFOlogy does not fool anyone, and certainly not professional scientists. The religious lava which seethes beneath, and only too often breaks through the thin containing skin of scientific rationality, is described in Chris Evans' book *Cults of Unreason*, and further in the booklet which he and I wrote together, *Science Fiction as Religion*. But of course C. G. Jung had already some time before identified and described that position in respect of 'flying saucers', as we shall see.

Anyone who believes that the current interest in the west in matters such as UFOs, ley lines, dragons, psychic healing, acupuncture, astral travelling, space gods, telepathy, clairvoyance, reincarnation, hypnotism and many, many allied matters is not very widespread, extremely intense and above all here-to-stay should study not only the sales figures of books on these subjects, but the content of the books themselves. He should note that an increasing number are written by highly qualified and often once hard-line scientists. He should also note the invasion of the serious scientific press and university courses by this material, and realize that here again an increasing number of those who came first to mock now stay to pray, as did Gauquelin and Eysenck in respect of astrology.

Without any doubt at all our society is in the grip of a full-scale religious revival. That its outward appearance is a little different from traditional revivals, and those currently taking place in Iran, Pakistan and Poland, should not blind us to its essence.

It has finally become clear that religion and religious belief are not commodities surplus to the requirements of the human condition or, more importantly, to its progress. On the absolute contrary, we find that people deprived of reasonable religious sustenance exhibit a condition which is best described as 'spiritual starvation'. As with many other forms of deprivation, both physical and psychological, the long-term result is an explosion of uncontrolled compensatory behaviour designed to redress the balance.

Perhaps we can see the effects of this 'spiritual starvation' most clearly in the behaviour and psychological processes of individual mental patients. Whatever physiotherapy and chemo-therapy we may rightly give them, we find that one necessary element in the patient's re-integration and rehabilitation is some kind of spiritual self-exploration and self-affirmation. Such was the core of Jung's teaching in particular, and it is precisely for such statements and insights that he has become one of the high priests of the new age. In passing here, we ought to emphasize that psychoanalysis itself and its many modern descendants is also part of the religious revival.

Religion and science are two diametrically different modes of human thought and being. The difference is best summed up in the epigram: in religion things have to be believed to be seen, while in science they have to be seen to be believed. This fundamental opposition has been repeatedly endorsed by a very wide range of writers – Jung, D. H. Lawrence, Fritjof Capra, Teilhard de Chardin, Carlos Castaneda, Lyall Watson, Tom Graves, Richard Elen, Jan Merta and so on. Here is what the physicist Fritjof Capra has to say on the subject in *The Tao of Physics:*

> Is modern science, with all its sophisticated machinery, merely rediscovering ancient wisdom known to Eastern sages for thousands of years? Should physicists, therefore, abandon the scientific method and begin to meditate?
> I think all these questions have to be answered in the negative. I see science and mysticism as two complementary manifestations of the human mind; of its rational and intuitive faculties. The modern physicist experiences the world through an extreme specialization of the rational mind; the mystic through an extreme specialization of the intuitive mind. The two approaches are entirely different and involve far more than a certain view of the physical world....Neither is comprehended in the other, nor can either of them be reduced to the other....Science does not need mysticism and mysticism does not need science; but man needs both.

Without doubt what took place in human affairs in mankind's recent history and pre-history was a high point in mystical development. By 'recent' I am talking about something like the last one hundred thousand years. And what we see in the last ten thousand years – the stone circles of Britain, the High Wisdom of Egypt, the hints of former glory among Central American Indians and the Australian Aborigines – all these are (in my opinion) but faint echoes and memories of a once very considerable mastery of the paranormal and the esoteric, a High Civilization of Dreams, so to speak, that flourished principally in the time of Neanderthal man. Such a civilization, founded and built on the inner life of mankind, necessarily left behind little in the way of material artifacts or great cities. Such were not the concerns of these ancients. Nature herself was their palace, and their concern during our brief human life was simply to increase and develop their understanding of the esoteric and eternal, in single-minded preparation for resuming the palace in the great wheel of eternity that our human physical existence so briefly interrupts.

There is no need to defend the possibility of such attitudes and such civilizations. We can witness them today as lived out in the life and beliefs of the occasional great mystics and visionaries of our times – Christ, Buddha, Mohammed, and the other true saints and holy men of the world religions, both living and dead. I once had the privilege of meeting such a saint, a Catholic nun working in a mission in central England. The radiance which shone from her face was as real as mountains.

But equally not to be doubted is that our present age – say, the last two thousand years – whatever its other shortcomings, represents an equally amazing high point in the development of the rational, objective mind. Our high point of scientific understanding and mastery of the physical world is quite certainly the equal (though of course the opposite) of any achievement by any mystical civilization or individual.

A very important question is whether the mystical-rational swing is a continuous, cyclic process. There are therefore two sub-questions. First, are we now about to enter a new age of high mysticism? Second, was the now past age of high mysticism itself preceded by outstanding rational achievements in the understanding and control of the physical world? I believe the answer to both questions is yes.

The new age of high mysticism would be the much-heralded and much-publicized Age of Aquarius. Is this idea merely a froth of nonsense to delight and seduce the gullible? Some of the evidence presented in this book will strongly indicate otherwise. And the 'gullible' include such outstanding thinkers and scientists as C. G. Jung:

> It is not presumption that drives me, but my conscience as a psychiatrist that bids me fulfil my duty and prepare those few who will hear me for coming events which are in accord with the end of an era...changes...which bring about, or accompany, long-lasting transformations of the collective psyche....We are now nearing that change which may be expected when the spring point enters Aquarius. It would be frivolous of me to conceal from the reader that reflections such as these are not only exceedingly unpopular but come perilously close to those turbid fantasies which becloud the minds of world-improvers and other interpreters of 'signs and portents'. But I must take this risk, even if it means putting hard-won reputation for truthfulness, trustworthiness and scientific judgement in jeopardy. I can assure my readers that I do not do this with a light heart. I am, to be quite frank, concerned for all those who are caught unprepared by the events in question and disconcerted by their incomprehensible nature. Since, so far as I know, no one has yet felt moved to examine and set forth the possible psychic consequences of this foreseeable change, I deem it my duty to do what I can in this respect. I undertake this thankless task in the expectation that my chisel will make no impression on the hard stone it meets.

What of our other suggestion, that the past age of mysticism was preceded by an earlier age of rational and objective achievement?

We can make out a good case for this position. Five hundred thousand years ago, for example, we find men living in warm, dry caves, using fire, cooking in pots and practising communal hunting. From that time on we see a steady improvement in, for instance, a quite remarkable range of flint and bone tools, including needles and combs. Fur garments have button holes for tying with leather or sinew thongs. Beds in these caves are a great heap of cured fur-skins. The deep caves are used for the refrigeration and storage of meat, especially in winter. Sixty thousand years ago we find a burial in Iraq that reveals an extensive knowledge of the curative properties of herbs (along with a care programme for the disabled). This knowledge, clearly, had not been achieved overnight. It must have been the outcome of a long process of trial and error.

As an illustrative aside here, a very recent study (in the 1970s) in China found the curative properties, in respect of cancer, of an age-old mixture of more than forty herbs to be more effective than all modern drug treatments.

Some of these inventions – needle and thread, for example – may not seem shattering today, but in their context they are as dramatic and as visionary a step as the internal combustion engine or the radio in our own time. Any step, once achieved, becomes commonplace, but its initial achievement is and has to be the work of a genius. Without such a visionary individual, the 'commonplace' discovery goes unmade. Thus the otherwise highly advanced civilizations of Central America (the Olmecs, Aztecs, Incas) never discovered the wheel, and never discovered iron (despite the fact that they grasped the magnetic properties of magnetite and understood its relation to haematite, both of which are oxides of iron). The Ancient Egyptians, notwithstanding their great knowledge of architecture and astonomy, never realized that the brain was the seat of intellect and consciousness. When they mummified a body, they preserved the stomach organs in carefully sealed jars, but they sucked the brain out by a straw through the nose and threw it away.

The period 500,000 to 100,000 years ago therefore really was a Golden Age of Conscious Discovery, of technological innovation, a time when man's mastery of his physical environment progressed by leaps and bounds.

Then, it seems, came the upswing of religious consciousness, in which context the movement of the magnetite compass was seen not as a harnassable property of the physical universe, but as a mystical indicator of the dwelling place of the great Spirit of the universe, a spiritual pointer to that motionless centre of the northern sky marked by the presence of the seven stars of the Great Bear (the Plough) and the Pole Star, about which the starry heavens wheel each night.

In this way we seem to discern in our history a continual macro-swing or macro-oscillation of the rational-mystical pendulum (probably incorporating also numerous similar micro-fluctuations). And, indeed, such a bi-polar movement (as well as a bi-polar basis to the individual human personality) is elaborately described in the yin-yang philosophy of ancient China. But a better image still than the pendulum is that of the ascending spiral, the circular, rising movement which returns always to its point of origin but at a higher level; or, perhaps, of the flattened, two-dimensional spiral which from its centre reaches always further out, embracing all its own previous movement and echoing again, at one remove, all its previous stations.

Was it this sensing of the spiral basis of evolution which placed the spiral maze and the spiral dance at the centre of ancient religion (as the designs in Figure 1 in chapter 1 illustrate)? We know now that the basis of all life, the giant DNA molecule, the double helix, has the shape of an ascending spiral, each rung of which is a pair of positive-negative opposites. We know how, from the time-lapse camera, that all plants grow in a spiral, turning each day a complete revolution in response to the combined influence of sun, moon and the earth's magnetic field. There is much more still to say on the symbolism and significance of the spiral.

However, one undesirable feature of the otherwise natural and, in principle, desirable oscillation is the element of extremism or exaggeration. Consider the act of breathing. If we breathe in and out very exaggeratedly for a minute or so we start to feel very ill indeed. Breathing is a perfectly natural, perfectly necessary phenomenon, but exaggerated breathing is a real danger to us. So it is with the oscillation between rational and mystical states of mind, and between rational and mystical civilizations.

When the mystical mode has been in control, the rational mode has always tended to be not simply ignored, but actively persecuted. Similarly, when the rational mode has been in control, the mystical has been actively repressed. We see an example of the first in the treatment which the Catholic Church gave to scientists in medieval times. They were tortured, imprisoned and executed for questioning 'God's laws' – in claiming, for example, that the earth went round the sun and not the sun round the earth. Galileo himself was only saved from torture and death by agreeing to abstain from all further astronomical work. We see the reverse of this process today, where the (temporarily) triumphant rationalist mocks and scorns the processes of religion. For the modern scientist, religion is synonymous with superstition and self-deception, as activity practised only by the stupid and educationally illiterate.

This persecution and counter-persecution becomes a more deadly and destructive process with every turn of the spiral, by reason of the greater power which persecutors have at their disposal. The religious terrorists in the Middle East today carry not swords, but machine guns, nor do they hesitate to use them in enforcing 'the true faith'. But there are yet more subtle and more deadly weapons still, like the mass media, whose full uses the Nazis first demonstrated.

A further harm we can inflict on the movement and ultimate purpose of the evolutionary process, and ultimately on ourselves, is that of attempting to revert to an earlier point of the spiral – a point below or inside our present position – instead of encouraging the establishment of the new, just emerging and more evolved position. In our present case, instead of taking up a new religious position consonant with the present evolution of life on this planet, many individuals and organizations are attempting to resurrect and return to the religious positions of a bygone age. This is essentially what is occurring in Iran and Pakistan at this time. The same desire and direction is also seen in the attempts of the present Pope to enforce prescriptions and dogmas which are totally out of keeping with humanity's present mood and needs (the forbidding of contraception, divorce and women priests, for example). These attempts are necessarily doomed, but while they last they can cause the gravest damage. They might even halt or disable the evolutionary process permanently as far as this planet is concerned, or at any rate as far as the human species is concerned.

The new 'Age of Aquarius', if there is to be one, must be genuinely new. It must involve a re-forming, a new expression of the religious impulse. And in any case, we must not permit the persecution and banishment of science and rationality. We see attempts at this not just in the religious groups already mentioned, but in many simple-minded left-wing and ecological groups. These 'revolutionaries' have no idea of the horrors which would be unleashed on the world by the wholesale banishment of science, technology and urban communities.

What we really have to do is to attempt a life-style and an ethos that have only rarely even been attempted successfully. It was perhaps achieved for a time in Ancient China, and resulted among other things in such marvels as acupuncture and the *I Ching*. This attempt involves somehow allowing continuous or rapid oscillation between the two modes of our being. (The models of the pendulum and the spiral can equally express the position: for example, the spiral-maze dance first goes into the centre from outside, then turns and comes outward again.) We have, so to speak, to occupy diametrically opposed positions on the spiral simultaneously. If you will, we need to organize matters so that we can have our cake and eat it. We have to have a fully-fledged scientific attitude and a fully-fledged religious belief at one and the same time. Fortunately, this paradoxical position can really be reached, for as Friedrich Schiller put it as long ago as 1793: 'It is true that these two tendencies do indeed conflict with each other but – and this is the point to note – not in the same objectives. And things which never make contact can never collide.'

So we can indeed hope for – and certainly we must attempt – the miraculous synthesis of the two modes of human existence. Whether or not we actually achieve it, one thing for the moment is quite certain. The ancient knowledge is coming in once again from the cold. And the changes it will bring with it are beyond our present imagining.

The body with a mind of its own

4 The startled body

A European couple had settled in the depths of the South American rainforest, well away from other human beings. The wife became pregnant. During a difficult birth, the wife died. In despair at the prospect of also losing his child, the husband put the baby to his own breast. After repeated attempts, the male breast began producing a steadily increasing supply of milk. The child survived and grew into a healthy youngster.

A woman had as a girl often been savagely beaten by her sadistic father. At the age of seventeen she had had a mental breakdown followed by extensive amnesia. Her emotional problems persisted. Now at the age of thirty-seven she came into the care of a London psychiatrist. During her psychotherapy sessions she would often slide into a trance-like state of dissociation. In this state she was able to speak in detail of the many beatings her father had given her. But now as she described the specific wounds the whippings had produced – on legs, buttocks, shoulders and hands – the bleeding wounds reappeared under the eyes of the psychiatrist. Some of these wounds were photographed, and others were also witnessed first-hand by another doctor. In all, these wounds appeared on thirty different occasions. They were wholly real, and had to be dressed and treated like any normal wounds.

The psychiatrist involved, Dr R. L. Moody, had previously observed a similar case. An army officer, aged thirty-five, was admitted to hospital for the treatment of persistent sleep-walking, a condition which had recurred at intervals throughout his life. On an earlier occasion ten years before he had also been hospitalized for observation and treatment of the same condition. On that occasion, and as an attempted solution, his arms were tied behind his back in the hope of preventing him leaving his bed. After falling asleep, however, he 'awoke' as usual into his dissociated state and attempted to get up. He now struggled violently for some time and finally succeeded in leaving his bed, but as a direct result of the restraint and the struggling both his arms were deeply marked and bleeding.

In psychotherapy ten years later, the patient was given an abreactive drug (evipan) but not restrained in any way. He duly went into his dissociated state and began by reciting fragments of poetry as he usually did. Then he placed his hands behind his back and began struggling and gasping. Under the eyes of the doctor, in full electric light, deep weals began to form on the patient's arms. By morning the wounds had begun to bleed, and these too were recorded on photograph.

The photographic evidence in both cases, along with detailed reports, were published in the British medical magazine, *The Lancet*. Moody reported also on two other patients who under psychotherapy reproduced injuries sustained in former years. In a man who had been buried by rubble in a bomb attack the ankle and head swelled dramatically in reduplication of his injuries. A woman of thirty-five who had fractured her ribs in a riding accident at the age of ten now spontaneously produced clinical bruising and subcutaneous haemorrhage along the same ribs.

These cases also call to mind the numerous reports right up to the present day of individuals who have spontaneously reproduced the 'wounds of Christ' on their own bodies.

In 1974 a young religiously-minded black girl began to bleed spontaneously from her left palm. This was in Easter week. Taken to a doctor, she went on producing blood four or five times a day from several different wounds. She bled from the hands, feet, chest and forehead. On at least one occasion the first welling-out of blood was actually watched. The onset of bleeding was also observed by a doctor in a different case involving an American-Italian woman. Sometimes, again, young religious women designated by the Catholic faith as 'brides of Christ' have produced a red, coral-like ring on the skin of their wedding-finger.

In passing, we now know that Christ was nailed to the cross not through the palms – as traditional religious pictures indicate – but through the wrists. Yet the religious stigmatist develops holes in the palm of the hand. This fact alone points to the wounds being the result of autosuggestion, rather than to any possession by the discarnate spirit of Christ.

There are other interesting cases which seem to form a bridge between the religious individuals just described and psychiatric patients. The psychiatric patients reproduce wounds which have actually once existed on their bodies, whereas the religious individuals produce wounds which they personally have never experienced. These second kind are widely claimed by religious people to be divinely produced, not self-produced. Gordon Rattray Taylor, however, reports a woman whose hip began to bleed whenever she saw her handicapped son putting on his hip-brace. This woman was exactly duplicating the behaviour of the religious stigmatists, but without any divine intervention. A slightly different case again, but one which once more illustrates the power of the human body to cause wounds to come and go at will, is that of Jack Schwarz. Like many eastern fakirs, he can push knitting needles through his flesh without blood flowing as a result, but can then make the blood flow, and stop again, on mental command. His ability has been recorded on film.

Finally, there are numerous fully authenticated experiments which have demonstrated on many different occasions the dramatic ability of the human body to wound itself in response to commands given under hypnosis. Hypnotized subjects, told that they had been touched with stinging plant leaves, rapidly produced the blisters associated with such contact. In reality they had been touched with harmless leaves. Another group, touched with genuinely stinging leaves, but told that these were harmless chestnut leaves, produced no blisters. In a different experiment a man was told he had been touched with a red-hot poker. He flinched violently and soon produced a very large blister filled with fluid. One woman has been found who produces blisters to order at previously stipulated locations on her body, without being touched with anything at all.

In yet a further experiment involving a patient suffering from warts, these were removed by hypnotic suggestion from one hand, while the warts on the other hand, deliberately excluded from the instruction, remained unaffected. Not just witches, but doctors often remove warts from young children without any hypnosis by telling them to perform a ritual perhaps involving their touching pieces of medical equipment. (This particular method fails to work with adults – and we need very much to ask why.) A wart, a benign tumour, is of course related to cancer, a malignant tumour. Here then we are also touching directly on the subject matter of the next chapter.

In addition to such visible results, body-effects can be produced by hypnosis of which the subject has no knowledge whatsoever. Thus, when hypnotized subjects are told they have just eaten a fatty meal, their stomachs secrete enzymes necessary to digest fat. But if they are told it was a high-protein meal, enzymes appropriate to protein digestion now appear in the urine. Here we are very close indeed to the 'phantom pregnancy' phenomenon discussed in the Introduction.

There have been many anecdotal reports of autosuggestion and hypnosis being successful in enabling women to enlarge the size of their breasts, plus a number of successful demonstrations of this feat under experimental conditions. In the most recent of these, in 1977, R. D. Willard used twenty-two volunteers aged between nineteen and fifty-four. Independently, a doctor measured the height, diameter and circumference of the women's breasts before the experiment began.

Then, in light hypnotic trance, the women were told to imagine warm water flowing over their breasts or a heat lamp playing on them. They were given a tape-recording of their instructions, to be used daily at home. After twelve weeks, twenty-eight per cent of the women had achieved the size of breast they wanted, and stopped practising. By this time, eighty-five per cent had achieved a measurable enlargement and forty-six per cent were now purchasing a larger-sized bra. Average increases were 0.65 inches vertically, 1.00 inch horizontally and 1.37 inches in circumference, although some women achieved double these amounts.

There were several relevant circumstances which supported the genuineness of these results. Forty-two per cent of the women had lost weight overall, so they had not just become fatter. And in fact every single woman in the experiment showed a reduced waistline. Some women had wanted firmer breasts, and some had wanted equal-size breasts. These specific aims were achieved. Three months after treatment ceased, eighty per cent of the breast gains had been retained.

In 1979 a remarkable case was reported in the British national press. A boy of fourteen, after a mishap, had been completely immersed in ice-cold water for three hours. He was given the kiss of life, and to everyone's astonishment began breathing again. He subsequently recovered fully, with no ill-effects of any kind. This instance is a particularly dramatic version of numerous other incidents where individuals have been totally immersed in water for periods well in excess of two to three minutes and have nevertheless survived unharmed. The precise wording of this last sentence is important, for after two to three minutes without oxygen the brain begins to undergo irreversible cell damage. Although individuals may often survive an immersion of five minutes or more, they are as a very firm rule indeed just living vegetables, in care for the rest of their lives.

This 'very firm rule' is, however, broken from time to time, frequently enough in fact for doctors to have proposed a 'diving reflex', which allows survival for 'up to half an hour' without oxygen and without brain damage. This is supposed to be the result of a very primitive reflex that normally comes into play during a difficult birth, to prevent suffocation of the child in the birth canal. Now, this proposed reflex cannot have any connection with normal breathing or its stopping, for until the umbilical cord is cut the baby does not need to breathe. And until and unless its lungs have once been inflated, it cannot breath. The only case we can be speaking of is where the umbilical cord is squeezed so hard that blood cannot pass through it. The 'half-an-hour' time estimate in particular is based on no clinical criteria at all. Really, the whole 'explanation' is just a vague concession on the part of doctors to a not understood but undeniable phenomenon. The quite exceptional three-hour immersion of the fourteen year old boy, in any case, reminds us far more of the Indian mystics, who are said to be able to survive many days of burial underground or in sealed cabinets.

This particular claim has not been verified scientifically, but other, equally improbable claims have. Before we come to a detailed demonstration performed by the Swami Rama under laboratory conditions, one other spontaneous case of 'impossible' survival must be mentioned.

In 1978 a young male stowaway travelled from America to Britain in the wheel compartment of a transatlantic jet. He was in this compartment, which is of course outside the cabin sections of the aircraft, for eight hours. He arrived in Britain not only alive but virtually unharmed. Doctors involved in the case were adamant that no human being could survive the temperature and other conditions of such a flight for even a small fraction of this time. That this young man was not just alive but unharmed was entirely impossible. Most interestingly, the stowaway had been unconscious throughout the trip.

The Swami Rama had claimed that he could vary his heart-beat at will, could produce the skipping rhythms of angina, could completely stop his heart at will – and now offered to perform this feat under supervision in a western medical laboratory. The laboratory involved was the Menninger Foundation in Kansas, America. Here the Swami Rama was connected up to a cardiotachometer. His normal heart-rate was established at 66 beats per minute. On request he now speeded this to 94 beats, afterwards bringing it back to 62. Such control, however, had already been achieved in the laboratory by Europeans after biofeedack training. But then the Swami showed he could increase one half of the normal 'flub-dub' heartbeat (which we usually experience as one event, although it is in fact two separate but very closely connected events). He now began producing, in effect, 'flub-DUB, flub-DUB'. He was manipulating one of the valves but not the other.

Now the Swami undertook to stop his heart completely. He offered to do so for three to four minutes – but the nervous scientists suggested they would be satisfied with ten seconds. Then abruptly the Swami's heart-rate rose from 70 to 300 beats per minute. This rate he held for seventeen seconds. A rate of 300 beats per minute is known as 'atrial flutter', a condition occurring when the heart has stopped pumping. The valves are not working and the chambers are not filling with blood. In this condition blood pressure drops dramatically and the person concerned invariably faints. But the Swami, having substantiated his claim, took off the electrodes and went out to give a lecture.

The phrase 'heart-stopping' leads, appropriately enough, to the phenomenon of 'time stood still'. Throughout human history people have claimed at moments of great excitement, drama or danger a strong sense of time disturbance. It is for them as if time slows to a crawl, or stops altogether. As it happens, I myself had this experience a good many years ago. I was driving with some other students on one of Germany's notorious 'herring-bone' cobblestone roads that are like ice-rinks in the wet. It was raining. The over-loaded car we had was an elderly Volkswagen which the driver, a Spanish boy, had bought that morning. We were making something like sixty miles an hour, when the car suddenly began to spin round out of control, while at the same time moving diagonally off the road. Later it was established that the front wheels had locked. Especially with the engine being in the rear, and four passengers in the back seat, the spinning movement was the result.

The road had no kerb. On either side the open common-land was dotted with bushes and trees. Our spin was ferocious and the whole incident must have been over in seconds. Yet to me we were waltzing with a dreamy slowness. Emotionally I was perfectly calm and detached, without the slightest sense of fear or alarm. I had all the time in the world to study the faces of my companions and the other cars around us. Idly I was wondering whether we were going to hit one of the trees or only the bushes, and I developed a detached interest in the answer to the question. Though some of my companions were shouting, and the car itself must have been making a good deal of noise, I could hear only faint sounds. The slowing of time seemed also to have muted sound. In the event we missed the trees and came to rest still on four wheels in a clump of bushes some distance from the road. Even now that events had returned to normal, I still felt entirely relaxed and cheerful.

Supposing, during the time-stop period, I had chosen to take some action? Would my movements have been accelerated in normal time, or would they have appeared just as slow to me as everything else did? The answer was supplied a couple of years later by a chance meeting with a man at a lecture, but even then I little realized that the truth had already been demonstrated experimentally many times. The man I met, Mr S, was a rock climber. He told me of an occasion when he and a friend had been climbing. Young and over-confident, they were taking inadequate precautions in order to climb fast. Suddenly the other man, who was above S, lost his hold and fell. It flashed through S's mind that although he was linked to his friend by rope, he was not going to be able to hold him, and that the two of them would plunge off the rock-face together to their deaths. But as his friend fell past him with apparently grotesque slowness, S seized a piton from his belt, hammered it firmly home, took the slack rope that was also falling past him, and wound it several times round the piton. What seemed some time later, S and the piton took the weight of the faller. The combination held.

Although S (backed up in relevant detail by his friend) knew that the event had occurred as described, he could not understand or explain how he could have moved so quickly. 'What I did was impossible' was his final comment. How delighted both he and I would have been to know that his experience had already been duplicated many times under experimental conditions.

In 1952 L. Cooper and M. Erickson published their book *Time Distortion in Hypnosis: An Experimental and Clinical Investigation*. Among other experiments, Cooper asked a woman violinist to practise on a hallucinated violin. She found she could play this non-existent violin much faster than normally. She did not feel, however, that she was omitting any value or quality or other aspect of the exercise. In the circumstances, of course, this feeling could have been just a subjective hallucination. But she also found that the hallucinated practice now gave her an overall grasp of the composition far superior to the grasp of it she had achieved in normal practice. Here, at least, was a real result of the 'hallucinated' practice, one which might lead to a belief that the woman had really gone through the whole piece in simulation, and much faster than was normally possible. Incidentally, in this kind of hallucinated test some subjects reported that they could achieve in ten seconds what usually took them half an hour. But Cooper did not leave matters there. Other subjects performed truly real, although simpler motor tasks under hypnosis, such as writing words and sentences. In these wholly real exercises normal output could be as much as doubled. In one experiment, one subject's real output in twenty-seven minutes, under hypnosis, equalled his real but non-hypnotized output for ninety-six minutes.

So Mr S was telling the truth.

Reports sometimes appear in the press and in books of individuals also developing superhuman strength in time of emergency. A typical report concerns a mother who is said to have lifted a saloon car from the body of her child – something she could not possibly achieve by any normal definition. As we have seen already, anecdotal reports such as these deserve to be taken seriously. So far hypnotic experiment has only shown that subjects under hypnosis perform at their absolute maximum strength, rather than at any average or unmotivated value. The case here, however (as so often in psychological experiments), seems to be only that we dare not duplicate in experiments the life-or-death situation which, in real life, produces truly unusual motivation and with it perhaps superhuman strength.

The report at the beginning of this chapter of the man whose chest produced milk to feed his new-born child comes to us from Alexander Humboldt, the famous naturalist and explorer, after whom the Humboldt current off the coast of South America is named. Commenting on the report, Ernst Haeckel the equally famous German biologist of the nineteenth century (to whom even Darwin acknowledged a debt) remarked: 'Similar cases have been often observed, even among other male mammals such as sheep and goats.' The use of the word 'often' is interesting, since I can find no reports of this event in this century. It is equally of interest to speculate why this particular manifestation of the startled body should apparently have disappeared. We must probably put it down to the development of long-distance communication (telegraph, telephone and radio). It is rarely possible for any of us to be or, importantly, to feel truly isolated today. But Haeckel's specific inclusion of animal cases means that the observations of these eminent biologists can be experimentally verified by us, as of now.

Dr R. L. Moody's reports on spontaneous wound generation were published in 1946 and 1948. All the other material we have examined is of a later date. We are therefore no longer speaking of the past. We are speaking of our own time and our own generation.

Any one of the cases so far discussed should cause any thinking biologist or doctor to call for a review of current theory and practice in respect of the human organism, in the same way as any slight crack in an airliner automatically results in a thorough inspection of every part of the aircraft. But when we see, and will see further, that the whole medical-biological edifice is literally covered with such cracks, then we very much have to begin to ask why the professionals concerned remain silent.

5 The self-healing body

The following case is known to me personally, though in the interests of privacy I have slightly altered non-significant details.

Mr Z, a British schoolteacher aged sixty-five, was on the verge of retirement. For most of his life he had been troubled by a severe duodenal ulcer, which involved an almost permanent diet of milk and boiled fish. The ulcer was almost certainly caused by his very stressful marriage, but Mr Z was a member of an orthodox religious community and in such circles you did not divorce or leave your wife. As he approached what we might think of as a rather bleak retirement, a mouth-sore was diagnosed as malignant. He was taken into hospital for treatment and after some weeks discharged under observation.

Now Mr Z did something amazing. He left his wife and house, and moved into a bed-sitter. This, it was commonly felt among much head-shaking, was to be the end. Who would cook his boiled fish and watch over his diet? Wouldn't the mouth cancer return? Wasn't he obviously now also becoming mentally unstable?

The reality, however, proved quite otherwise. In the hope of writing occasional articles for educational magazines, Mr Z called on several. One of them agreed that he should write a trial article about aspects of his method of teaching geography. But while he was in the office one day, on impulse the editor asked his opinion about two different types of desk that the magazine was reviewing. A few weeks later the magazine rang him again, this time to ask his views on some new wall charts. Within a year Mr Z was not simply being widely consulted about educational equipment, but was trading in it. By the end of another year he was involved in import-export. Nor was he any longer just dealing in educational and office equipment. He was concerned with every kind of business furnishing, both as finished articles, and in respect of raw materials.

Today, at eighty years of age, Mr Z is an international business man of very considerable means, an international jet-setter, much in evidence at economic conferences. You will have often seen him on newsreels and in documentaries. Apart from his work, he has a vigorous social life that most twenty-five year olds would not only find hard to cope with, but be glad to have. Needless to say, Mr Z today has no cancer, and no duodenal ulcer.

Moyra Caldecott is the wife of Oliver Caldecott, a well-known London publisher. Moyra Caldecott is herself a successful novelist, published in hardback and paperback on both sides of the Atlantic.

In her mid-forties Mrs Caldecott became unwell. She began very easily to get out of breath. If she hurried upstairs she experienced a squeezing sensation in her chest. Although a hospital electrocardiograph (ECG) showed no sign of heart trouble, the symptoms, however, grew worse. At this point she was given an exercise ECG, in which the heart is tested while the patient performs vigorous exercise.

It was now established that Mrs Caldecott was suffering from angina. Angina pectoris is a progressive heart disease, whose outward symptoms are violent, cramping chest pains after exertion, and general lassitude. These result from an inadequate supply of blood or oxygen to the heart muscle, caused by the narrowing or degeneration of the coronary arteries – for example by the accumulation of scleroid tissue. The amount of exertion needed to produce an attack is a guide to the severity of the condition. In the advanced form even the act of turning over in bed will be enough to produce crippling spasm and severe pain. There are drug treatments which reduce some of the effects of attack, but they do not cure the underlying condition. Ultimately, the only cure is an operation to bypass the blockage. The success rate of the operation, itself often fatal, is not high. Without the bypass operation, however, sooner or later the unchecked condition leads to a fatal heart attack.

For the next two years Mrs Caldecott had a series of tablet treatments at a London hospital. Far from improving her condition, these treatments merely produced a series of painful side-effects – a result which is not uncommon – and instead her condition deteriorated steadily. She began collapsing on the way to hospital. Eventually she became completely housebound. The slightest movement, such as picking up a cup, would set off an attack. The seizures were now so severe that she almost invariably collapsed. She was, by this time, more than semi-invalid.

Following an especially bad seizure, Mrs Caldecott was admitted to hospital. Discharged after a period of rest and treatment, she collapsed again immediately and was readmitted to hospital. She was now at real risk of a fatal attack, and it was proposed that she undergo the bypass operation as a last hope.

While facing this decision, Mrs Caldecott was told by a writer working on a book for her husband about a psychic healer in the west country. She wrote to the healer asking if he could help. He arranged to put her on his 'absent healing' list, and told her that her condition would

55

improve slightly as a result. The procedure in absent healing is that the healer concentrates on the person concerned at a particular time of day, at which precise time the patient also turns his or her thoughts to the healer.

Perhaps only as a result of auto-suggestion, Mrs Caldecott's condition did improve slightly. The bypass operation was postponed and she returned home. A few months later she felt well enough to be driven down to see the healer in Bristol. Then, some months later again, came a complete relapse and a very severe attack. Now the bypass operation was a certainty. The healer, however, had spoken of the possibility of a 'psychic operation'. Risking a possible fatal seizure, Mrs Caldecott was driven down again to Bristol.

The 'psychic operation' was performed. It involved the healer simply going into light trance, speaking with his 'spirit voice', and passing his hands over Mrs Caldecott's fully clothed body, without actually touching her.

As he made these gestures, Mrs Caldecott says she felt a fluttering movement about her heart 'as if a trapped butterfly were trying to get out'.

'That's it,' said the healer, coming out of the trance. He remarked that her condition would clear up entirely 'in the next few days', but that meanwhile she should rest and be quiet.

The last was easier said than done. The busy house in London was full of visitors in and out. On the fourth day after the trip new visitors were due, and these were to stay. Mrs Caldecott realized that there was nothing like sufficient food in the house. She would have to go to the shops. Getting out of her rest chair, and picking up her shopping basket, she set off. Only when she was half-way there, crossing a busy road, did she realize what she was doing. She had not been out shopping for years.

From then on she went from strength to strength. A further visit was made to the healer about a year later for a kind of topping-up 'operation', just as simple as the first.

Today Mrs Caldecott leads a fully normal life and any visitor to the house sees only a bustling woman looking younger than her age, full of normal good health.

It was Oliver Caldecott's intention to have a book writen about the whole sequence of events. The healer, however, declined any suggestion of publicity. He takes no payment whatsoever for his work, and by day is a store-keeper in a factory. He already has more patients than he can reasonably handle, and says that in any case his spirit guides have forbidden publicity. These reasons seem honourable enough.

But the hospital medical staff, while privately agreeing that some kind of miracle had occurred that they were unable to explain, refused to make any public comment, or to disclose any of their records, or even to be named. Their reasons, one suspects, are less than honourable.

Ichthyosiform erythrodermia complex is a congenital, structural disease of the skin present from birth. It is also aptly enough called 'rhinoceros' or 'crocodile' skin. It is a thickening, hardening and darkening of the skin. The condition is resistant to all forms of treatment and is progressive, reaching maximum around the age of fifteen, when it either remains static or deteriorates with secondary complications.

This case concerns a boy aged sixteen. By this time a thick, black, horny layer covered his entire body, except for his chest, neck and face. This layer itself was densely covered with rough protrusions rising between two and six millimetres above the surface. Some of these warty excrescences were as much as five millimetres across. To the touch the skin was as hard as a finger-nail. Any bending or flexing of any part of the body led to a crack which oozed blood-stained serum. These numerous cracks were chronically infected and extremely painful. As usually happens the condition also gave rise to an objectionable smell, so bad that other schoolchildren and teachers could not tolerate it. Continuous treatment thoughout the patient's life had been of no avail. Skin grafts from the unaffected chest area to affected areas, for instance, had themselves rapidly developed the full condition.

On 10 February 1951 (at the Queen Victoria Hospital, East Grinstead, England) the patient was hypnotized and told that his left arm would clear. For experimental reasons, the instruction was deliberately confined to this one area. Five days later the horny layer softened, broke up and fell off. The skin below was slightly inflamed, but normal in texture and general appearance. The inflammation faded in a further few days. At the end of ten days the arm was completely clear from shoulder to wrist.

At this stage, to forestall any later doubts by the medical profession, a sample of horny skin was taken from the calf of the leg and sent for independent analysis to King's College Hospital, London.

Professor H. A. Magnus' report was as follows:

> The specimen consists of a roughly elliptical piece of warty tissue measuring 1.5 by 0.7 centimetres. Section shows a massive degree of hyper-keratosis [layers of horny overgrowth], the average thickness of the keratin layer being 1.5 millimetres. The keratin [a fibrous protein found in nails, hair and horns] is laminated [arranged in plates] and has produced many fissures in the underlying epidermis, which is atrophic [wasted] and in places thinly drawn out into the keratin. The papillae [protrusions] are elongated and narrow (alpine papillae). There are no other changes

in the corium [lower skin] apart from a marked deficiency in elastic fibre, only occasional fragments of which are present. One hair follicle and the somewhat atrophied duct of one sweat gland are present. This histological picture is similar to that described as being present in *ichthyosis congenita*.

With the presence of this congenital structural disease independently confirmed, beyond any question, the boy's right arm was now treated hypnotically, then the legs and finally the trunk.

At the end of treatment the arms were 95 per cent cleared, the back 90 per cent, the buttocks 60 per cent, the thighs 70 per cent, and the legs and feet 50 per cent.

A. A. Mason, the Senior Registrar of the Queen Victoria Hospital whose case this was, writes:

> The improvement in the patient's mental state has been as dramatic as his organic improvement. Previously his schooling and social contact had been reduced to a minimum, his sensitivity towards his smell and appearance causing him to become lonely and solitary, with a hopeless attitude towards future friendship and employment. Now he has become a happy, normal boy, though still educationally retarded, and is already being employed as an electrician's assistant.
>
> From this response to hypnosis one of two inferences may be drawn. Either there is a hitherto unsuspected psychic factor in the aetiology [causal history] of the disease or this is a case of congenital organic condition being affected by a psychological process. A combination of both these factors is of course a third possibility. Whichever is true, the improvement in this case seems to be totally unprecedented, and was effected after the failure of all recognized methods of treatment.

The case was also commented upon by Dr F. Ray Bettley, who independently observed the progress of the treatment. Describing the cure as 'astonishing' he goes on to emphasize these vital points:

> *Erythrodermia ichthyosiform* is a congenital disorder in which structural abnormality is more important than functional deviation; it is as much an anatomical mal-development as is club-foot. It is surprising that it should respond to any kind of treatment; that it should respond to hypnotic suggestion demands a revision of current concepts of the relation between mind and body.

The disease, then, is *genetic* in origin. Some fault in the basic genetic cellular code has led to a basic structural defect. This is no hysterical illness involving the *mal-function* of an otherwise *structurally sound* organ, such as we see in hysterical paralysis, and in the stigmata produced by religious devotees, and in the onset of hysterical pregnancy. What we see in the case of this boy is a reaching down into

58

the microscopic depths of the genetic organism, down to the springs of the life-force itself – with an order to scrap the existing basic design plan, and to rebuild from scratch. This is the staggering implication of this case: the body, under the direction of a mind, can, in principle, re-structure a club-foot, close a spina bifida, or alter the brain of a Mongol child.

The achievement of Chief Rolling Thunder, a Shoshone medicine man, may seem a pale one by comparison, yet it is also a vital brick in the wall of evidence. Like Swami Rama's heart-stop, the following incident was observed at the Menninger Foundation in Kansas. Rolling Thunder claimed to be able to heal genuine wounds instantaneously. A man was brought to him with a genuine, large bruise sustained on the leg in the course of work. Rolling Thunder applied his mouth to the bruise, sucked vigorously, then ran across the room and vomited. The bruise had gone. The scientists examined the vomit in amazement. It contained nothing it should not have contained.

This case differs in two ways from those we saw in the last chapter where, under hypnosis, subjects on command developed and then cured a wound in their own bodies. Firstly, the wound Rolling Thunder dealt with was not an hysterical wound, it was a real wound. (Although already we must start being very careful in our use of the word 'real', for there is certainly more than one kind of reality. These realities are not inferior or superior to each other in any value sense, just very different.) Rolling Thunder, then, not only caused a real wound to disappear instantaneously, but he did so in a person who was not hypnotized.

R. D. Laing also reports a case of very rapid, if not instantaneous, real wound healing in a mental patient. In the course of the day this man would sometimes cut or otherwise wound himself, either in workshop accidents, or perhaps during outbursts. But the next morning, after sleeping, these wounds were entirely gone. Once again, we are not dealing here with any kind of 'mere' hysterical or subjective reality. We are involved indisputably with objective reality.

Does this now exhaust the cup of wonders? No, not in the slightest.

Eugene Osty was a French doctor and psychiatrist practising in Paris in the earlier part of this century. He became deeply interested in paranormal phenomena, and spent twelve years of his life not just researching the field, but conducting experiments himself. He drew heavily also on the work and reports of other doctors, psychiatrists and psychologists known to him. The results of his work he published in a remarkable book *Supernormal Faculties in Man*. This appeared in Paris in 1922, and in Britain a year later.

It is not just astonishing, but very saddening, that this book and with it Osty's work has been so completely lost from sight. On the British side this may be in part due to the appalling translation, quite the worst I have ever seen. (I am hoping to produce a new translation of the book in the near future.) Yet why was this outstanding impetus not followed up in France? Here, after all, was a community not of cranks, but of doctors and psychologists of impeccable backgrounds. The ideas of Osty himself are particularly original. In many cases he is documenting matters which are currently being produced as 'new' discoveries, such as seeing with the fingertips.

Osty himself fully believed that his work would be taken up. In his Preface he writes: 'The biological problem set out [in this book] is so important in itself and its implications that I have no doubt the scientific community will itself be most anxious to confirm my experiments. I hope that men of science will not stand indifferent, or merely as passive spectators of the drama unfolded in these pages....In publishing the results of my personal research I now place on the scientific community the duty of repeating these experiments, on one of the most profoundly interesting problems presented to mankind....Such confirmation of my findings would have the effect of bringing into the domain of science phenomena that have hitherto lain outside it because they have been considered (without examination) to be absurd....Further investigation by competent experimenters will rapidly produce fruitful results.'

Alas, Osty and his colleagues failed to appreciate the intense prejudice that exists in these areas.

In the case which follows, Osty is citing not his own work, but that of three other doctors (Comar, Buvat, Sollier) who – like Freud and Charcot – were using hypnosis in the treatment of neurotic illness. In so doing these doctors stumbled on a phenomenon they called 'autoscopy'. This is the ability of a patient in trance to observe and report on the condition and structure of his own internal organs, *in some cases down to the microscopic level.* These individuals were totally lacking in any medical training, and were in some cases uneducated altogether. The doctors in fact note that these abilities were far more often present in 'simple' people, and much less often among the sophisticated.

One such untutored patient of Dr Sollier described, in her own non-technical vocabulary: 'her veins, heart, lungs, bronchia down to the pulmonary vesicles, intestines, ovaries, Fallopian tubes, uterus and appendages, muscles, tendons and skeleton, including that of the face, and finally the brain. She had no normal knowledge of the outer form of these organs nor of their structure; nor of the ovaries and the brain, of which she described the microscopic structure.'

We are now going to look at one of these fascinating cases in detail. It comes from Dr Comar and was published in the *Presse*

Medicale of 17 January 1900. Indeed, all these accounts were published in the most respected medical and psychological journals of the time – the *Revue de Neurologie*, the *Gazette des Hopitaux* and so on.

The girl involved here is using her own simple language. She calls the appendix (and the blind gut) the 'little end', and the membrane of the intestine, particularly that of the blind gut and appendix, the 'little skin'. I will explain the full clinical position at the end of the extract, and we shall see that the girl, under hypnosis, had a knowledge of body anatomy and function that not even a (non-medical) university graduate possesses. I did not know it myself until I checked the items in a medical textbook. The translation here, as above, is my own:

Extract from a Doctor's Diary (*Presse Médicale*, January, 1900)

> M. was a patient with major hysterical symptoms whom I was treating by hypnotherapy. She was suddenly taken ill with fever. Her temperature rapidly rose to around 105°, but her only other symptom was pain in the right iliac [appendix] region....In the absence of any apparent explanation for the fever, I assumed it would prove to be hysterical, with perhaps some sympathetic inflammation in the cecal [again, appendix] region. The delirious condition subsided in fact after three weeks. During this time the patient, under hypnosis, spoke to me several times of the 'little skin' [membrane] of the intestine, which she said was inflamed, especially in one area. With rest and the application of ice all apparent symptoms abated. The patient began getting up, but did not resume a normal diet. I kept her on liquids, but after some days the original symptoms reappeared even more strongly, accompanied by nausea, swelling of the abdomen, constipation, stabbing pains at the level of the appendix and high fever.
>
> When her temperature again reached 105°, I gave her cool baths. Any movement caused an increase of pain, and on the third day she suffered a severe attack of cramps. During this seizure she told me that the membranal lining was more inflamed than ever, and that the 'little end' of the intestine was especially bad. I pressed her, still in the hypnotic state, to tell me exactly what she could see.
>
> 'I do not see the little end very well. I do not see where it finishes.'
>
> 'Why do you not see it?'
>
> 'I cannot see it because I cannot feel it. I see my bowel and the skin [membrane] of the bowel because I can feel them, but I have never felt the little end part.'
>
> 'Well,' I ordered, 'feel it now.'
>
> Her abdomen twitched, and these movements were obviously accompanied by sharp pain, because she cried out.
>
> 'Oh, it will be pierced, it is so very thin. The skin of the little

61

end sticks and is folded. In the folds is a sort of thick, dirty liquid. It sticks and unsticks whenever I move. It is going to tear apart. It's like a whitlow on the finger, and that whole part is inflamed. All the skin in my stomach is inflamed, but especially on the right.'

I ordered her to feel still more. Her abdomen began moving again. The pain seemed to increase. She cried out:

'Oh, the little end is full of dirty matter. Oh, how clogged it is! But it's been like that a long time. That's what hurts me. It can't get away.'

'Try to feel more specifically.'

'Ah! Yes! I can see the end [appendix] now.'

Another quick movement, which stopped suddenly. Then she said:

'It pricks me.'

'What pricks you?'

'There is something in the end.'

'What?'

'I can't see very well. It's buried in the pus. It hurts me, and I daren't move in case it bursts.'

'In case what bursts?'

'Why, the little end. There is some pointed thing irritating it, but it's so full of matter that I can't see clearly what it is. But if I move, I'm afraid that the point will pierce the intestine.'

'Very well – go on feeling slowly, but take great care that the point doesn't pierce.'

M. now resumed the gentle abdominal movements she had been making in order to feel or experience the bowel, and then announced:

'It is moving. The little end of the intestine twists about like a worm, and moves the material in it...that goes up...it scrapes me in passing...now it is out of the little end...it is in the big intestine.'

She continued to make movements for a time, but then stopped, saying it hurt her too much. I thought it inadvisable to proceed further that day, fearing more serious complications. And since the patient had stopped of her own accord, I thought it better to follow her impulse than to force her against it. I had no proof that any of what she had said was literally true – but the safest course was to assume that it was. By that evening her temperature had dropped slightly.

Next day I hypnotized her once again and asked if she could still see the intestine.

'Yes. And the little point that hurt me yesterday is still in the same place.'

'Very well, please activate your bowel.'

Her abdomen began visible movements, and she announced that the whole intestine was in motion. She reported likewise that the 'little point' was also on the move, and that the encrustation of matter around it was less. I asked her to try to feel more, and a moment later she said:

'I begin to see it more clearly, but I only see one end of it. It is like a piece of bone about a centimetre long and pointed at one end.' So saying she indicated a place in the transverse colon.

'Continue to feel.'

Her abdominal movements went on, and I asked her where the point was now. She indicated her left iliac fossa [see diagram below].

'Are you sure?'

'Yes. I see it quite clearly.'

'Then please stop, and don't try to feel any more.'

I now administered an injection of water into the intestine while she was still under hypnosis. On recovering this water from the bowel, I filtered it and found a small piece of bone of the form and size the patient had described. I then asked her if she could still see the little point. 'No,' she said. 'It went out with the water.'

From that day on her temperature fell steadily. Under further hypnosis the patient declared that the intestinal linings and membranes were less inflamed, and that the pus and dirt which had caused the adhesions was dissipating. Daily she reported a continual diminution of the inflammation, and the absorption of the harmful matter from the appendix and cecum.

There are many remarkable aspects to this account. Under hypnosis the patient was for example able to effect movements of the intestine, something which is entirely out of our conscious control, and in particular movements of the appendix itself. The piece of bone she precisely described proved to exist, and was exactly as described. The girl was literally able to give herself an operation for appendicitis – without a single cut.

But the bone itself does not exhaust the evidence. Figure 2 is a simplified drawing of relevant sections of the human intestine. As can be seen from the diagram, the ileum, which is the end of the small intestine, opens into the cecum, also known as the blind gut, which is a cul de sac about two and a half inches deep. In the wall of the cecum is the appendix, another little blind alley, which is vestigial and useless in man (although it has functions in one or two animals). After leaving the small intestine (the ileum) and entering the cecum, the contents of what is from here on the large intestine move *vertically upwards* for about a foot through what is called the ascending colon. They then turn left and cross to the other side of the abdomen through what is called the transverse colon. Then they turn downwards at right angles into the decending colon, whence they finally enter the rectum and are excreted.

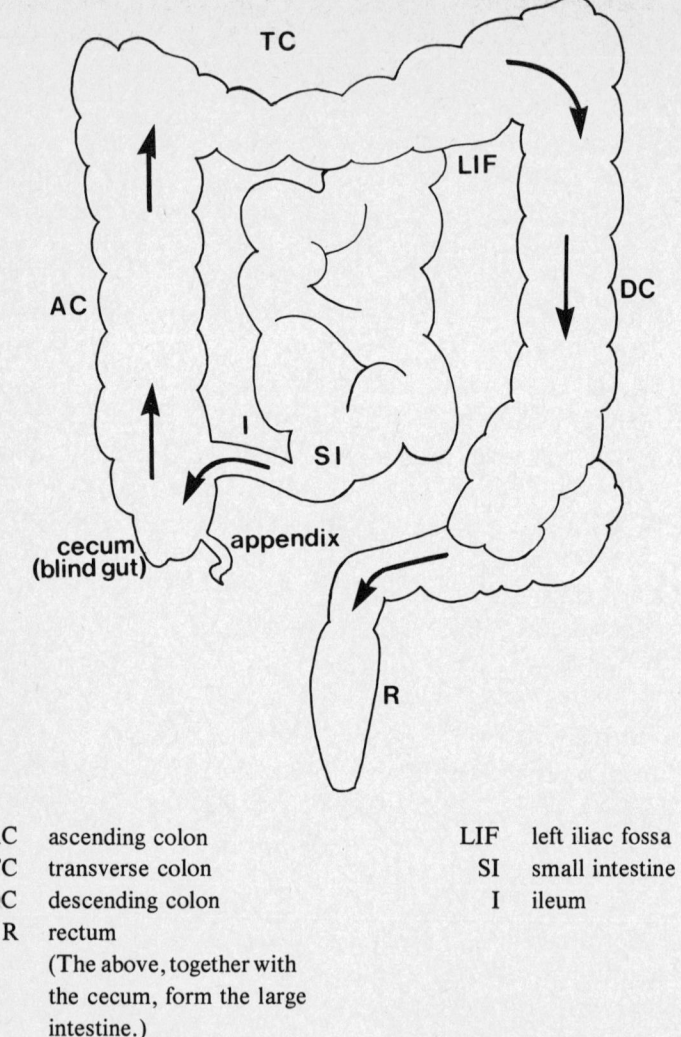

AC	ascending colon	LIF	left iliac fossa
TC	transverse colon	SI	small intestine
DC	descending colon	I	ileum
R	rectum		

(The above, together with the cecum, form the large intestine.)

Figure 2   Simplified diagram of structures of the small and large intestine.

Like most people, I was till recently ignorant of the geography of the human intestines. I had never heard of the blind gut, nor did I realize that the appendix was a further blind alley running off it. Least of all did I realize that the contents of the intestine at that point move vertically upwards. It is entirely fair to assume that this uneducated girl also knew none of these things.

Yet consider her words 'that goes up'. She correctly reports that the material dislodged from the appendix and the cecum moves upwards into the large intestine. The large intestine *begins* at this point

– she got that right too. Later she places the bone, correctly, in the transverse colon, and finally at the head of the descending colon (the left iliac fossa). From here of course Dr Comar is easily able to wash down the item into the rectum and out of the anal opening.

I find myself thunderstruck by this whole report and its implications. Such detailed internal self-viewing is, however, exactly the literal underpinning we require in respect of the precise body changes which occur in hypnosis and hysteria.

Self-healing?

The title of this chapter is 'the self-healing body', but were not some of the people we have discussed healed by others? This is perfectly true, and yet the chapter heading is still accurate. However, first let us establish that in this chapter we are not talking about the spontaneous remission of hysterical symptoms. That result can be triggered by any factor whatsoever, anything that the person concerned, for any reason at all, considers can bring it about.

Let us take the hypothetical case of a young boy who has become inexplicably paralysed from the waist down. Doctors can find nothing organically or structurally wrong with him. There is no objective reason why the legs should not function normally. The boy has what is called an hysterical symptom. Psychotherapeutic investigation establishes, say, that the boy's parents are about to separate. The therapist privately draws the conclusion that the boy's paralysed legs are his unconscious attempt to keep the parents together. Their pity for him in this condition and his need for constant nursing may well delay or even altogether prevent their separating. Gently the therapist suggests this interpretation to the boy. Suddenly the youngster has a fit of uncontrollable weeping. But now, equally suddenly, he can walk again normally.

This is a specific case involving a specific unconscious wish. We could have a more diffuse situation with a much more complex and obscure causation, such as now follows. But still, even here, one event can bring about the abrupt disappearance of the hysterical symptoms involved.

A young woman has *anorexia nervosa* (that is, she is completely unable to eat normally). She also has an acute skin condition, red and itchy, especially around the breasts, stomach and genital area. She suffers from cramps and pains, and occasionally outright paralysis of the fingers. She cannot sleep. She has difficulty in urinating and evacuating. These functions also cause further pain and irritation.

The woman does not consciously know that her physical symp-

65

toms are caused by a deep sense of fear and guilt about her own sexuality. It does not matter, for our purposes, how this situation has come about, but it was a common enough one in repressive Victorian homes, for instance. Now, this woman is a severe case, who would be totally resistant to any suggestion that her symptoms were the outcome of sexual fear. (How could that be, she would ask, when she has no interest in sex?) Nor would she seek psychotherapy, though she may take medicines from her doctor.

Now she meets an extremely personable and magnetic priest or evangelist. He tells her that her symptoms are God's way of showing her that her life is wrong. She must dedicate her life to God, and after that she will be cured. There and then the woman decides to become a nun and to give herself to Christ. And, lo, the next day all her symptoms have gone! What a wonderful proof of God's power, and of the rightness of the priest's prophetic diagnosis.

If we could see inside the woman's head we might observe that she spends a good deal of time thinking about the priest and also about Jesus himself, in a rather concrete and not altogether ethereal way. Perhaps this woman will be one of those who develops the coral ring on her wedding finger (see p. 47).

Hopefully these two examples give some idea of what hysterical symptoms are. They are the bodily expression or outcome of some problem in mental life, a problem of which the person concerned is often consciously unaware, although sometimes there can be a good theoretical grasp of what is happening. But in these cases the conscious knowledge does not seem to be able to communicate itself to the body. It is a purely intellectual knowledge that remains 'unexperienced'.

The important point to grasp is that the hysterical symptom is a functional disturbance, not an organic or structural fact. So there is a high fever, but no bacteria or poison in the blood. There are the symptoms of pregnancy but there is no baby in the womb. Yet, on the other hand, the hysterical situation is in no way a conscious pretence or a trick. It is real enough – subjectively. It is just not independently real.

Much of the material of the previous chapter was hysterical in the sense just described, but not all of that was by any means negative. The ability to perform motor actions accurately but at supernormal speed is unquestionably a positive development. And in any case, positive or negative, the working of the hysterical process is a marvel in its own right, one that the scientific establishment, sadly, refuses to take seriously. We shall nevertheless be taking it very seriously in the remainder of this book.

But the *additional* miracle of the cases we have looked at in the present chapter is that they involve organic and structural illness. They involve real illness, in the truly objective sense. That is what makes these cases so much more remarkable still than the hysterical cases. Even scientists who acknowledge the astonishing implications of hysterical phenomena fight tooth and nail when it is proposed that the mind can also control purely objective situations. So let us have one more objective illness and cure, just to underline the point.

Dr Alexis Carrel, a distinguished French scientist and Nobel Prize winner, died in 1944. In 1902 Carrel became interested in the subject of psychic healing, and in 1903 took charge of a group of patients visiting the shrine of Lourdes as part of the National Pilgrimage. With Dr Carrel on this expedition went a young patient of his, Marie Bailly. All this girl's family had died of tuberculosis, and she herself was now in the last stages of tubercular peritonitis. She was literally dying, and had hours rather than days to live. The girl's case and prognosis had also been confirmed independently by two other physicians. Marie had tubercular lesions in her lungs, disseminated tuberculosis throughout her system, and tubercular sores on her body. In this condition she was now taken before the Grotto. And those watching saw a truly miraculous change. Marie's pulse and respiration returned to normal, her distended abdomen shrank, and her colouring likewise normalized. Carrel and three other physicians then examined and clinically tested Marie that same evening. Not the slightest doubt or reservation was expressed by any of them. The girl was totally and permanently cured, and entirely free from every trace of disease.

Further comment on this case is really superfluous. I would say only that when sceptics persist in their scepticism in the face of evidence such as this, what then comes into further question is not the evidence, but the mental condition of those who reject it. After his event Carrel openly declared his belief in miraculous cure. For this stand he was expelled from his position at the Lyons Faculty of Medicine, and left France to take up a post at the Rockefeller Institute in New York. For his work there he was awarded, in 1912, the Nobel Prize for Medicine.

One question which remains for us is whether the shrine at Lourdes really gives out some kind of radiation or influence, as of course the old religions have always claimed, or not. But back for the moment to the question of the self-healing of organic disease (*not* hysterical illness), as against what seems to be the healing of organic disease through the agency of someone else. Examining a large number of cases, it looks very much as if those who are healed 'of themselves' cannot heal other people; while those who heal other people, that is, who function as healers, do not seem able to produce the effect in themselves. I personally know of one or two healers who are actually in a rather poor state of general health. Many, certainly, cannot get rid of their own headaches or arthritis, and instead go to other healers or conventional doctors for attention to such ailments.

Is there any well-established distinction between any pair of psychological types that might correspond to the two healing conditions, self and other? The personality opposites of introversion/extraversion seem tailor-made for our purpose. Briefly, the extravert is an outgoing, sociable type, while the introvert is inward-turning and enjoys solitude. (These characteristics tend to show up more under pressure, and a quick test you can apply to yourself is whether, when you feel depressed or unhappy, you tend to seek the company of someone else, or prefer to be by yourself.)

As far as I know, the following proposal has not been carried out, but it would be of the greatest interest if psychic healers were shown to score highly on standardized tests of extraversion. We would also want individuals like Marie Bailly to score equally highly on introversion. As it happens, Mr Z, with whom we opened this chapter, would almost certainly score *low* on introversion. But no matter: in psychology we are always talking of tendencies and group averages, not of watertight divisions or absolutes.

It needs to be emphasized that what passes between the psychic healer and his patient is some kind of tangible energy. That much has been shown beyond doubt in several large-scale laboratory experiments, supervised by doctors and biochemists, where psychic healers have effected cures in animals and plants – and even in microscopic enzymes.

In one large-scale laboratory experiment carried out by Dr Bernard Grad at Canada's McGill University, a psychic healer (Oskar Estebany) in three weeks produced significantly faster healing in experimentally wounded mice, not by actually touching them, but simply by placing his hands against their cages for a few moments each day. Mice that were not treated at all, and other mice 'treated' by medical staff doing exactly what Estebany did, both showed the same lower rate of improvement. In later experiments Estebany caused plants to grow faster, taller and with more leaves simply by 'healing' the solution with which the plants were fed; and later again (at the Human Dimensions Institute in New York) raised pancreatic enzyme, de-natured by exposure to a magnetic field, back to its natural level of functioning. Another unnamed psychic healer, at the University of Chile, produced a significant retardation of tumour growth in mice injected with malignant tissue, as compared with those not treated by the healer.

Since such experimental animals, plants and enzymes cannot be said either to have faith in the healer, nor to have been suffering from hysterical symptoms, we are obliged instead to think in terms of some kind of energy-exchange from healer to sick organism. I often call this energy 'libido', which was Freud's name for the energy of the unconscious mind. But perhaps instead we ought to take a leaf out of Colin Wilson's book and call it 'energy X'.

For whatever reason, and in whatever way, it seems that 'energy X' arises in individuals like Mr Z, who was spontaneously self-cured of an organic illness, or who are hypnotized into spontaneous self-cure, like the boy with rhinoceros skin. Could the hypnotist in the boy's case have functioned like a psychic healer? Was there an exchange of energy? It seems unlikely. Could a hypnotist treat mice or enzymes, for instance? The case of Marie Bailly is a rather bigger problem. Was she cured by the shrine at Lourdes radiating some kind of energy at her? Or did the reputation of Lourdes trigger her own inner energy discharge and self-cure? We probably have to suspend judgment on this question, though the idea of Lourdes working by reputation does involve fewer theoretical assumptions, which is usually the best approach when heading into the unknown.

In the case of self-cure, energy X seems only available, internally, to the person generating it. But in the case of psychic healers, energy X is available for use by others – and in fact, it seems, only by others. Again, in the usually good cause of making as few assumptions as possible, I am inclined to consider at least as a working hypothesis that only one kind of energy is involved in both these kinds of cases. On this basis self-healing and other healing are just two sides of one coin. But there remains of course the possibility that we are dealing with two different energies.

What we can do at this point, however, is to answer quite emphatically one part of the general question why the medical and scientific establishment as a whole stubbornly refuses to pursue the wonders we have already more than sufficiently documented. It is not at all because those in charge think that these happenings are false. It is because they know they are true.

6 Biochemistry as mind

We have already seen a great deal of evidence that the body, in the absence of any form of normal consciousness, can go about its affairs not just miraculously – and that is not the point here – but coherently and purposefully. These elements of coherence and purpose are actually even more significant than the miraculous aspect itself.

We have seen (and shall see further) that during unconsciousness, coma, sleep, hypnosis, and many other forms of trance the body itself can institute events of the most complex and subtle kind. Nothing seems to be beyond its capacities. It can produce large-scale or purely local changes. It can do a simple cosmetic job that, even with its superficial impressionism, will pass a moderately careful inspection. Alternatively, if the contract so specifies, it can totally scrap or alter existing structures and rebuild from base upwards. In such cases no detailed specification, however fine-grain, is too much for it. On record, too, it has every detail of old wounds and conditions, and can reproduce any of these to order. Or, if required, it can produce completely new wounds in new places, given even a rough hint of the product required – as in the case of religious stigmata and 'coral wedding rings'. It excels in rush jobs (from terminal, disseminated tuberculosis to full health in a matter of hours), yet can equally well sustain complex long-term projects like phantom pregnancy. But in either case the outstanding quality of workmanship is the same.

My account is deliberately picturesque, but in no way does it go beyond the facts. Some doctors and scientists who are not at all dismissive of these various events are nevertheless bewildered as to how they should make a start in coming to terms with them. And many non-scientists and non-medics, who are quite happy to accept these phenomena of our secret lives in their own right, would nevertheless still be glad of some explanations – if only to be better able to face up to sceptics. Both these groups are helped by a look at four areas of biochemistry: hormones, the immune system, biofeedback, and hallucinogenic drugs.

Hormones are chemical substances produced within the body by a range of glands and organs, including the pineal, hypothalamus, pituitary, thyroid, parathyroid, thymus, pancreas, adrenal, and ovaries/testes. These precise details do not concern us too much. The point is that the substances involved directly affect *behaviour*. In a sense, they *are* behaviour. They are a clear and straightforward instance of biochemistry functioning as mind.

Androgens are substances produced by the male testicles which govern masculine behaviour. Estrogens are substances produced mainly by the ovaries which govern female behaviour.

If an adult male is given large doses of estrogen his masculine behaviours are inhibited and female behaviours appear, while if an adult female receives androgen the reverse occurs. The male will show less general aggression, for example, and be more submissive in sexual encounters (show reduced sexual aggression). Homosexuals, whose general behaviour most people would describe as more feminine, have a lower androgen-estrogen ratio than sexually normal males. The effects of the two groups of hormones are best seen in animal studies where, say, a male animal is castrated and then supplied with estrogen. This animal now makes sexual advances to other males, using the instinctive body movements of the normal female. Scientists do not perform experiments of this kind on human beings, but some adults themselves choose to undergo sex-change operations, followed by reverse hormone injections. The results are similar to those obtained in animal studies, though never perfect, for a great deal more is involved in human sexuality than hormone profiles.

Whenever we become excited – by the prospect of a holiday, a promotion or whatever – the adrenal glands produce adrenalin. As a result the heart-rate speeds up, extra sugar is poured into the bloodstream, and the oxidation of the body is increased. This is the body preparing for action (which it assumes to be both real and imminent). Conversely, if in a calm, relaxed mood we are injected with a dose of adrenalin, we become excited. It is not just that our eyes dilate and our pulse quickens and so on, but our mental thresholds are also lowered. We start to take more note of what is happening around us. Our thoughts begin racing. Precisely the opposite effect is produced by the hormone insulin, which is made by the pancreas. Increased amounts of insulin are, for instance, produced in the autumn by animals which hibernate or remain dormant through the winter. If we breed pure strains of tame mice, we find that these mice have smaller adrenal, thyroid and pituitary glands – and a more active pancreas than normal animals.

An entire book would have to be written to illustrate the numerous and often very subtle effects of a long list of hormones on our behaviours and moods and thoughts. Instead, we shall simply underline the fact that our internal chemical environment – our biochemistry – is a potent factor in shaping and colouring our mental life.

The body with a mind of its own

The immune system is the collective name given to the body's natural defence systems against invasion by microbes and poisons. This is a very broad concept with no well-defined edges. New items are being added to it almost daily. The term immune system necessarily further includes in addition to first-line defence the body's natural powers of tissue healing or replacement, and general recovery from illness.

Most people know that the blood and tissues of the body contain a variety of substances that are capable of killing a very large number of microbes, and that the white cells of the blood are particularly active in this respect. The pus that forms around an open wound is the dead bodies of white cells that have died in our defence. The number of white cells in our blood increases significantly during exercise, when the risk of hurting ourselves is greater than when resting. Some other cells scavenge through the blood the whole time, digesting and destroying particles of foreign matter. Antibodies are specific protein substances formed in response to invasion by these foreign antigens. Certain cells, having examined an antigen, then on the spot build and release a quite specific antibody to deal with the invader. It does not matter that the cells have not known that particular antigen before. Antibodies play a very significant role in our natural immunity.

The capacities of the body in this last respect have been formally harnessed in the procedure known as vaccination. Here a doctor deliberately injects us with a mild form of a disease. In defeating it – a process that takes a few days – the body prepares a more or less permanent reserve of appropriate antibodies. Now should a powerful, killing version of the same disease try to invade us, it will be immediately stopped in its tracks. The first vaccination ever devised was that of giving a person a dose of cowpox in order to immunize against smallpox. In a splendid tribute to the discoverer, Edward Jenner, the World Health Organization has recently announced that smallpox has been totally eradicated from the world.

The particular form of biochemical activity on view in the working of the immune system does not seem to have any *direct* counterpart or reflection in our mental life. But there are two points. One is that here in the immune system is a ready-made army just awaiting direction. And – the second point – it looks as if 'someone' or 'something' steps in and directs it during paranormal healing. For if normal consciousness is not directly affected by the immune system, the immune system is certainly very directly affected by our conscious life – and often in a wholly destructive way. Mental stress, as well as other 'bad behaviour' on our part, like eating too much or drinking too much, can radically harm the working of the immune system.

There is a currently fashionable view among progressives that 'all illness is mental illness', but such extreme views are not really justified, as we shall see in a moment. A more extreme view which is, paradoxically, far more likely is that the human body-mind will one day be able to monitor itself perfectly.

However, if we want to claim that it is never an outside cause which generates disease – either in the form of poison or microbes – then we are hard put to explain why certain diseases are far more common in particular environments. So radiologists develop more leukemia than normal, outdoor workers more cancer of the skin, nuns more breast cancer and miners more silicosis. (The reason why nuns have a significantly higher rate of breast cancer seems actually not to be due to their not breast-feeding babies, but to their not having children. Breast cancer apparently results from a long-term effect of two of the estrogens, an effect which is modified by other hormones produced during pregnancy.) In China, where the population is far more rooted to birth place than in any western country, doctors have been able to show that, for instance, types of cancer are firmly attached to very precise areas – to the banks of a particular river, to the soil of one particular valley and so on. In one area *one in four* (that is, twenty-five per cent) of the local population were dying from cancer of the esophagus or gullet (and so were the chickens). Children showed the same incidence as adults. Yet a couple of hundred miles away the disease was non-existent. The complex causation chain of this disease involved first a specific mineral lack in the local soil. Hence plants were low in vitamin C and high in nitrites (a known cancer agent). The cooking methods of the local people further concentrated the nitrites. And finally the preparation of bread and sauces involved letting the food go mouldy. The fungi involved again further raised the cancerous potential – two of them were carcinogens in their own right. The net result of all these factors was an epidemic rate of cancer of the gullet in the human population, and in the chickens who were fed with scraps from the table. (We aren't going to claim, are we, that the chickens had some mental health problem?)

There is therefore plenty of evidence to show the independent role the environment plays in causing illness and disease. And yet three-quarters of those Chinese did not develop esophagal cancer. Why was that? And if we think back to Jacques Cartier's crew (see chapter 3), out of a hundred and three sailors, one hundred developed scurvy (and twenty-five died of it). But three did not get scurvy. Why? It would be fascinating to have a detailed description of the physical and psychological backgrounds of all the sailors and especially of the three who escaped illness. Alas we do not. Were the three men deeply religious? Were they keep fit fanatics? Were they non-smokers? Were they teetotallers? Or were they just bullies, who took food from their weaker companions?

But of more direct concern to us is the role of mental stress as a causal factor in disease, either as sole agent or as a significant additive which often finally tilts the odds against our own defence systems. And we are concerned here with the direct effects of stress, not indirect ones. If stress causes a person to smoke heavily, so producing lung cancer, that is an indirect outcome, as is the gastric ulcer which develops in a harassed business man who eats too many processed and fat-soaked 'fast food' meals.

Direct stress, operating as a single factor in its own right as a direct producer of illness, has been demonstrated experimentally on many occasions. For instance, monkeys were trained to operate machines in response to incoming signals. These were quite complicated instructions, for a monkey, and required constant alertness to avoid mistakes. Now, as a next step, whenever the monkey concerned made a mistake, he received a painful shock. The monkeys were under constant tension and constant threat during their working hours. Within weeks all developed duodenal ulcers. (Other monkeys, who operated similar machines and who were shocked, randomly, just as often, but whose decisions, right or wrong, did not influence the shock process, developed no ulcers.) This is an unpleasant experiment, but at least it removes the question of the harmful effects of stress from the area of debate, and into the area of solid, proven fact.

The direct effect of stress in the production of illness is therefore part of what I already called 'self harming'. Self harming is the reverse of the process of self healing. They are two sides of one coin.

Why is a particular organ affected as opposed to some other? Sometimes it is undoubtedly because 'tension knots' occur at specific and quite logical points in the body. When we are tense or frightened, for example, the digestive process is disturbed, our throat becomes dry and so on, as the body redeploys its resources to face attack (again real, physical attack as far as the body is concerned). We know too, for instance, that the acidity level of the blood rises in stress and that acidity is directly involved in a range of conditions from stomach ulcers to cavities in teeth. Such considerations aside, is it not really just a case of saying that, in stress or depression the general level of health is reduced overall, but that any organ which is constitutionally weaker (for any of a variety of reasons) gives way first, just as the weakest link of a chain snaps first? Again, that too is sometimes fair argument.

But in psychotherapeutic and psychoanalytic work we frequently find that the organ or organs singled out for illness or malfunction have significant guilt or fear associations for the patient. A Japanese girl in

74

Britain on a course of study was living with an acquaintance of mine. She told me that if this fact were known in the little town she came from she would be considered a prostitute, and no longer acceptable to her family and neighbours. Subsequently the girl developed very severe herpes of the genital region (a form of the cold sores many people get on their lips). The boyfriend had no history of the disease, and both of them claimed not to have been sleeping with anyone else.

In case that one swallow does not seem to make a summer, doctors who work in VD clinics are now satisfied that the irritant disease known as non-specific urethritis can arise spontaneously in couples (often just one partner) who are sexually entirely faithful to each other. It is also generally accepted that the disease is an indicator of some kind of marital or psychological discord. The literature of psychotherapy is in fact filled with cases where the illness of a specific organ seems clearly the result of a specific psychological attitude to or association with that organ. The organ is sometimes being used as a weapon (of defence or attack), is sometimes actively being punished, or in some cases acts merely as a mute witness to the truth and the unconscious associations involved.

In the case of the boy discussed in the last chapter who developed hysterical paralysis of the legs, his parents *were* planning to 'walk away' from each other. His sacrifice of his own mobility was, by no coincidence, the means his body-mind chose to limit the parents' mobility. The Japanese girl, by developing herpes of the genitals, for the time being freed herself of the guilt of sexual intercourse. (I suspected also that at another level she was witholding sexual favours from the boyfriend to see how he would react, testing the non-sexual temperature of his involvement with her; and even, paradoxically, putting pressure on him to marry her.) Another friend of mine was separating from a girlfriend he had lived with for several years. An earlier girlfriend whom he had previously lived with for several years had committed suicide in a particularly unpleasant way. Now my friend developed a fungal infection of the scalp for which he received medical treatment. 'But it's not serious,' he insisted. 'It's only along the parting.'

Often, as I said, it is equally clear that the affected organ is being punished. The unconscious anger or despair of the patient is being directed against it. (So, once again, was the case with the Japanese girl.) This mechanism, incidentally, can be seen working openly in young children who will sometimes smack a leg that has hurt itself, or a hand that has just stolen a cake. The procedure can go as far as the death of the organ. There is a horrifying case in the literature of an initially healthy woman who became mentally ill and began developing malignancies (cancers and gangrene) in her peripheral limbs and organs, helping the process along with occasional accidents in which she lost parts of her anatomy, gradually moving in towards the centre. As each organ was removed she seemed happier for a while, but then became severely depressed, and another part would have to go. Eventually she was left minus both legs and arms, parts of her face and several internal organs. Finally she died.

The punishment or suicide effect may be a significant factor in those cases of cancer which we cannot resonably assign to environmental causes. In her book *Preventing Cancer* Dr Elizabeth Whelan estimates that up to thirty-three per cent of cancer is unaccounted for in terms of environmental factors, personal habits and heredity. This outstanding thirty-three per cent might be assignable to stress – Dr Carl Simonton in America certainly thinks so. At his clinic he takes only severe cases, for which he uses all the known methods of cancer treatment – radiation, drugs and so on. But in addition the families and friends of the patient as well as the patient have to agree to undergo forms of psychotherapy, such as the following.

> The unconventional tool I use in the treatment of cancer...is 'relaxation and mental imagery'....In regular sessions with a patient I ask the patient to practice simple muscle relaxation, focusing on breathing. Then I have him mentally picture his cancer – picturing it the way it seems to him – and the way he views the treatment, how he sees the body and the body-cells operating against the malignancy, and so on. I try to get him to produce mental descriptions of all aspects of the disease. Through these techniques the patient begins to activate his motivations to be well and to arouse emotions and problems into consciousness.

Dr Simonton has an impressive cure rate of seemingly terminal cases.

In support of his view that mind plays, or can play, a crucial role in the genesis of cancer, Simonton quotes the words of a former President of the American Cancer Society, Dr Pentegrass:

> I personally have observed cancer patients who have undergone successful treatment and were living and well for years. Then an emotional stress, such as the death of a son in World War II, the infidelity of a daughter-in-law or the burden of long employment seem to have been precipitating factors in the reactivation of their disease, which then resulted in death.

Dr Whelan herself quotes two reports from the eighteenth and nineteenth centuries respectively which show that the mind/body cancer link has long been observed.

> Mrs Emmerson, upon the Death of her Daughter, underwent great Affliction, and perceived her Breast to swell, which soon after grew painful; at last it broke out in a most inveterate Cancer, which consumed a great Part of it in a short Time. She had always enjoy'd a perfect state of health.

> The Wife of a Mate of a Ship (who was taken some Time ago by the French and put in Prison) was thereby so much affected, that her Breast began to swell, and soon after broke out in a desperate Cancer which had proceeded so far that I could not undertake her case. She never before had any complaint in her Breast.

We started here by considering the actions of hormones and the immune system as if these effects were purely mechanical, were merely aspects of blind reflex systems at some level far removed from mind. But such a view soon becomes inadequate to account for what we can observe taking place both in illness and in cure. My hope is that by the end of the chapter, previously sceptical medical personnel will come to feel that body really is also mindful, and that the logic and powers of observation and reaction that the body itself – somehow – possesses are not in any way inferior to those of a conscious, rational mind.

C. Maxwell Cade, a distinguished physicist with both medical and psychological training, has recently initiated a breakthrough which I believe will carry conviction to a great many previous doubters. Working with Geoffrey Blundell, an electronics technician, Cade has devised a display-amplifier of electrical brain patterns, which he calls the Mind Mirror. In use, the head of the subject is taped with electrodes at strategic points. These monitor the electrical waves emitted by the brain, which are then translated into visual signals and displayed on a television screen. Each cerebral hemisphere is monitored separately, but the final picture presents the two readings side by side as a single, though bilateral, image.

Several extremely important objective facts emerge. First, yogis and swamis from the east who both themselves claim to have reached, and are regarded by their followers as having reached, advanced levels of awareness, in combination with marked abilities to produce psychic healing, all show a particular brain wave pattern. This pattern, called level 5 by Cade, is quite unmistakable (see Figure 3). No one can refute the objective force of this demonstration that advanced swamis, quite independently of each other, when they put themselves into their meditational-healing state, produce a particular brain wave pattern on a machine which they previously had no idea even existed. At that point, however, a sceptic could still argue about what, if anything, the state signified – but more evidence remains.

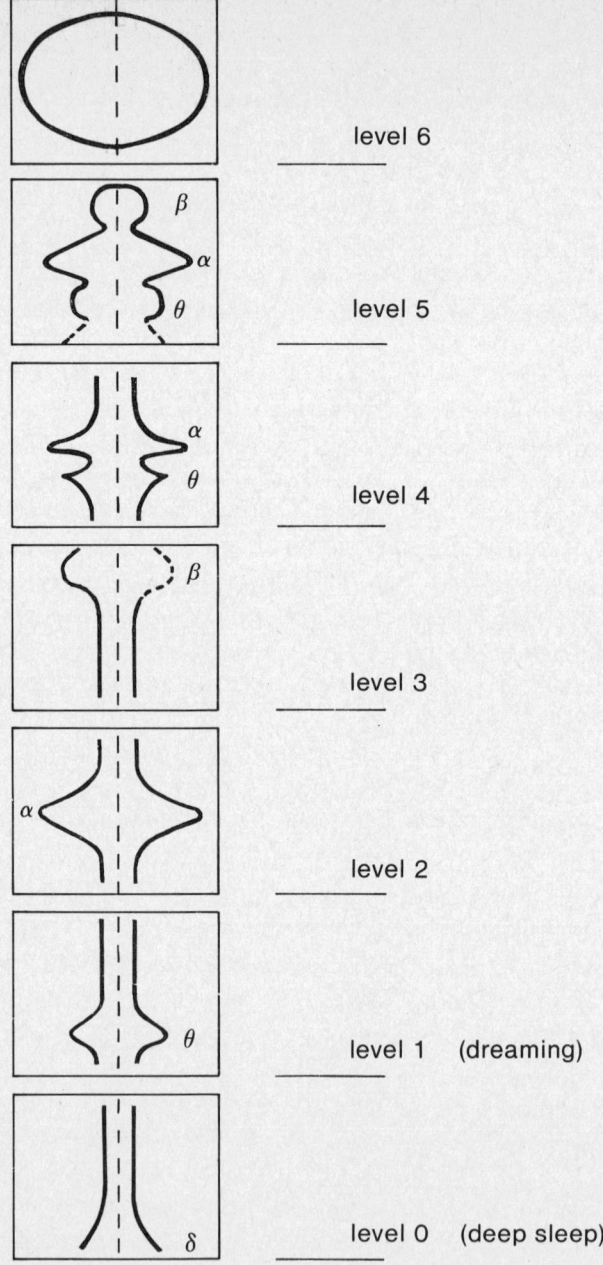

Figure 3   Simplified table of seven 'levels' of consciousness identified by Maxwell Cade's 'Mind Mirror' device (from *The Awakened Mind* by C. Maxwell Cade and Nona Coxhead).

A word, though, about 'levels'. The term 'level of consciousness' is one that Cade has adopted from mystical tradition, in which it is claimed that advanced yogis have 'ascended' the path of enlightenment to reach 'higher' levels of consciousness on their way to union with the 'all-high' or supreme consciousness. These terms are question-begging, in the sense that they imply some kind of *objective* positioning in the brain or mind, or even in the universe, whereas it is likely that the sensations (of moving upwards and so on) are purely subjective. These points will be elaborated in chapter 12. For the moment we note simply that the phrase 'differing mental states' would be much less question-begging. But we keep Cade's general use of the world 'levels' for the moment in order to present his material without unnecessary complications.

Another evidential finding by Cade and his co-workers is that as his modern students of meditation (using biofeedback devices as training aids, rather than the extended monastic training methods of traditional esoteric teaching) progress 'up' the path of development, all independently pass through the developmental stages in strict sequence. Other regular body changes, like increased electrical skin resistance, are also observed. Moreover, the purely subjective sensations reported during each stage – 'a sense of great peace' or whatever – also correlate appropriately with brain patterns.

But potentially more impressive, and potentially of very considerable help in unravelling the mysteries of the secret life, are still other circumstances. I have had to use the world 'potentially' in the last sentence, as there are one or two probably trifling weaknesses in Cade's design which must be mentioned.

Cade has found that a patient undergoing healing by a psychic healer rapidly reproduces the brain wave pattern being generated by the healer. In principle this is the fifth level pattern (or alpha-beta-theta triad, as Cade also calls it, referring to the types of electrical waves involved). Moreover, the amplitude (strength) of the pattern decreases in the healer and increases in the patient when the actual healing is occurring – reported verbally by the patient as an easing of pain, and so forth. A yet further confirming circumstance is that in cases where the healer was known to be tired or overworked, not only did no healing occur in the patient, but a reverse flow of amplitude occurred. The healer appeared to be drawing strength from the patient instead of vice versa. After these particular sessions the patients spontaneously reported not feeling any better at all.

All this material is remarkably coherent and seems to offer clear evidence of some kind of objective energy interchange between healer and patient. The design weakness, however, is that many, and perhaps all, of the subjects (the patients) used by Cade had had biofeedback training, and understood what the Mind Mirror was supposed to register. It is not clear from Cade's account whether totally naive or untrained patients were ever monitored. A hardened sceptic might argue that these trained patients were responding as expected, but quite independently of the healer, because of unconscious auto-suggestion. Although some of the patients Cade monitored at Bruce MacManaway's clinic may have been naive in the sense we are discussing, Cade does not make this completely clear.

In practice, however, we can rule out methodological error effects in Cade's experiments by reference back to those conducted by Drs Grad, Smith, Onetto and Elguin (see chapter 5), where psychic healers produced objective changes in plants, animals and enzymes. We are therefore already quite certain that some kind of objective energy flows from the healer to the healed. What Cade's work gives us is apparently a print-out record of this event for all to see. Still more than that, his methods and devices not only enable the miraculous to be seen, but allow everyone the possibility of taking part in such experiences.

The phenomena connected with the psychic Matthew Manning can now also be slotted in. Manning recently worked in America with a number of scientists in carefully monitored experiments. In one experiment he was able to kill cancer cells in a glass container by concentrating on the vessel. Numerous photographs were also taken of Manning when he claimed to be producing healing energy. One of these shows an extensive diffuse white radiance shining from his hands. When Manning directed his healing attention to someone across the room, a piece or ball of this radiance, moving across the room, appeared on film. It is true that photographs can be forged, or conjuring tricks performed to produce phoney effects, but in the context of Cade's work and the other hard evidence for the existence of healing energy (energy X) as an objective fact, we have no grounds here for suspecting trickery.

In other experiments Manning was able to quieten restless hamsters in an adjoining room, and alternatively to rouse resting hamsters to vigorous activity, simply by turning his thoughts to them. Similarly, Maxwell Cade again has shown that his healers can also produce their effects at the distance of a room or two. An important question, though, is just how far these effects can reach.

Let us turn aside for a moment to consider poltergeist phenomena. Poltergeist phenomena are disturbances in the local environment which can include furniture moving, small objects flying about in the air, objects falling from shelves and walls, and cracks and breaks appearing in likely and unlikely materials. We are as certain as we can be in view of the will-o-the-wisp nature of the events involved that these happenings always occur in the presence of one particular individual, and not in his or her absence. Such events surrounded the young Matthew Manning to a remarkable extent, and numerous independent witnesses have testified to their authenticity. It has long been my belief that poltergeist phenomena and psychic healing are closely connected, that in fact the same energy is employed in both. Making an analogy with electricity, I suggested that psychic healing is like electricity docilely and obediently lighting an electric bulb, while poltergeist phenomena are like that same electricity exploding a fuse box and setting a house on fire. Pursuing my belief, I proposed some years ago that powerful physical mediums like Matthew Manning and Jan Merta ought to be tested for healing ability. Now Manning has spontaneously turned to psychic healing full-time, with very impressive results. 'Coincidentally' the poltergeist phenomena are no longer in evidence. The theoretical position here looks like a strong one.

In earlier chapters I further suggest that 'self healing' and what I call 'self harming' might also be two sides of one coin. Both involved energy X, I proposed, but this was available only internally, being used and usable by the individual concerned only within his own body, but either for positive or negative ends. This internal use of energy X might be a function of the introverted personality type, while the psychic healing of others, and poltergeist phenomena, which are both external energies, might be a function of the extraverted personality type. Now what if, instead of speaking of 'positive' and 'negative' internal energy, we spoke again of 'controlled' and 'uncontrolled' energy? This schema would give us the following interrelationship between the energy and the general personality shown in Figure 4. (Obviously, the bottom right-hand box is taking us in the direction of what is usually called 'black magic'.)

Let us stay for a moment with the suggestion that poltergeist phenomena and psychic healing are connected. One careful investi-

	controlled or integrated energy X	uncontrolled or unintegrated energy X
introverted personality	self healing	self harming
extraverted personality	psychic healing of others	poltergeist phenomena; ?and psychic harming of others

Figure 4   Possible interrelations between energy X and personality type.

gation of a poltergeist attack, by J. G. Pratt and W. G. Roll, showed the following: that heavy objects moved less readily than light objects; and that objects nearer the individual who caused the outbreaks moved greater distances than objects further away. This in itself very normal feature of these unusual events strongly suggests that poltergeist influence, or paranormal energy of the physical kind, diminishes proportionally to the distance involved. If now Maxwell Cade and those working with Matthew Manning could show that psychic healing and the ability to quieten or disturb animals also diminishes with distance, we would have another strong parallel – and further evidence that only one form of energy is involved in these various phenomena.

But what of 'absent healing', which can allegedly work across hundreds or even thousands of miles and which we possibly saw in the case of Moyra Caldecott? What we might have here is not an indefinite extension of psychic healing energy by the healer, but something very different. The knowledge that the healer is (apparently) working on one's behalf and is (allegedly) transmitting energy possibly triggers one's own internal healing powers, just as hypnotism often triggers it, and as (perhaps) Lourdes triggered Marie Bailly's.

We have by no means finished with the triggering of internal energy. It arises again in connection with the first of two remaining aspects of biochemistry, placebos and hallucinogenic drugs.

The word 'placebo' in Latin means 'I shall please'. It is the name given by doctors to the well-known effect that if you believe a medicine will do you good, or cure a particular condition, it probably will, even if the 'medicine' is actually just a piece of bran or a bottle of coloured water. Such a placebo relieves pain in about forty per cent of cases as efficiently as morphine. Even thirty-five per cent of cancer patients experience relief from pain simply from placebos. An endless list of factors can add to or diminish the placebo effect: the colour of the alleged medication, whether it tastes bitter or sweet, whether one has been told that it is powerful or weak, and so on. But the main effect of a placebo derives from the fact that it comes from a highly respected source, usually a hospital or a doctor. There is no doubt that many of the cures of witch doctors and medicine men are due to placebo effects.

Some of these effects can be demonstrated in animals also. If rats or mice who have been injected a few times with a genuinely tranquillizing drug are then injected with salt solution, the tranquillizing effect still occurs. Such experiments clearly demonstrate that some level of the rat's nervous system has recorded all details of the original experience. Now any repeat of part of the experiment – specifically, the injection with a liquid – causes the nervous system to re-institute all the associated effects. We are nudging here something like the spontaneous regeneration of old wounds shown by Dr Moody's patients (see chapter 4).

The medical profession is in no doubt about the genuineness of the placebo effect. It bedevils all attempts to test the objective properties of drugs and medicines. There is probably no hospital in Britain that is not currently treating a random sample of its patients just with placebos. The medical profession frankly admits itself at a loss to explain the placebo effect. And because these matters are very widely publicized, medical personnel sceptical of some of the other matters presented in this book can begin their conversion by reflecting on placebos. No member of the profession can or will reproach them for that.

Our last instance of biochemistry as mind (and, naturally, vice versa) concerns the so-called hallucinogenic drugs. Of these, there can hardly be anyone who has not at least heard of marijuana, heroin and LSD. These substances induce strong and colourful visions, often of an ecstatic nature and not infrequently of a general religious nature. So much is this last point true that one religious group in the United States uses marijuana as its sacrament, and so far has managed to avoid arrest and prosecution for the otherwise illegal use of marijuana. Many Middle Eastern, Eastern and South American peoples have used and in some cases still do use the 'magic mushroom' in order to experience religious enlightenment and contact with the gods.

Just in passing we should note that visions and hallucinations can be produced also in a variety of other ways – by alcoholism, starvation, sensory deprivation, mental breakdown, hormone imbalance, sniffing glue and so on. For our present purposes, however, we shall take these as read.

At first many religionists tried to deny that drug-induced visions had anything to do with 'genuine' religious vision. But they were on a losing wicket, and it is now generally accepted that hallucinogenic and religious visions are closely related. The religious vision or enlightenment is now defended rather differently, and not altogether unacceptably. Taking drugs, it is said, is rather like reading the last few pages of a book without reading the rest. You know how it ends, but you don't know how the characters have developed, or what experiences brought them to the decisions they have now made. Or it is like taking a closed cable car to the top of a mountain, instead of climbing the path. It is the same top of the mountain in both cases, and it is the same view. But the slow climber has benefited from all kinds of interim experiences. He knows the nature of the mountain and he has seen the view gradually develop. Or, more prosaically, it is like trying to go from bottom gear to top gear in a car (or from top down to bottom) without shifting gradually through the intervening gears. Only a fool would think the two procedures were the same, and that no damage has been done to the engine.

This is all fair enough. Also, the swamis who cooperated with Maxwell Cade could summon up the various mental 'levels' at will, and could maintain them while engaging in the affairs of this world – debates, healing sessions or whatever. The drug user, however, cannot summon up his visions at will without the drug. On the contrary, he or she becomes increasingly dependent on ever stronger doses of the hallucinogen; and the ability to handle the affairs of the world while 'under the influence' is very severely impaired. Nor can a drug user even predict in advance what kind of altered state he will find himself in. He can never know whether he will have a good or a bad trip. But the swami does know.

Yet while agreeing all these differences, we must not lose sight of the basic truth which the drug experience teaches. It is that religious visions, like those also of madness and deprivation, are produced by changes in the internal chemistry of our bodies. In that sense, religious visions *are* the biochemical changes. So the Kingdom of God *is* within us.

Summary

What we understand from this chapter is that the body, apart from being an energy system itself anyway, also possesses a kind of energy service system. The basic energy of this service system seems to be energy X. Observation suggests that energy X can be poured into the normal immune/maintenance system – which, left to its own devices, routinely functions at a level typical for the individual concerned, retailing the defence mechanisms and stratagems which evolution has bred into the human organism. But energy X can, first of all, galvanize the whole immune/maintenance system to work more vigorously and efficiently. This is what seems to happen when a psychic healer gives healing to a patient. The laying-on of hands is really like using jump leads between two cars, one of which has a flat battery and one of which hasn't. The jump leads enable the second car to be started by the first.

But some people at least, and even very, very sick people, can generate a great flood of energy X from within themselves. (They do it not only under hypnosis, but under a wide variety of other stimuli. The treatment known as acupuncture is one of them.) This internal flood of energy seems to produce the same kind of effects as those which the psychic healer brings about.

Yet these already remarkable statements are only the least part of the story. The really astonishing part of the story is in the specificness of the reaction. When the boy with rhinoceros skin was told to clear his left arm, this was all that happened. If some general immune response had been triggered (via the bloodstream or whatever) then the illness would have retreated all over the body. How does the body understand and say to itself – say to its cells and its molecules – 'OK, lads, just the left arm this time, if you will, and look sharp about it'? And what of the woman who can produce blisters to order on any part of her body, where they have never been before?

With this we are into 'self harming', where the business is more daunting than ever. It is one thing to think of an immune – i.e. a healing and protecting system – being galvanized into increased action, but how on earth or in heaven or anywhere else do you instruct such a system to produce damage? How does the system respond to the order: 'OK, lads, I want gangrenous sores to form under this woman's wedding ring, so that she is forced not to wear it' (an actual case on record)? And last of all, how does all this take place when no such conscious instruction has ever been issued? The woman we just spoke of had a very unhappy marriage, but her training and religion forbade her to even contemplate divorce. Yet some part of her, some inner system to whom a nod is as good as a wink, said to itself: 'OK, lads, wedding ring off'.

With the range and type of example we have had so far both in this chapter and throughout the book, we are obliged to accept not just that the body is – or possesses – an incredibly sensitive and localized monitoring system (capable of both positive and negative flow, of both construction and destruction), but that it has also a thinking, self-governing, responsive, forward-planning, record-keeping, wish-fulfilling, curse-fulfilling, independent existence of its own, in any way you care to define those terms. What we are talking of here is, I think, the ka of Ancient Egypt, the semi-immortal soul, the etheric double, the astral body, the subtle anatomy. Does it survive our own death? Yes, perhaps. After all, the stowaway in the jet undercarriage was supposed to be dead. The boy who spent three hours under water should have been dead. Marie Bailly was almost dead when she reached Lourdes. But some part of her was very much alive. And when it snapped its fingers – in response to what precise cue we do not know – she too was alive again.

7 The planetary aspects of astrology

During the last twenty years an amazing event has taken place. In terms of its shattering effect on the orthodox scientific community it is equalled only by recent developments in dowsing, which we look at in chapter 9. The 'amazing event' is the result of one man's monumental efforts. That man is French psychologist and statistician Michel Gauquelin. What he and his later co-workers have shown, in absolutely objective scientific terms, and beyond any shadow of doubt whatsoever, is that the precise position of the planets of the solar system in relation to our planet Earth at the time of an individual's birth is an extremely significant indicator of later outstanding professional achievement. This is such a totally unnerving idea for westerners brought up in the belief that 'astrology is rubbish' that we need to approach it cautiously.

Gauquelin's findings and precise details of his methods have been published in a series of scientific papers and monographs from the late nineteen fifties onwards, and also in several books written for the general reader (these include *Astrology and Science, The Cosmic Clocks, Cosmic Influences on Human Behaviour* and *The Spheres of Destiny*). Gauquelin's revolutionary evidence quickly aroused the at first mainly hostile interest of other scientists, but the involvement of these other scientists (such as Hans Eysenck in Britain) has simply confirmed and extended the work. Notably the traditionally very sceptical Belgian Committee for the Scientific Study of Paranormal Phenomena (a body made up of leading scientists) undertook the independent duplication of Gauquelin's findings. To everyone's astonishment, not least that of the scientists involved, the committee's independent research produced findings precisely in parallel with Gauquelin's own.

The accuracy and authenticity of the work we are now discussing is beyond question. It now forms part of the established body of scientific knowledge – which, alas, is not quite the same as saying that scientists everywhere have incorporated it into their thinking.

A very brief survey and sample of Gauquelin's results is as follows. First Gauquelin combed standard reference works like *Who's Who* in order to produce lists of many thousands of actors, soldiers, doctors, writers, sportsmen, scientists and other professionals whom the community considered to be of outstanding excellence or fame in their particular profession. This was an objective criterion: Gauquelin himself did not say who was or was not famous. He allowed standard reference books to do that for him. As a control group he now made lists of thousands of *non*-famous actors, soldiers, writers and so on. These were working members of the profession concerned. But, though competent, they were not noted for outstanding work. Now Gauquelin compared the position of a number of planets at the time of birth of every individual in the study.

Seen from Earth, every planet has its own 'day' just like the Sun. The planet rises, reaches a peak, sets, and passes below us to rise again next 'day'. Gauquelin divided the planetary cycle into twelve equal sections. But in practice he found only four points equidistant from each other on the full circle to be important: the point of rising above Earth's horizon; the high point of upper culmination; the point of setting below Earth's horizon; and the point of lowest culmination below the Earth. For the sake of simplicity, we shall call these points 1, 2, 3 and 4.

In the case of the control groups – the non-famous scientists, doctors, politicians and so on – the position of each particular planet at the time of birth proved to be random. It could and did occur absolutely anywhere in the twelve sections of the original scale. But in the case of the famous, the planet was found at two of the four points described (points 1 and 2) enormously more often than chance allows – at odds as high as five million to one.

In summary, then, Saturn (at points 1 and 2) is found to be a highly significant planet for doctors and scientists; Mars for sportsmen and soldiers; Jupiter for actors and soldiers; Venus for writers; and the Moon for writers and politicians. There is an equally consistent negative aspect to the findings. The Moon, for example, tends to be found significantly less often at points 1 and 2 among famous sportsmen and soldiers. Saturn is found significantly less often at points 1 and 2 for notable actors and writers.

Further analysis of the original data has yielded additional supportive evidence – and resolved one or two apparent anomalies. As an example of anomaly, Jupiter, as well as being significant at points 1 and 2 for actors and soldiers, is also significant at those points for writers. Yet the Moon, which is highly significant at points 1 and 2 for writers, is only negatively significant for soldiers.

Various refinements were suggested to Gauquelin. For instance, in their biological profiles in the standard reference works some scientists were described as shy and retiring, while others were said to be aggressive, courageous, sociable and so on. Would it be possible to divide scientists into two groups, introverted and extraverted? This was done. It was now found that Saturn is observed significantly more often at points 1 and 2 in the case of extraverted scientists, and significantly less often at those points for introverted scientists. (For introverted scientists the significant positive positions of Saturn are points 3 and 4 which, as one might expect, are also positions of negative significance for the extraverts.) Here, incidentally, is one more independent validation of the concepts of introversion and extraversion, discussed in the last chapter.

It was also proposed to Gauquelin that there were exhibitionist, highly social actors but also a (perhaps smaller) group of shy, modest actors. When these traits were isolated and tested, it was found that exhibitionist actors were born twice as often as shy actors when Jupiter was at points 1 and 2. A similar result was also achieved in respect of Mars and strong-willed versus weak-willed champions. Mars is present at position 1 for only 33 per cent of all run-of-the-mill sportsmen. It is found at position 1 for 64 per cent of strong-willed champions – but for only 29 per cent of weak-willed champions. What these detailed analyses show is that it is personality as much as profession which the planet dictates. If we combine the two factors, personality-type and chosen profession, the predictive basis is now more reliable still than for profession alone.

We must come to the question of how the planets could possibly be responsible for these observed effects. But first two other surprises.

Gauquelin has so far found no significant effects whatsoever for the Sun, Mercury, Uranus, Neptune or Pluto. However, Gauquelin has not yet by any means studied all the professions. The influence of these other heavenly bodies may show up in later studies. The effect of Venus for writers, for example, has only recently been established. But if no influence should be forthcoming long-term for these other heavenly bodies, that is going to make very hard work indeed for any attempt at explanation of the planetary effects already established.

But perhaps the really major surprise in all this, beating the effect itself by a short head, is that the effects or character traits Gauquelin has derived in respect of the planets we have been looking at very closely parallels the traits assigned to them by ancient peoples. Here are a few examples, taken from Geoffrey Dean's massive reference work *Recent Advances in Natal Astrology 1900-1976* (a text absolutely indispensable to anyone seriously interested in astrology):

	Traditional values	Values empirically derived by Gauquelin
Mars	aggression	aggressive
	courage	courageous
	energy	energetic
	impulsiveness	reckless
Jupiter	cheerful	happy
	generosity	prodigal
	joviality	good humoured
	nobility	authoritarian
Saturn	cautious	reserved
	self-restraint	modest
	steadfastness	conscientious
	taciturnity	silent

So we find ourselves squarely back in the business of praising the achievements of the ancients. Gauquelin's work has involved the careful sifting and observing of tens of thousands of cases, as well as complex analysis of acres of astronomical tables. Clearly, the ancients also either managed to perform this operation successfully or had some more intuitive, but equally impressive method of their own

At all events, we are faced with explaining what is in logical terms an altogether unnerving position. A planet that can only be seen with difficulty against the backdrop of stars – even if you know where to look – rises, reaches its culmination, and sets. And in the course of so doing it determines complex psychological qualities in babies undergoing birth, leading to clear-cut behaviour (in fact to very obvious and very remarkable behaviour) that persists throughout life. But then again, only in some babies.

Presumably we can rule out as a factor the light waves emanating from the planet, since these are insignificant and unable to pierce even slightly overcast skies (though see p. 91). That leaves us with a magnetic or gravitational effect – an incredibly slight one again, although in this respect the material of chapter 9 is encouraging. So perhaps, then, magnetic or gravitational impulses trigger the release of a hormone or hormones in the baby (as well as by the baby in the mother, since it looks too as if the planet induces the birth itself). These then have a persistent effect on motivation, perhaps even on intelligence. But why does the planet have this effect only when it is at the horizon or when it is at its maximum height above the horizon, but not in between? And why only on some babies? And why is this effect neither a necessary nor a *sufficient* cause – which means, why is it possible to become a champion sportsman without the help of Mars, and fail to become one even with its help?

Is perhaps the position of a particular planet the accidental accompanying factor of some other real cause? For instance, the summer flooding of the Nile which brought life and wealth to Ancient Egypt was the result of the spring melting of the snow in high mountains thousands of miles away. But the Egyptians, in their ignorance, looked for and found other 'causes'. During a thousand years or more the first annual dawn rising of Sirius, the brightest star in the sky, occurred just before the flooding. The Egyptians thought the rising of this star triggered the flood and worshipped it accordingly.

Is some similar effect operating in respect of the 1 and 2 positions of certain of the planets? Is the real effect perhaps back in time, nine months earlier, at the moment of conception? It is an attractive idea, particularly if we imagine, say, the Moon to be involved at that point. The Moon is after all very closely concerned with the female menstrual cycle, as we shall see.

The otherwise excellent *Recent Advances in Natal Astrology* claims it is difficult to calculate the moment of conception, but this is not the case. The length of a normal human pregnancy is know to be rather precisely 9×29.53059 days. The second figure is the length of one lunation, that is, one complete cycle of the Moon. The events taking place in the sky at the moment of birth may show a spurious correlation with the events in the sky of nine months earlier, just as the rising of Sirius seemed to cause the flooding of the Nile simply because it coincided with that event. (Anyone who has studied statistics, however, has the phrase engraved on his heart: correlation is not cause.) Maybe it is the events in the sky at the moment of conception that tell the real story, and perhaps they do away with the puzzles we find when we study the sky at birth. Perhaps the Moon, in particular, has the secret to it all.

So the question to Michel Gauquelin, Geoffrey Dean and their colleagues is this: where was the Moon and what was it doing 9×29.53059 days before, in the place where the husband and wife were living or, of course, staying at that moment? Or still better: what were the Moon, the Sun and all the planets doing – because we must not exclusively favour the Moon in advance of any facts. Yet certainly the importance of the Moon, nor just in connection with the human female ovulation-menstruation cycle, but in connection with the very evolution of mankind, cannot be overestimated.

It is absolutely clear that what first caused the apes to come into existence (and we are one of the apes) out of the ranks of the monkeys was the development by the female apes of a physiological response to the cycles of the Moon. The evidence for this altogether remarkable event is indisputable. The length of the menstruation cycle of all female apes, humans included, is very close to the length of one lunation (the progress of the Moon from zero through all its phases and back to zero again). As we have already seen, one lunation lasts 29.53059 days.

Here is the average menstruation cycle, in days, of the various ape species: Gorilla, 30.5 days; Orang-utan, 30.5 days; Gibbon, 30 days; Human, 28 days; Chimpanzee, 36.5 days. Some typical menstruation cycles in monkeys, however, are: Saimiri, 10 days; Capuchin, 18 days; Howler, 23 days.

In modern woman the menstrual cycle is often seriously distorted. But numerous studies have now shown (see for instance Louise Lacey's book *Lunaception*) that the human female cycle can be regularized to a 29 day cycle (the figure of 28 days given just now is an average value of an event that in most modern women swings wildly on either side of that mark) if the woman concerned will keep an electric light bulb burning in an open cupboard in the bedroom, while she sleeps, during the fourteenth to the seventeenth nights of her own cycle.

It is clear that the bedroom light is functioning as the Moon, from whose light civilized man has for so long been cut off. Our distant ancestors, of course, evolved in tropical climates where clear night skies were the firm rule, and they slept in the open in trees as do chimps, orangs and gibbons to this day. As for human females, it has been observed that women who live together tend to menstruate together, and this is particularly true where the bedroom light normalizing procedure has been followed. Can it be that all the women of each individual tribe once menstruated in unison? It seems a strong possibility. The totality of these circumstances would be a very fruitful basis for the evolution of a Moon religion. As we have already noted, 'Moon' happens to be the same word as 'mother'.

This chapter has dealt with many matters on which the last word cannot be said. But all in all the planetary teachings of ancient astrology, whatever the full explanation behind them may prove to be, are further potent examples of the body with a mind of its own.

The stellar aspects of astrology, however, are a very different matter.

8 Bashevis Singer and paranormal fire

Henne Fire is the title of a story by Isaac Bashevis Singer. Here is how the story ends:

> Finally they broke the door open and what they saw should never be seen again. Some time before Henne had bought an upholstered chair from a widow. It was an old piece of furniture. She used to sit in it drinking and babbling to herself. When they got the door open, sitting in the chair was a skeleton as black as coal....The chair itself was almost intact, only the material at the back was singed....Nor had the linen on the bed caught fire... everything was undamaged....'It's impossible,' the doctor replied. 'If someone were to tell me such a thing, I would call him a filthy liar.'

Singer's story concerns a case of the 'spontaneous combustion' or 'auto-oxidation' of a human being by means unknown. Two other well-known writers, Captain Marryat and Charles Dickens, relate similar stories. Are these accounts purely fictional, or where did the writers derive their inspiration? It seems they derived it from real life.

Michael Harrison has written a book, *Fire From Heaven,* about a large number of authenticated cases of this astonishing phenomenon. There are in all several hundred on record. A number date from the last few decades, so it is not a matter of a once observed phenomenon that is no longer observed today (and therefore unlike, say, the one-time alleged production by mediums of the substance called ectoplasm). What will perhaps carry most weight with many people are the official photographs taken of the remains, which were the subject of coroner's inquests. There are three such photographs in Michael Harrison's book, one dating from 1958 and another from 1963, although the third is taken from the *British Medical Journal* of 1888. Francis Hitching's book *World Atlas of Mysteries* has a fourth, taken in 1966.

The phenomenon seems remarkably consistent, widespread and well-documented. The fact that the general public, and especially the well-educated general public, hears so little of it seems to be yet another tribute to the blanket censorship of all matters relating to our secret lives by establishment organizations. The events of spontaneous combustion do at first sight seem wider than anything we have so far examined, but at second look they relate rather meaningfully to items we have already clearly identified.

What occurs in these cases of spontaneous combustion, or auto-oxidation, is that the victim suddenly finds him or herself on fire. But it is not one's clothing that is burning. It is oneself. The occasional eyewitness accounts of the event say that burning begins at a specific point on or in the body, and then rapidly spreads throughout.

Phyllis Newcombe was waltzing in a public ballroom. Suddenly she glowed with blue flames and, while the other dancers looked on in horror, was 'within minutes a blackened mass of ash'. Father Bertholi, a cleric, was heard to scream in sudden agony. He was found enveloped in blue flames, which the others succeeded in beating out with their coats and hands. The examining surgeon found that part of one arm had been totally consumed and that there were extensive burns on the re-mainder of the body. The wounds rapidly mortified, and were accom-panied by extreme thirst. Father Bertholi died a few days later. A professor of mathematics, Professor H, felt a sharp pain in his left leg. He looked down and saw a bright flame several inches in length sprouting from his trousered leg, rather like a lighted gas jet. He slapped at it and then cupped his hands around the flame to keep oxygen from it. At this, it went out. Doctors who subsequently examined the professor confirmed unusual features of the wound which remained, including its extreme dryness.

There are two very consistent features of the cases: (1) Little or no damage is done to immediately adjacent combustibles such as clothing, bed-clothing, paper, wood, furnishings or whatever. Almost never, as far as one can tell, does the occurrence result in any kind of general fire. (2) The body is almost totally consumed, apart from extremities like the hands, feet and skull, and sometimes the skeleton. Nevertheless, any remaining bones are reduced and dry. Of the flesh and organs, all that is left is a small residue of grease and ash.

As in Singer's story, the circumstances of the scene defy all known logic. Thus Mrs Johnson of Sydenham in London was found, having just returned from the local shops, as a pile of calcinated bones inside her unburned clothing. Actual clothing is, in fact, fairly often burned or scorched. But other adjacent combustibles are as a very firm rule left intact, often not even showing scorch marks.

The victim is often an isolated and lonely individual, frequently given to solitary drinking. From these circumstances, as well as from direct reporting, we can deduce that a majority of these people were suffering from depression. And, indeed, there are two cases of individuals bursting into flames while in the act of committing suicide.

Mr G. B. Denney (in 1952) had cut his arteries in the kitchen, for there was much blood. But when found he was burning on the bedroom floor. As is standard in these cases, no other object in the flat was burned in any way – nor, although the coroner ruled that the man had set light to himself, were any matches or any liquid combustibles found. Quite how a man with cut arteries, burning from head to foot, could manage to dispose of such alleged items was never explained. B. T. Peterson had connected a hose pipe to the exhaust of his car, and was seated in the car in his garage going through the classic carbon-monoxide method of suicide. But before he died he became a victim of spontaneous combustion, which charred parts of his body to a crisp, while leaving his clothes undamaged.

Most of the victims of spontaneous combustion are women. This is a most interesting observation, particularly when we consider that more women than men suffer from hysteria and neurosis, that more women than men are mediums, and have more spontaneous psychic experiences than men, dream more than men, and so on. Very, very few of the victims, throughout history to the present day, have been of a social class higher than lower middle class. One is reminded here that most of those individuals reported by Drs Sollier and Comar as being able to produce autoscopy (see chapter 5) were simple and uneducated, i.e. from the working classes. In this general connection it has long been my own view that Neanderthal qualities and characteristics are concentrated in the lower urban classes and agricultural workers (or what used to be called peasants).

Instead of being extinguished by water, the flames of spontaneous combustion are actually encouraged by it. Writing in 1838 in their book *Elements of Medical Jurisprudence,* T. R. and J. B. Beck state the 'well-known fact' that water, far from extinguishing the fire of spontaneous combustion, 'aggravates it'.

Sleep appears to be a predisposng factor in the onset of human auto-oxidation. In a majority of cases the victims were either known to have been asleep or can reasonably be inferred to have been. Many were certainly also drunk or tipsy, or, like the two suicides mentioned, in some kind of dissociated state. This general circumstance of dissociation, along with much else already mentioned, dovetails well with some of the observations made in earlier chapters.

At this point we can now make some rather incisive proposals about the true nature of spontaneous combustion. But first one other possibly associated matter. It has been observed that certain otherwise normal individuals give out a luminosity in the dark. G. M. Gould and W. L. Pyle mention two cases in their book *Anomalies and Curiosities of Medicine* (published 1937). An asthma patient in hospital in Italy produced a flickering bluish glow around her breasts while she slept at night. This emanation was visible for several seconds at a time, and was accompanied also by an increased pulse rate and profuse sweating. Another woman patient, in America, suffering from cancer of the breast, produced such a powerful glow from her chest that a watch could be read by its light. These two reports are authenticated by doctors and other officials, but there are similar cases on more informal record. In one, the body of a recently dead young boy was observed to be glowing with a blue light. This particular emanation actually scorched the sheet on which the body was lying.

The following proposals seem to meet at least some of the observed facts of auto-oxidation.

The body, whatever else it may be, is a complex electromagnetic energy system, as the next chapter most vividly shows. Apart from its solid constituents, the human body is composed of seventy per cent water. That means that a one hundred and fifty pound man comprises one hundred and five pounds of water. Water itself is a compound of two elemental gases, hydrogen and oxygen. If an electric current is passed through water, in the common-place procedure known as electrolysis, it splits back into its two gaseous components, hydrogen and oxygen. When together these two gases provide a mixture that is not merely inflammable but explosive. How would it be if some freak of electricity (whether internally or externally generated) set the process of water electrolysis in motion within the body? And supposing this process was somehow contained by the body's own electromagnetic field (that is, by the etheric or subtle body, which may well persist for a time after the body itself is dead). We can then think in terms of a rapid, contained chain reaction (A. Devergie, a French medico-legal writer describes the onset of auto-oxidation as 'a bluish flame seen to extend itself little by little, with an extreme rapidity, over all the parts of the body affected') which is nevertheless shielded from normal contact with adjacent inflammable materials by the body's electromagnetic field.

Electrolysis of the body's seventy per cent water would leave behind most of the body's solids (some thirty percent of normal body weight) as a dehydrated deposit, including the body's fat minus its water (fat being only about fifteen per cent water). Now we seem to have all the traditional features of the case: the extremely dry remains (let us also not forget the unusual dryness of Professor H's wound, and the great thirst of Father Bertholi) admixed with a greasy residue. Electrolysis, plus combustion, also accounts for the bluish flame. And the process would generate enormous heat, which in fact is also in evidence in many cases. Sometimes nearby plastic and metal objects have melted – though, as continually emphasized, there is almost never combustion.

In a few cases the heat or other energy involved has 'burnt' a hole right through the floor immediately under the remains, so that the ash of the body has trickled to a small, neat pyramid on the floor below, but the floor and wooden floor-boards in which the hole has appeared have not caught fire, as they certainly would have done in any normal circumstances. In the precise kinds of circumstance we have just been considering, the auto-oxidation occurrence seems less wild and improbable than it appeared at first. The bluish flame, the extreme dryness, the greasy residue – all can make sense in the context of the controlled electrolysis of body water.

We could go on picking up such cues almost indefinitely. The bones, where these survive the catastrophe, are dry and shrivelled. In one well-authenticated case the skull itself was considerably shrunken (a woman's skull reduced 'to the size of a baseball'). Bone contains 32 per cent water. Removal of that water, plus the general cell collapse in the heat, could produce this observed result. And when, conversely, water is thrown on a combusting victim, it 'aggravates' the situation. That might be because some of the water is drawn into the process of electrolysis, so adding fuel. Or it might simply be because water is an excellent conductor of electricity. This added free water might perhaps allow the electrolytic process to proceed more rapidly, body water of course being locked in body cells and not so readily available.

What exactly causes the spontaneous combustion process to begin? Is this, perhaps, an extreme case of self harming? It is, perhaps, a kind of 'inner poltergeist' attack, the ultimate *inward* version of that ultimate *outer* phenomenon (see Figure 4 in chapter 6). Interestingly enough, outward poltergeist attacks can affect electrical fittings. Lights may flicker or fuse, for example. In the famous Rosenheim case in Germany, apart from more usual phenomena, lights continually exploded, and the office telephone monitoring system in the building where Anne-Marie Schaberl, the girl concerned, worked began registering calls that were never made. 'Someone' was dialling the speaking clock for hours on end. A specially installed voltmeter registered inexplicable surges of current in the building's whole electrical system.

Or perhaps the 'inner poltergeist' attracts electromagnetic energy from the atmosphere or some conventional source of electricity, and this added element then triggers the inner combustion. There are a number of cases on record of mediums and deeply religious evangelists attracting (or generating) balls of St Elmo's fire (we even call that poorly-understood electrical phenomenon after a saint) and other kinds of spontaneous flashes and lights. The Welsh evangelist Mary Jones is a well-known instance. Balls of fire or lightning were frequently seen above or near churches where she was preaching.

In all this, too, have we some kind of explanation for the Shroud of Turin? As most people know, this piece of undoubtedly ancient cloth bears the detailed likeness of a man burnt or radiated into it, in a way conventional science can neither explain nor duplicate. The image appears to be a likeness of the dead body of Christ. In his book *The Turin Shroud* Ian Wilson emphasizes that other shrouds bearing the rather less well-defined likenesses of saints and martyrs have been reliably reported. Presumably these shrouds have not survived into the present, although Wilson is vague on that point. But no matter, for we have, for instance, the case of the corpse of the young boy, whose body 'scorched' the sheet on which it was laid (p. 95).

In the case of an exceptionally powerful psychic and healer like Christ we can certainly postulate an extremely powerful body-mind (i.e. ka or etheric double). Persisting for a time after normal bodily death, as the subtle body may well do, and being at least electro-magnetic in its properties, could it not impress itself on a winding sheet? This seems a not unreasonable hypothesis, and, what is more, one that echoes and dovetails well with much other strange evidence concerning the body-mind we have so far collected.

Would it be possible to persuade powerful psychics living at this moment to attempt to impress their own image on a winding sheet after their death? It would be a famous experiment.

9 The magnetic body

Individuals who can paranormally locate underground water, minerals and a variety of other items, with or without the use of a divining rod, have existed throughout the ages. They are usually called dowsers or diviners. There are many, many testimonies to their powers and a number of first class diviners are alive and practising today. The diviner usually claims that he (or she) senses some kind or emission or ray from the underground object or material he is seeking. And in recent decades serious scientific attempts have been made to identify what rays or radiation, if any, the diviner and dowser are responding to. An obvious suspect in the search was magnetism.

In the 1950s the development of the proton magnetometer enabled very faint magnetic fields to be measured very precisely. Yves Rocard, Professor of Physics at the Ecole Normale in Paris, reported that some of the individuals he had studied could detect almost unbelievably minute changes in local magnetic fields. The report was greeted with incredulity by most scientists. But then from 1968 onwards Dr Zaboj Harvalik, for twenty-five years Professor of Physics at Arkansas University, began demonstrating that Rocard had in fact grossly *under*estimated the sensitivity of his human subjects.

The Earth itself is a gigantic although not powerful magnet. Its magnetism arises from the flow and movement of the liquid materials that make up the Earth's core. The strength of this Earth-magnet varies from 0.3 of a gauss to 1.5 gauss – a gauss being a unit of measurement of magnetism – and is usually described as having an average strength of 0.5, or half a gauss. We gain some idea of the weakness of the Earth-magnet by realizing that an ordinary child's magnet has a strength of one thousand gauss.

And yet, thanks to the work of Rocard and Harvalik, we now know that certain human beings can sense changes in a magnetic field of 1/1,000,000,000 of a gauss; in words, one one thousand millionth of a gauss. No wonder many orthodox scientists registered outrage, astonishment and despair at this news (depending on their various temperaments). About five per cent of the population, apparently, can detect changes of one millionth of a gauss. One man has been discovered, a German dowser named Wilhelm de Boer, who was still detecting changes when the instruments stopped being able to monitor him. He had beaten the most sensitive instrument so far devised. But in fact de Boer must share his record with any number of animals and plants. These incredible levels of sensitivity to magnetism are widespread thoughout the life-forms of our planet and probably universal.

A major breakthrough on the animal front came in 1975, when Richard Blakemore, who was studying sea bacteria, realized that the microscopic organisms he was examining in a drop of water were orienting themselves by reference to magnetic fields. He then discovered that each of these creatures contains a minute string of magnetite beads. (So once again that material worshipped worldwide by 'superstitious' ancient peoples forces itself on our consciousness.) At about the same time as Blackmore's discovery, other workers were discovering that the heads of homing pigeons contain 'tiny unit magnets of magnetite' on the inner side of the skull. It had been known for some time that homing pigeons could be rendered helpless by tying a tiny bar magnet to their heads. Here now was the final proof that homing pigeons navigate by a literal, internal magnetite compass.

Nor is this magnetic sensitivity of the bird simply one of north-south directionalism. The homing pigeon senses nothing less than a grid-map of the Earth's magnetic field. By reference to this grid-map it knows exactly where it is on the globe, and which way it must head for home.

Discoveries on this general front are piling in thick and fast. Honey-bees are now known to contain large numbers of 'superparamagnetic crystals of magnetite'. Writing in *Science* magazine, C. Walcott, J. Gould and J. Kirschvink also tell us that 'many organic molecules are weakly paramagnetic'. From the study and isolation of various chains and groups of beads of magnetite, meghemite, haematite, as well as paramagnetic compounds comes the final confirmation of work begun by pioneers like Frank Brown in America, and Alexandr Presman in Russia, that probably all organisms in the world – oysters, beans, snails, sharks, rays, tulips – are sensitive to local and general magnetic fields. The fields 'talk' to organisms continuously.

Frank Brown had shown in the 1950s that the humble potato, shut in darkness in experimental rooms, was precisely aware of and responded to the passage of the Moon. This in one sense prosaic demonstration was in another sense even more unearthly than the proof that fiddler crabs kept in total darkness showed two periods of activity per day, which exactly coincided with the twice-daily low tides at their place of capture. This point is when the crab can best scavenge for food. The Moon, it seems, 'imprints' the new-born fiddler crab magnetically with a tide timetable appropriate to its specific location.

The Earth's magnetic field goes through a continuous inter-weaving pattern of regular daily fluctuations in intensity, regular monthly fluctuations, and a regular winter-summer cycle. These changes are in addition to the varying intensities of field at different parts of the Earth's surface. Organisms refer to this vast and complex timetable for a wide range of information – position on the globe, depth below water, height above sea-level, time of day, time of year, the movements of the tides, the imminence of bad weather, earthquakes, and heaven knows what else. They, and we, are always riding this field.

A young, growing plant, photographed by a time-lapse camera, is seen to move upwards with a constant spiralling movement, which takes the head of the plant through a full circle every twenty-four hours. One might once have supposed the plant to be simply following the moving light of the sun, except this would not explain its completing the circle at night. Now it seems that the plant is responding to the daily magnetic cycle.

We have time-lapse cameras, the ancients did not. But did some of the ancients sit in day-long contemplation of the growing plant (perhaps the origin of the in some ways pointless contemplation by mystics now of a mental rose or a mental lotus), and did they thus observe the 'mystic spiral' of growing vegetative life, and enshrine this in their religious descriptions of the universe?

As already more than implied, the Earth's magnetic field is in no way insulated from the rest of the solar system. In fact the rhythms of the Earth's field are in large part cosmically, not locally, determined. The Moon's influence has already been mentioned, but the Sun pours out a continuous although fluctuating wind of electrically charged particles. When severe, as during sun-spot activity on the Sun, this virtual storm buffets the Earth; and the Northern Lights glow more vividly in visual answering response. All organisms are affected by these solar events, human beings no less than others. Mental breakdown, as calculated by rates of admission to mental hospitals, is more frequent during times of high sun-spot activity than when the Sun is quiet.

In this context we can now see that the idea of a distant planet like Jupiter or Saturn or Mars triggering a specific response in a human embryo, or a human egg, is not something absolutely to choke upon. Abruptly, this idea is no longer preposterous. It is not even unreasonable.

What part or parts of the human body respond to magnetic influence, and how exactly? This is not an easy question to answer, because we can never wholly insulate or shield against magnetism, as we can against electricity. The best we can manage is to shield parts of the dowser's anatomy substantially from magnetic influence, to see how this step affects his sensitivity and accuracy. Such experiments produce two apparent results. Zaboj Karvalik reports that some dowsers he has studied sense or feel their information in the solar plexus, while others seem to receive it in the head in the region of the temples. Interestingly, not a few people (who are not necessarily dowsers) see light when an ordinary bar magnet is held against their temples in a darkened room.

There are, perhaps, two aspects to the question of magnetic influence. Some specific part or parts of the body may and probably do react or vibrate directly in response to incoming stimuli. But this information then still has to be transmitted to consciousness itself – presumably somewhere in the higher brain centres. Dr Jan Merta, himself a gifted psychic and dowser, has actually made a somewhat revolutionary suggestion. He has proposed that the dowsing information is first received directly and clairvoyantly in the brain. This information is then transmitted, in a fraction of a second, to the muscles of the arms, stomach or whatever, which respond with a twitch or some similar reaction. (The idea is very like William James's suggestion that we feel fear because we run away, not run away because we feel fear.) Merta has devised a very sensitive piece of electronic measuring equipment which appears to support his claim. For those interested this equipment is described and diagrammed in Christopher Bird's book *Divining*. (Also occupied with these problems, Professor John Taylor has suggested that perhaps all the cells of the brain connected end to end might function as a giant aerial.)

There is no reason in principle, however, why every single cell of an organism should not be receptive to, and perhaps also itself emit, magnetic radiation. Each cell of the body is certainly a complete electromagnetic structure in its own right, 'a tiny electric battery generating its own current by chemical action'; and blood cells in the living body rotate on their axis, as in the laboratory they can be made to rotate by the application of magnetic fields.

Meanwhile, however, there are some important comments to make about health, illness and magnetism.

Since the late 1950s Dr Robert Becker in America has pioneered the use of electromagnetism in the treatment of illness. Various parts of the human body show differing electromagnetic potentials (as is generally agreed). Already in the 1930s Dr H. S. Burr was measuring such local surface potentials, and correlating abnormal potentials with the later development at those sites of cancer. But Becker has been concerned with healing. He has found that the application of weak electric current at a site of illness significantly speeds up the healing process. He has succeeded in healing both skin and bone conditions more rapidly than normal. In one spectacular case doctors, using this technique, cured a rare bone disease (pseudarthrosis) in a boy who would otherwise have lost the limb. The sleep of patients has also been significantly improved by such stimulus. Meanwhile, in Russia Alexandr Presman reported increased rates of growth in mustard seedlings, or decreased rates, depending on the type of electromagnetic field applied.

What an astonishing parallel these two kinds of work show with the effects achieved by psychic healers. Psychic healers (also working under scientific supervision) likewise produce accelerated rates of healing in people and accelerated growth rates in plants (see chapter 5). Do psychic healers function by altering the electromagnetic potentials in organisms? Surely this is close to a certainty.

But the evidence continues. Several doctors and scientists (Dr E. Stanton Maxey, for example) claim to have located a regular pattern of electromagnetic potentials at the sites designated as meaningful in the Chinese healing method of acupuncture. Dr Becker himself has found that the application of weak electric currents further stimulates the known beneficial effects of acupuncture.

In acupuncture, silver needles are inserted at strategic points in the body, designated as such by traditions that are lost in the mists of time and at least four thousand years old. The insertion of needles at such points has long been used in China to treat an enormous array of illnesses and disabilities – malaria, pneumonia, sciatica, arthritis, rheumatism, fractures, sores, epilepsy, insomnia, deafness, dumbness. Can we now doubt that acupucture also works electromagnetically, particularly when we hear that the needles are often twiddled to increase the effects? Such movement of an inserted needle could disturb and/or regenerate electrical potential at that point, as also throughout the total energy body.

For those unfamilar with acupuncture, it is not a 'faith-healing' system. It works whether you believe in it or not. Apart from producing cures in illness, it is nowadays also widely used as an anaesthetic. Major surgery – such as the removal of lung tissue and stomach organs – has been performed on patients anaesthetized only by having a few needles placed at strategic points in the body. Such operations have been filmed and shown on western TV.

There is still an enormous amount for us to understand, but as we proceed, a very strong sense of coherence is beginning to manifest itself in these at first sight very diverse phenomena, particularly in respect of magnetism.

More startling than the cures effected by Dr Becker is his demonstration that applied electric potential can cause the partial regrowth of amputated limbs in *mammals*. Note that we are not talking of amphibians and reptiles or other lower animals in which limb regeneration is sometimes a normal and natural part of their biological equipment. We are speaking of the order of mammals – our own order. Mammals have partially regrown amputated limbs. Meanwhile, encouraging results have recently been reported from Britain on the regrowth among children of fingertips severed in accidents. Dr Becker himself believes that human beings will one day be able to generate lost limbs completely. This hope is not in any way unfounded.

There is a clutch of results from experiments around the world that ought to be mentioned in passing. They would be well worth discussing in more detail, except that these particular experiments have proved difficult to repeat. They include both positive and negative influences. What they all show is the incredible potential that exists in this general area. And so the application of magnetic fields that differ from those normally experienced (either of lower or higher or weaker or stronger, cycles) has been shown to retard the ageing process, to reduce the incidence of breast cancer, to cure or substantially reduce other cancers, to produce higher activity rates coupled with less eating (suggesting a more efficient energy-use of food), to increase learning, to increase ageing, to produce psychological stress, to produce stunted offspring into the third generation, to delay human reaction time to stimuli – and in short, to influence virtually every biological function of organisms.

Returning now specifically to dowsers and diviners, firstly all kinds of interesting physiological corrections are found in the dowser while divining. There are changes in electrical skin resistance, for example, which Maxwell Cade also noted in meditation states. Wilhelm de Boer found he could increase his dowsing ability tenfold if he drank a couple of glasses of water before beginning. This point touches two other matters. One is the apparently significant role of water in cases of spontaneous combustion. The other is the ancient tradition among mediums and psychics that water should be drunk before giving clairvoyance, and that a bowl of water should also stand in the room where the seance or sitting is taking place. (Again, we are reminded of Jan Merta's belief that dowsing and clairvoyance are one and the same – and he, after all, is both a clairvoyant and a dowser.) And, lastly, it is noted that dowsers work better when the heart is turned towards a source of magnetic influence. Often a dowser's test scores drop to zero when the heart is turned away from the source. In the tests, of course, the dowser is not himself aware in any normal sense of where the magnetic source is located.

It must be emphasized most strongly that professional dowsers do not just search for and locate water, and other minerals and geological strata. They also successfully locate underground tunnels, including collapsed tunnels, former ditches, earthworks and buildings now buried, lost pipelines and cables, treasures and graves, in fact any kind of hidden or buried object whatsoever. Such objects and artifacts, or the faint traces in the ground of their former presence, produce almost inconceivably minute variations in the local magnetic field. This fluctuation it seems is nevertheless detectable by the dowser.

But even if these altogether daunting achievements are accepted, it is still not enough. There remains the matter of map dowsing.

Map dowsing

There had for some time been reports of individuals who could find water, lost tunnels or whatever, not by going to the site, standing over it and trying to detect vibrations (with or without a dowsing rod) but simply by looking at a map of the area. These individuals could be thousands or tens of thousands of miles from the actual site. It seemed to make no difference.

Francis Hitching set out to test this remarkable claim in a scientifically controlled experiment, working with the dowser Bill Lewis (who incidentally uses a pendulum, not a dowsing rod). This experiment and the results are described in full in Hitching's book *Pendulum: the Psi Connection.* Lewis had already achieved success in non-experimental situations, such as locating from England underground water in an arid area of Australia.

Hitching's experiment was concerned with locating ancient Indian megalithic stones on the North American continent. Numbers of these have already been found, but there are plenty more to be discovered. Maps, not showing any ancient sites, were obtained from US map and survey suppliers. Bill Lewis did not see the relevant map until a particular experimental session started. Hitching, opening the map, would put particular questions to Lewis like: where is the largest standing stone in this area? Is there a burial chamber that I can comfortably walk to?

Lewis then 'felt' his way into the situation, keeping up a running commentary, and building a detailed picture of the site he alleged would be found. 'A burial chamber with spiral markings, you want?....How about this?....Right in the neck of a river bend....You won't even have to get your feet wet....It's all silted up....Mound's visible alright, you can see it above the ground....Capstone's all broken and silted up....'

At the end of the series of prediction sessions, Hitching had a list of twenty-two sites, containing sixty-three specific predictions.

As a control, a member of the Society for Psychical Research,

John Stiles, had taken the same map and guessed similar predictions after looking at it. If Bill Lewis had guessed a standing stone of a given height in a given area, for example, Stiles would then place a similar stone of similar height, say, half a mile from Lewis's spot. These guesses were called 'check sites'.

Now Hitching physically went to America to look for and at the sites proposed. Circumstances did not permit him to look at all of them, but he was able to visit a substantial number.

The full results of the experiment can be studied in detail in Hitching's book, but in summary the control, John Stiles, scored *one* per cent correct predictions. This is chance level, in statistical terms, whereas Bill Lewis's score was a startling thirty-five to forty per cent success rate. He scored thirty-five per cent in terms of placing of site, and forty per cent on specific description.

This experiment, along with all the informal, yet astonishing and evidential successes that dowsers have achieved using maps only, places the phenomenon of map dowsing squarely outside the realm of the hypothetical and inside the realm of the actual.

In trying to account for map dowsing, especially if we wish to retain an electromagnetic view of the phenomenon, we necessarily have to burst beyond even the extended frame of reference we have already been forced to adopt.

Electromagnetism – or what?

The electromagnetic explanation of many of the events covered in this chapter is such a good one – and at least the involvement of magnetism in these events is indisputable – that we should take it as far as we possibly can. Magnetism is a tried and tested runner, and moreover one that orthodox science can in the long run accept, however astonishing the details seem at first meeting.

How, then, does the following sound? How would it be if the gifted dowser (and, perhaps, potentially all human beings) is somehow in touch permanently and continuously with every part of the total electromagnetic field of this planet? And not just with the broad outlines of the field, but with its fine-grain detail, down to minute local magnetic effects produced by a single standing stone placed over an underground stream?

It does sound completely mad. And yet a homing pigeon, taken hundreds and sometimes thousands of miles away from its home to a place where it has never before been, can, after one or two circling flights of the strange place, pin-point the location of its home and fly in a straight line towards it. One pigeon released in France flew home to

105

Saigon, a distance of 7,200 miles. The journey took 24 days, representing an average log of 300 miles a day. Yet if en route that pigeon should fly over an underground deposit of magnetite or other ferrous oxide, or any other kind of local magnetic fault, it will lose its orientation until it finally flounders out of the influence of that tiny local anomaly. So the degrees of sensitivity we are postulating exist even in a simple organism like a pigeon. Nor is that ability confined to homing pigeons. A shearwater, kept as a pet, was taken from an island off the coast of Wales to Boston in America. It returned to Wales in 12½ days, a distance of 3,300 miles. Starlings, swallows, storks, terns, gulls and petrels have also demonstrated such untrained homing behaviour.

But let's be more outrageous still. Let us suggest that every individual organism in the world has its own electromagnetic 'finger-print'. This personal electromagnetic field, then, like ordinary finger-prints, would have features and peculiarities special to it and no other. And let us also propose that once we have registered another person's or organism's magnetic fingerprint, we can thenceforth locate and communicate with that person, at the magnetic level, no matter where they go in the world.

Such an arrangement would give us an electromagnetic explanation for an extremely important and well-authenticated paranormal phenomenon, that of 'psi trailing'. This event is usually considered under the heading of mental or clairvoyant phenomena. Certainly we *are* nudging something very like clairvoyance here, and eventually we are going to be forced to deal with clairvoyance on its own terms – but not quite yet.

Psi trailing

There are a large number of cases of psi trailing on record at the Parapsychology Laboratory in America, authenticated beyond any possible doubt. All these cases have been independently investigated by organizations like the RSPCA, and also involve large numbers of reliable witnesses.

The occurrence takes various forms. Usually it involves an animal (other than a bird in the cases we are considering now) that has been lost or left behind, finding its way to its owner's new home as much as thousands of miles away; or, finding its way back to its usual home, after being abducted. But there are other variations on this theme: animals, for instance, which have been taken by their regular owners to a new home, but have nevertheless elected to return to the old one.

One of the most famous cases, and probably also the most moving, involved a Collie dog called Bobbie. He was lost by an American family while they were in Wolcott, Indiana, on 6 August 1923. He reappeared at home in Silverton, Oregon, six months later on 15 February 1924. The distance involved is around three thousand miles, as the crow flies. The dog's condition showed that it had suffered very considerable hardship – after all, it had come through the American winter. Subsequently advertisements were placed in newspapers to try to establish whether anyone recalled seeing or feeding the dog en route. Several people came forward to testify that they had fed and temporarily housed the dog in his pathetic condition. He would stay with these new owners for a few days, gathering his strength. But as soon as he was half well enough to walk and his paws had healed, he set off again.

A similar case involves Tony, a mongrel. The family moved from Illinois to Michigan, and gave Tony away before so doing. Six weeks later the dog appeared on the new doorstep. He had licence tags on his collar from Jackson County, through which he would have passed.

In a story from Britain and the First World War, Private James Brown went to France with his regiment. Two months later his dog Prince, which had pined badly, disappeared from the house in London. A fortnight later the dog ran up to James Brown in the trenches at Armentieres in France. Although the case was thoroughly investigated, it was never established how the dog managed to cross the channel.

An anonymous cat easily topped this feat. A ship sailed from Australia on 22 November, leaving behind its ship's cat. On 20 January the cat walked aboard the ship in the London docks. There are, in fact, plenty of stories of such hitch-hiking cats and dogs on record. A book has been written about one of them, by Captain Kenneth Dodson of the US Navy, entitled *Hector, the Stowaway Dog*. Hector was first observed boarding four separate ships in the docks in Vancouver by a ship's officer, H. Kildall. Kildall watched the dog for a while, but then went about his duties. His own ship, the *SS Hanley*, now sailed. But next morning Kildall was confronted with Hector. The dog was cared for, but would not make friends among the crew. Its studied indifference, however, was replaced by excitement as the coast of Japan was approached. At the end of her voyage, the *SS Hanley* dropped anchor in Yokohama. The nearest ship, a Dutch vessel, was about three hundred yards away, but Hector was watching it with excitement. A boat put out from the Dutch ship and passed the *SS Hanley*. Hector sprang into the water and swam to it. In the boat was Hector's owner.

The case of Sugar, a Persian cat, is again more 'conventional'. The family were moving from California to Oklahoma. They intended to take the cat with them, but it was terrified of cars, and struggled insanely every time they tried to put it aboard. So the cat was given away to neighbours. Fourteen months later Sugar jumped on Mrs W's shoulder in the garden of her new home. When contacted, the neighbours reported that the cat had stayed only eighteen days with them, but they had not had the heart to tell the Ws of the loss. Sugar, incidentally, had a known deformity of the hip and it is this kind of detail which clinches the authentic stories. There is no question of some local 'look-alike' cat at the new location coincidentally appearing on the scene. The record distance for a psi trailing cat, overland, is two thousand five hundred miles. That trip took two years and six weeks, and the cat concerned was almost dead on arrival.

There are one or two other cases of a slightly different nature. An English family motored from Surbiton near London to Devon to their new home, and took their cat Peter with them. Shortly after arrival he disappeared. He reappeared ten weeks later back in Surbiton, having negotiated one hundred and eighty miles. Yet another cat returned a mere sixty miles from a new home to an old one, but brought with her three kittens, born at the new home, and only at the crawling stage. She must have carried each one a few hundred yards, deposited it, and gone back for another.

A boy had found a homing pigeon, which he kept as a pet. It had on its leg a seamless aluminium band with the number 167. Later the boy was taken to hospital. Three days after arrival there, the boy called to a nurse to let in his pigeon, which was outside the window, in the middle of a raging snowstorm, trying to get in. The nurse confirmed the number on the leg-band, and the family confirmed that the pigeon had been secure at home when they first returned from the hospital trip. In another touching case, in Sweden, a teacher reported that a magpie had flown in through an open window and perched on the shoulder of one of a class of forty boys. The boy exclaimed: 'It's our summer bird!' It was an initially wild bird that the boy had befriended, some fifty miles away, when the family had been on summer holiday. It was quite clear, the teacher said, that the bird knew the boy, and he was excused school to take it home.

The differing elements of these various cases are as follows. (1) A pet finds its way home across great distance from a strange place. (2) A pet travels such a distance across, again, unknown territory, this time from an old home to an entirely new and unknown one. (3) A pet finds its way back over considerable distance from a new home (which apparently it does not like) to an old home where, however, its owners no longer live. (4) A pet finds a *wandering* target (its owner or friend) not just across land but where necessary even across water. In this category come Prince, who found his master in France, the ship's cat who hitch-hiked from Australia to London, and the two birds who tracked their young human companions.

We can see that the idea of an 'electromagnetic fingerprint' for every individual living organism (the idea of a place having a fingerprint, as it may do, is irrelevant in most of these cases) is the least assumption we can make, if we are to explain these events in electromagnetic terms. On that basis one organism has to be able continually to register the magnetic whereabouts of another organism. There must be a signal 'I'm here, I'm here' repeated over and over again without break. Does the 'talking' magnetic field of the Earth carry that information to one who is able to listen? It seems that such must be the case.

We can, of course, abandon electromagnetism as an explanation at this point. But it seems such a good friend to us when we are trying to account for matters like psychic healing, acupuncture, the regeneration of bones and limbs, and so on, that one is reluctant to let it go.

These cases of psi trailing have much in common with the many authenticated cases of pets registering the distant death of their owners, and the rather fewer, though no less startling, cases of owners registering the distant death of their pet. And we can salvage an electromagnetic explanation in these cases too, providing that both sets of events take place in the present. But there are cases which involve a knowledge of future death, and then we are finally forced into labels like 'precognition' and 'clairvoyance', behind which it is hard for us to see any explanations that could fit with even the most elastic objective science.

The best anchor

The magnetic end of the Siamese-twin spectrum of electromagnetism is at present the best link we have between the conventional and unconventional worlds, between the normal and the paranormal. Magnetism comes specially recommended in a number of ways. Not only do organisms respond to it far more subtly than they do to electricity, but in itself magnetism is a more subtle creation. For example, it is not possible to build such screens in respect of magnetism. There is no such thing as a magnetic insulator. Appreciable magnetic fields can be created in non-magnetic materials, and even in a vacuum, whereas when we speak of a non-conductor of electricity, we mean precisely what we say. In the case of magnetism we can create 'paths of low reluctance' which absorb or deflect most of the field, but not all of it. We can therefore never completely hide ourselves away from magnetism.

Yet magnetism is not the end of the possibilities for a scientific explanation of paranormal communication.

Scientists consider that there are four forces in the universe: nuclear force, radioactivity, gravity and electromagnetism. It was once thought that there were more, but at every stage so far physicists have been able to write new equations which link together apparently differing forces, so reducing the overall number needed to describe the events of the physical world. A majority of scientists believe that one day soon an equation will be written that brings together all the remaining four forces into one framework, but that day is not quite yet. The production of a 'unified field theory' defeated even Einstein.

What we can tentatively assume, however, on the basis that there is a unified field theory waiting to be found, is that any event in any of the four forces named will probably produce effects in each of the others. While electromagnetism is at present providing us with the best leads we have for a scientific (and in that sense conventional) explanation of the paranormal, we are in no way exclusively tied to electromagnetism.

We have at our possible disposal the whole massive world of gravitational energy on the one hand, and the bewildering universe of sub-atomic particles on the other. Here there are neutrinos, strange particles without mass, most of which pass right through our planet Earth without touching it. There are other slightly more solid particles that nevertheless make easy work of space travel. And there are positively and negatively charged ions. Just suppose that organisms broadcast patterned streams of ions, where the positive or negative charge functions like the binary (the 'on or off') system of a computer. There are no limits to the amount or complexity of information that could be transmitted in this way.

But even within the framework of electromagnetism itself, the possibilities are almost unbounded. Francis Hitching speaks of the 'infinite spectrum' of electromagnetic waves, and repeats 'this range is literally infinite':

> At the low end of the scale, at around one Hertz (that is to say, one oscillation per second, when the electromagnetic wave is so slow that it is virtually indistinguishable from static magnetic or static electric fields) the length of the wave equals approximately fifty times the radius of the Earth. Astronomers think they have discovered waves that last for forty seconds, which would give each wave a length of seven million miles. At the other end of the scale are the cosmic and gamma rays that bombard the Earth from outer space, their wavelength so short that a million side by side could pass through the eye of a needle.

So we are not short of possibilities.

Coming now back from the infinite to the finite, there are two concluding points.

Dowsers say that in the neighbourhood of megalithic standing stones, be these single or arranged in circles, they sense the harnessing or channelling of currents of electromagnetism. In the simplest case, a stone may have been erected above an underground stream. Such a stream generates a weak magnetic field. The stone can serve to gather or amplify some of the energy. In turn a human being may then be able to re-charge or re-vitalize his or her own internal energies.

Aside from their undoubted role as astronomical observation and measuring devices, the more complex stone circles may be functioning more as a battery, or as a series of transformers or amplifiers. Perhaps this is why the stones are of different sizes or heights, and not always equidistantly spaced from each other. They may be coping with the vagaries of a variable local field or fields. Possibly the stones were once placed very carefully and precisely, but with time and misuse have slightly shifted their exact relative positions. So perhaps they are like out-of-tune pianos, still producing notes, but without the proper harmonies.

In short, the stone circles, properly in tune, may once have been healing clinics. Perhaps the vibrations they produced could significantly raise an individual's level of energy X – or perhaps they only helped the psychic priests to be more clairvoyant.

Even as this chapter was being written science confirmed that not just gifted dowsers, but every single human being does indeed continuously respond to and monitor the Earth's magnetic field. In a long series of experiments Dr Robin Baker has shown that blindfolded human subjects, taken up to fifty kilometres from their homes by winding and deliberately confusing routes, can nevertheless (while still blindfolded) correctly indicate the direction of their homes. These results were confirmed by several experimental refinements. For example, subjects (the same subjects) did far less well without blindfolds. It is clear therefore that they were not consciously or unconsciously making use of information such as the position of the sun – though in any case results for clear and overcast days were compared. But most importantly of all, when subjects wore helmets containing magnets they were entirely disoriented – just as are homing pigeons with small magnets attached to their heads.

The evidence for an electromagnetic basis to many paranormal phenomena continues to mount.

One final comment. Acupuncture also works on animals.

111

The brain with a mind of its own

10 Electrical, chemical and magnetic brains

Many of the secrets of our secret life are undoubtedly hidden in the body. And even if in the final analysis we choose to think that there are aspects of mind or spirit which are separate or fundamentally different from body, there is always going to be some kind of correspondence and correlation between them. When talking about the one we shall always have to keep half an eye on the other. Even if there really is some fragment of a human being that survives bodily death, and even if that fragment is truly immortal, nevertheless it is clear that when the body dies, the mind or soul is obliged to go its own way. The manifestation of mind or spirit in the objective world, however, seems to require a body – otherwise why do we have a body at all? – and this body undoubtedly determines many of the qualities of mind.

Better than any philosophical discussion of this very basic issue is the simple practical demonstration not just that bits of body are very closely linked to bits of mind (as we saw already in respect of drugs and hormones) but that whole structures of body, and of brain, are linked to whole structures of mind. Here, first, are some generally agreed points about the structure of the human nervous system.

The human nervous system is physically divided into two main sections, called the central nervous system and the autonomic nervous system respectively. The central nervous system is governed by the part of the brain known as the cerebrum (the material immediately visible when the top of the skull is removed), and specifically by the two cerebral hemispheres. The central nervous system, in totality, comprises the so-called striped muscles (the ones so clearly on view in body-builders like Mr Universe), the skeleton and the external senses. All voluntary movements are made by the central nervous system, and in the cerebral hemispheres resides our normal, waking consciousness. Specific parts of the cerebral cortex (the uppermost layer of the cerebrum) receive extensive 'projections' of nerve pathways from our external senses – the eyes, ears, nose, skin and so on. Into each projection area nerve fibres run from each external sense organ – and stop. Although the true situation is actually more complicated, the general position is that if these fibres, or the part of the cerebral cortex into which they run, are damaged, we lose the sense involved. We go

114

blind, for instance. The central nervous system is, in very many ways, concerned with the outside world and our relationship to it.

The autonomic (self-governing) system, by contrast, is concerned with our internal environment. Basically, it runs the internal economy. So it is concerned with matters like digestion, sleep, breathing, body repair, the functions of glands and internal organs, the distribution of blood where most needed, sexual arousal, the smooth muscles (like those of the heart), keeping cool (sweating), keeping hot (goose pimples and shivering to make us warmer) and so on. All the millions of internal operations and reactions continuously required to keep the body functioning are handled, as a rule quietly and without fuss, and without our having to give any conscious orders, by the autonomic nervous system. It has emergency powers too: in crisis it can take over the striped muscles, causing us for instance to withdraw our hand from a hot object even before we are consciously aware that it is hot.

The autonomic nervous system (ans), like the central nervous system (cns), has its own headquarters quite literally – the ans is 'master-minded' by the cerebellum. This organ lies in the lower rear part of the skull and looks like the cerebrum, only is apparently much smaller, and like the cerebrum has two hemispheres, a cortex, and so on. It too has projection areas. The cerebellum is altogether very complex and very special – so special that it deserves a chapter of its own (chapter 11).

The autonomic nervous system is itself sub-divided into two parts, called the sympathetic nervous system and the parasympathetic nervous system respectively. These are rather useless names, but we are stuck with them. The sympathetic system is mainly concerned with states of arousal and aggression (with spending energy) and the para-sympathetic system mainly with states of rest and quiescence (with conserving energy). But the two are very closely and complexly connected, both being involved in the sex act, for instance. In many operations and states the sympathetic system actually helps out the parasympathetic, and vice versa. The two are therefore not necessarily antagonistic to each other, though in practice they often are. When we get involved in a fight, for example, the digestive processes are interrupted, and after we have eaten a very heavy meal, we tend not to feel like fighting.

These brief descriptions have been undertaken so that we can make some general and very important points. It is already clear that it is the autonomic system much more than the central system which is involved in matters such as paranormal healing and hysterical illness. The French girl who gave herself an appendix operation (chapter 5) was behaving very much like an autonomic system that had somehow acquired a voice and a consciousness. Intestinal sensation and move-ment of the gut and bowel, like everything else connected with digestion, are very much the concern of the ans and outside normal conscious control. Or again, when a person develops hysterical paralysis of the legs, hands or whatever, it very much looks as if the emergency control which the ans can exercise over our striped muscles has got itself not just switched on, but locked in position. On a more general level, we know too that neurotic patients, and people suffering from obviously psychosomatic diseases like ulcers, skin rashes, asthma and so on, very often show considerable disturbance of autonomic function quite apart from their specific complaint. So they variously sweat too much, blush, tremble, become constipated, show irregular pulse rates, shed more hair than they should, are often tired but nevertheless have insomnia, or conversely cannot keep awake, have eyes which are too bright or too dull, cry for no apparent reason, blink too much, produce too much or too little hormone, eat too much or too little – and so on for an endless range of autonomic reactions.

There are related items about which we have to be less emphatic. These are complex matters that cannot be dealt with adequately in a sentence or two. Nevertheless, it looks as if there is a connection between the pair sympathetic-parasympathetic and the pair extravert-introvert (or the out-going versus the inward-turning personality). The sympathetic system is the aggressive system. If energy X is an energy of the ans and if extraverts are, as suggested in chapter 6, those who project energy X outwards (in extreme cases in the form of poltergeist attacks), the idea then ties in well with the suggestion of it being extraverts who have a strong sympathetic system. Similarly, if intro-verts are those who turn energy X inward upon themselves, one might expect to find in them a strong *para*sympathetic system, concerned as it is with conserving and retaining energy.

All these matters are of importance. But our main attention must necessarily turn to the brain itself, for it is here that consciousness resides. Yet isn't consciousness a phenomenon of the whole organism, body included? It is and it isn't. The evidence is twofold. First, people who have limbs amputated often report that they can still feel the arm or the leg as if it were still there – the so-called 'phantom limb' effect. (Some unfortunate individuals continue to feel severe pain in the phantom limb, others a strong itching, which necessarily they cannot scratch.) Conversely, however, if I cut or anaesthetize the main nerves from your arm to the brain while leaving the arm otherwise intact, I can then cut the flesh, but you will feel no pain. Some individuals are born with a defect of nerves near the brain and cannot feel pain at all. They can put a hand against a red-hot stove, and watch and smell the flesh burn, but feel nothing. Especially as children, such individuals have to be very carefully protected, for unless they watch closely they are unaware of injuring themselves. Cutting a joint of meat, they may also cut right through their own hand.

So in the final analysis it is in the brain itself where everything takes place for us, even though, subjectively, our consciousness resides in our fingertips, in our skin, in our muscles, and so on. (But just to add to the paradox, the brain itself feels almost nothing. You can cut the brain in a fully conscious person without pain.)

There are a number of ways in which we can examine the operation of the brain itself, ways which bring us closer to the phenomenon of consciousness. As we have already seen in connection with Maxwell Cade's Mind Mirror, the brain, whatever else, is certainly an electrical apparatus. Close to the head is found a patterned field of electrical emission made up of waves of differing length, which vary rather consistently with states of mind. Various parts of the brain reliably produce known patterns of waves when particular activities of our minds are taking place – working on a maths problem, dreaming, day-dreaming and so on. At the microscopic and cellular level also, many connections and interconnections between the millions upon millions of brain cells are made electrically. No fewer than five distinct kinds of electrical transmission occur. This particular complexity is a recent discovery.

Also of recent understanding is the brain as a complex chemical phenomenon. One or two 'chemical messengers' working within the structure of the brain itself had been identified and known about for almost fifty years, but in the last two decades at least five families of chemical regulators have been discovered. (The brain even has its own immune system.) It is only in the last two decades that brain chemistry has emerged as a new and profoundly complex science. To quote Rattray Taylor's summary: 'Today more than forty active substances are known to be present. Among them are the catecholamines (like dopamine and norepinephrine); the indoleamines (like serotonin and tyramine); the amino-acids (like taurine); the prostaglandins; the small peptides; the endorphins; the purine nucleosides; the brain hormones; and various odds and ends such as P-substance, histamine, and sundry substances with unpronounceable names.'

The shattering importance of chemicals in the brain is only just beginning to be assessed. This knowledge will in due course be of great concern to students of the secret life, for it is already known, as we saw, that the presence or absence of some of these substances can produce hallucinations and visions. Substances like LSD and heroin work directly on brain chemistry, as do the many modern drugs used in the treatment and control of mental illness. Electrical brain studies themselves are meanwhile entering a new phase whose extent and implications cannot yet be visualized. This new work involves considering the brain not just at the cellular level, but at the molecular level. At that level the human brain may prove to be a computer of virtually infinite capacity.

Shattering in their implications, and unlimited in their possible long-term consequences though these electrical and chemical advances are, there is a further recent development of still more concern to us – the discovery of the magnetic brain. Figure 5 shows a stylized diagram of the field of magnetic force surrounding the human brain. Lines of force exist from the left of the head, curve and pass over the top, to pass back into the right side of the head. We can assume, without problems, that the lines of force travel continuously through the inside of the head, emerging once again on the left side.

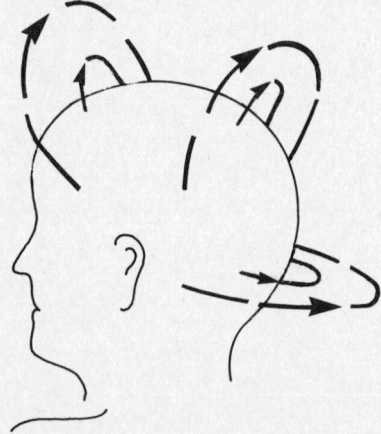

Figure 5   Lines of magnetic force produced by the normal human brain.

We come back now to the stone heads and statues of the ancient Olmec and Mayan civilizations of Central America. We have spoken already in chapter 2 of the large turtle head carved in basalt, in which the natural lines of magnetic force run together in a point in the snout. There are other remarkable stone statues also, huge pieces of work, referred to jokingly as 'fat boys'. For us, however, interest centres not in the artistic merit or demerit of the statues, but in the fact that the lines of magnetic force run together at the navel and at the temples of the head. How absolutely delightful, then, to discover from Francis Hitching that Zaboj Karvalik, using magnetic deflectors, claims to have established two centres of reactivity in the dowsers he tested – in the solar plexus and the temples. Also 'a Swiss dowser has completely lost his ability after having his right kidney and renal gland removed'; while 'Robert

Leftwich...when his forehead is directly above a centre, his rod flips upwards'. Hitching comments: 'It is too early to be certain just how accurately Zaboj Harvalik has identified these two sensory areas for dowsers, or if there may be more.' The head centre, however, appears to be 'somewhere along a line taken through the brain just above the ears and behind the temples'.

Back to Olmec and Mayan statues. Apart from the complete figures, there are also enormous carved stone heads, some of which are ten feet in height. These heads look as if they are wearing American football helmets, which are elaborately carved. Near the heads have been found numbers of perforated magnetite beads, many with more than one hole. It is as certain as anything can be in archaeology that the beads of magnetite were strung on cords and nets, which followed the pattern on the helmets, and were therefore probably placed over the helmets.

There may or may not have been human-size helmets, or bowls, of basalt, which individuals who were giving clairvoyance or healing wore on their heads along with nets of magnetite. (If so, these helmets have not yet been found.) Or it may be that the 'helmets' on the carved heads are merely stylized and concrete renderings of a sensed force-field around the skull. Perhaps the Olmec and Mayan psychics simply draped magnetite nets over their own bare heads.

As already noted, it has been established in modern times that some individuals see light if a bar magnet is placed against their temples in a darkened room. And since the early 1960s Russian scientists have demonstrated that horseshoe magnets placed near parts of the human head produce changes in the mental states of hypnotized subjects. Did the Olmec and the Maya make these same discoveries by applying pieces of lodestone (magnetite) to the head? Did they discover the magnetic properties of basalt rocks by floating a very thin sliver of magnetite on the surface of a cup of water (just as, with care, we can float a steel needle on water) and holding the cup against the rock?

Or did the ancients make such discoveries rather by some direct intuitive means? Were their sensitives able to pass their hands over individuals and rocks alike, and so map the force-fields and currents within? This must seem likely, in view of the existence, in far away ancient China, of the science of acupuncture.

The formal basis of acupuncture is a detailed and fine-grained map of hundreds of points at which needles may be inserted to produce, on demand, prescribed and reliable curative effects. These points are defined with an accuracy of a millimetre or so. Astonishingly, a few needles in the outer edge of one ear enable a man's stomach to be removed without pain. One needle in the right forearm is sufficient to permit surgery of the chest. To treat a woman's ovaries, needles are inserted at the wrist.

Obviously, once the principle of acupuncture was established, it could be further refined by a certain amount of trial and error. But the question is, how do you establish it in the first place? How do you first get the idea that the body has (or is) as intricate network of invisible energy, which can be tinkered with and tapped to cure disease, not at the site of the disease, but at some far-removed and apparently irrelevant point? And then, what is more, you devise an elaborate philosophical explanation of how the whole thing works, ultimately based on the notion of the two polarized opposites of yin and yang, which are really the negative and positive poles of modern electricity, or the north-south poles of the conventional magnet. All this is taking place, incidentally, at least four thousand years ago, but almost certainly the system is far older than that. And although silver needles have been used in recent times, effects can also be achieved with bone or wood slivers, and even with simple pressure of thumb or fingernail. We must, it seems, necessarily fall back on the idea of the direct, intuitive perception of the basis of acupuncture by sensitives and psychics – diviners and dowsers they no doubt also were – who had also a very fair grasp indeed of the overall electro-magnetic properties of our planet, and the ways in which electro-magnetism permeates and directs life.

Let us return to the magnetic brain. As we saw in Figure 5, a clockwise magnetic field encloses the skull and the brain within it. Now, as it happens, we can – and do – produce just such a clockwise magnetic field whenever we pass electrical current through a wire. This magnetic field is formed at right angles to the direction of the current. It forms instantly and always. (Whenever and wherever electricity appears, it is always accompanied by magnetism. And, in turn, a spinning magnet itself generates electricity – this is precisely what a dynamo is. Because of their Siamese-twin relationship we speak of the 'electromagnetic spectrum' as virtually a unit.) Figure 6a shows a wire carrying current and its magnetic field. And there is a very important further point here. Although in theory the magnetic field could and should be totally static, and absolutely at right angles to the current, in practice the magnetic field gradually corkscrews forward in the direction of the current, as shown in Figure 6b. It seems that here we have yet another version of the 'mystic spiral'.

Looking back now at Figure 5, must it not be the case that within the head there is a 'wire' carrying an electrical current? It seems certain. Figure 7a diagrams this possibility. Necessarily, the direction of the current must be towards the forehead, since this is demanded by the

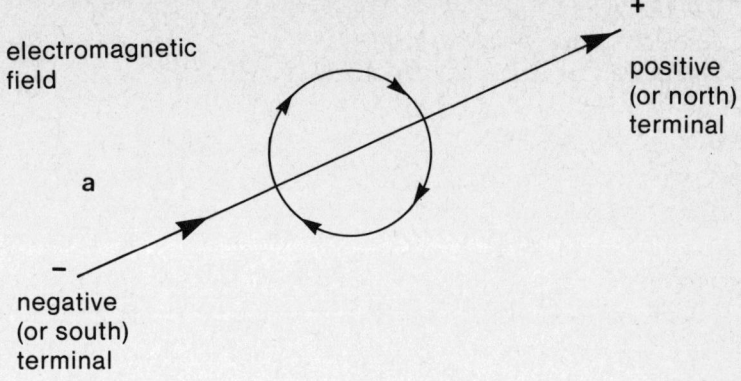

electromagnetic field

a

positive (or north) terminal

+

negative (or south) terminal

−

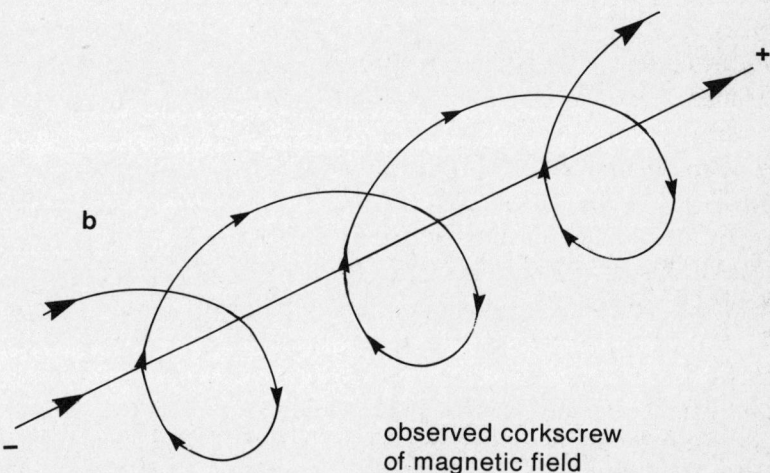

b

+

−

observed corkscrew of magnetic field

Figure 6 (a) magnetic field formed at right angles to a wire carrying current; (b) forward corkscrew motion of the magnetic field, in the direction of current flow.

clockwise direction of the magnetic field. Figure 7a is concerned with the head only, but Figure 7b includes also the spinal cord. The brain itself, of course, both anatomically and in evolutionary terms, is only an extension of the spine. Brain is just highly evolved spinal cord. In the diagram the cerebellum (and spine) is logically assumed to be the negative terminal, and the cerebrum the positive.

At this point we can make a most interesting cross-reference to one of the mystical claims of yoga. In this Hindu tradition, the 'spirit-power', or kundalini as it is properly called, lies curled at the base of the spine. Its full upward tendency, in the normal human being, is blocked.

121

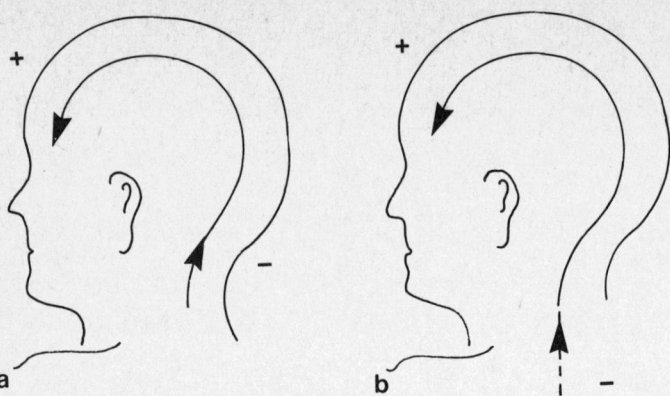

Figure 7   Possible flow of electrical energy (a) in the human brain and (b) in the brain and spinal cord.

Years of yogic, meditation and devotion, however, can remove the block so that the energy can flow up freely into the brain. The 'block' often finally gives way very suddenly after many years of discipline, with quite unmistakable accompanying symptoms, which themselves do suggest that some kind of dam or barrier has indeed been breached. The various accounts of the kundalini experience speak of a, literally, physical sense of energy pouring up the spine into the head. Within the head a blinding white light is manifested which, psychologically, sweeps all one's senses and normal orientation with it. (It looks, of course, very much as if kundalini is what we have called energy X, or at least one form of it.)

A typical kundalini breakthrough is described by Gopi Krishna in his autobiography *Kundalini: the Evolutionary Energy in Man*. Krishna had been meditating for many years and was now thirty-four. The exercise he was performing was the contemplation of the 'lotus of light' in the crown of his head, said to be the highest of the mystical chakras, which are allegedly sited in various parts of the body. Krishna takes up the story: '...I suddenly felt a strange sensation below the base of the spine, at the place touching the seat. The sensation was so extraordinary and so pleasing that my attention was forcibly drawn towards it.' But Krishna found that withdrawing his attention from the lotus of light, to attend to the sensation at the base of the spine, caused the sensation to disappear. So he resumed his contemplation of the lotus:

> With great effort I kept my attention centred round the lotus. Suddenly, with a roar like that of a waterfall, I felt a stream of liquid light entering my brain through the spinal cord...the illumination

grew brighter and brighter, the roaring louder, I experienced a
rocking sensation and then I felt myself slipping out of my body,
entirely enveloped in a halo of light....I was no longer myself...but
instead was a vast circle of consciousness in which the body was
but a point, bathed in light...in a state of exaltation and happiness
impossible to describe.

What this description most suggests, if we look for a normal
framework for it, is a subjective experience of an electromagnetic
phenomenon.

But extremely instructive and useful though these kundalini
experiences are for us in a theoretical sense, there are grave doubts as to
whether such an extreme path should be followed. Gopi Krishna was in
a severely disturbed state for several years after his kundalini breakthrough, and Itzhak Bentov, in his book *Stalking the Wild Pendulum*,
gives details of several other individuals who have suffered severe
physical and psychological symptoms after achieving kundalini. The
following case involved a woman aged fifty-eight:

A continuous loud sound appeared inside her head. Soon
there were cramps in her big toes, followed by vibratory feelings in
her legs. Overnight her big toenails darkened as if hit by a hammer
and eventually partially separated from the flesh. The tissues in her
legs felt 'torn through' by vibratory sensations. The vibrations
spread to her lower back and swept over her body from lower back
up to her head, forming a sensation of a band around the head just
above the eyebrows. Then her head started to move spontaneously.
Later her body moved sinuously, and her tongue pressed to the roof
of her mouth....At times her eyes seemed to move separately, and
the pupils felt like holes that bored into her head. Then she felt a
tremendous head pressure...which affected the eyes and vision had
deteriorated....

This case incidentally, like the next one, has all the classic marks of so-
called 'demonic possession', and the 'band around the head' perhaps
reminds us of the helmets on the Olmec statues.

A man, aged fifty-three, developed gross thrashing movements:
'at one time...violent uncontrollable spasms came on...he was aware of
sounds in his head, mostly of high-pitched whistling and hissing'. He
saw floods of white light in his head, as if his skull were lit up from
inside. Another mature woman (also fifty-three) had a far more serious
set of experiences. She was no doubt a powerful natural psychic, to
judge from her childhood experiences. Like the first woman, she
underwent the 'mild ' symptom of spontaneous blackening of the
toenails. But over the last thirteen years her symptoms have grown
more severe. Now her optic nerve has deteriorated, she has a thyroid

disorder, and considerable paralysis, coupled with anxiety and severe pain.

The similarities in this last case both to the hysterical conditions, and to the more extreme forms of self-harming we have looked at, are striking. And altogether in the kundalini record, we seem to be getting close to the 'inner poltergeist' attack which can result finally in spontaneous combustion and auto-oxidation.

Most if not all of the kundalini cases do in the very long run become stable, with a greatly increased psychic sensitivity, and so forth, and perhaps only in a minority of cases is there permanent physiological damage. Nevertheless, the extremes of the typical kundalini initiation are neither desirable nor necessary. A gradual, controlled development of inner psychic and healing power is always possible. The swamis and healers that Maxwell Cade and the Menninger Foundation studied had all achieved such careful progress. Provided a would-be developer trains with experienced and non-fanatical teachers, no harm results, and the benefits are many. Probably the most important point of all to remember is that one is dealing only with an aspect of oneself and one's own personality, not with any separate or discarnate force, let alone any discarnate spirit.

That profound *physical* changes can and do occur in the course of psychic self-discovery and development should not be doubted. The tremendously thrilling message from all the material we have looked at so far is that there are, at present, no foreseeable limits to what our body-mind and our brain-mind can achieve.

In California, a professor of psychology, James Donahoe, has for many years been investigating unusual aspects of dreaming, in particular their paranormal connections, and his two books reporting his experimental work (*Dream Reality* and *Enigma*) have recently become available in Britain. Professor Donahoe's major contribution has been in establishing the existence of 'mutual dreaming'. With training it is possible for two or more individuals to share the same dream at night, although physically far distant from each other. But Donahoe also reports one or two other dramatic developments among his students which are very relevant to the material we have been discussing. These items involve permanent physical changes also evident to others.

One of Donahoe's students (a girl, Pam Yellen) says that at the height of her psychological 'transformation' her face seemed to change in appearance. She could feel her cheekbones becoming less prominent, the lower part of her chin thinning out, and her forehead expanding slightly outward in rounded form. She had told no one about these changes, but less than a week after their occurrence, three of her friends each told her separately that they noticed these specific differences in her face. Ms Yellen concludes: 'My face still looks as it did at the end of that week.'

Professor Donahoe took some 'after' photographs of Pam Yellen, but realized that these were not going to carry much evidential weight. One could simply say that Pam's expression had changed. So he now asked Pam if she could try to produce some noticeable physical change in *him* by way of experiment. Donahoe writes:

> Some days after my work with transformation started, I felt odd sensations in my forehead, as if it were swelling slightly in size, just above my eyebrows. These sensations came on suddenly, lasted several minutes at most and then disappeared. By about the third time, I felt a buzzing vibration localized above my left eyebrow, accompanied by the distant sensation that my forehead was beginning to bulge slightly. As with Pam, several friends noticed the change without my mentioning it to them. Others recognized it once it was pointed out to them. The total change was small, but distinct and noticeable....I still have the formation above my eyebrows.

Finally, Donahoe reports the independent and corroborative experience of Dr Arnold, with which we opened chapter 1. The Arnold account is especially fascinating in view of the fact that Neanderthal man had very pronounced ridges projecting far out over his eyes. Neanderthal man, as it happens, also had a much larger cerebellum than modern man. And as it again happens, there is a phenomenon called 'the correlation of growth', apparently first described by Darwin, but reported since by other biologists, though no systematic investigation of it has taken place and no explanations are forthcoming. According to Darwin's observation, certain features of an organism are found always to be accompanied by certain others, even though there seems no logical connection between them. Thus pigeons with short beaks always have short feet, cats with blue eyes suffer from deafness, cats with no tails or naturally stubby tails have long hind legs, and a black sheep and a white sheep, even when both produced by the same parents, possess a differing resistance to certain natural poisons. Can it be, then, that a large cerebellum in human beings correlates with pronounced brow ridges, as well as perhaps with many other natural features, like projecting eyebrows, and a resistance, in men, to baldness (see for discussion my books *The Neanderthal Question* and *Guardians of the Ancient Wisdom*)? And can it be that when we activate the cerebellum, as we may be doing in pursuing the paranormal, we activate those other correlated features also? This query leads us neatly enough to the central mystery of the cerebellum. Is it the originator and controller of all the phenomena we have collected?

11 The forgotten brain

There are three areas of human experience not found in psychology text books. Anyone can check this claim by spending a few minutes in the psychology section of a bookshop or local library and examining the indexes at the back of volumes.

The first set of terms to look for in this informative game of 'search the index' includes trance, possession, automatic writing, hypnosis, mediumship, somnambulism, acupuncture, meditation and religion. To be absolutely fair here, you may find once in a while a whole page on hypnotism, or an entire paragraph on sleep-walking (somnambulism), but other than that, there is simply a great void where these items should be. And we have to stress should be, because although an academic psychologist might quite legitimtely want to offer very different explanations for these matters from those usually found among the general public, he has no right whatsoever to ignore the phenomena. He has no justification for ignoring them. They are his 'bag', as we say. They are events which indisputably occur and exist, and which indisputably fall into the psychologist's area of of reference.

The second set of terms includes the following: telepathy, clairvoyance, precognition, levitation, astral travelling, lucid dreaming, reincarnation, psychic healing, prophecy, visionary experience, fortune-telling, poltergeists and psychokinesis. Here the academic psychologist has a cast-iron defence for his position: these items do not exist, they are just words for non-existent events. So psychic healing, and psychic harming, don't exist. Marie Bailly was not cured at Lourdes. The 'rhinoceros skin' case never happened. Moyra Caldecott did not recover from terminal angina. R. L. Moody's patients did not spontaneously reproduce the wounds they received in childhood.

The third missing list is in many ways the saddest of all. It reads like a list of casualties; and certainly it has much to do with the impending death of civilization on this planet. It includes loyalty, friendship, love, hope, courage, wishing, believing, sacrifice, kindness, duty, concern, despair, affection, nostalgia, tenderness, wistfulness, amazement, striving, poetry, happiness, mind, mindfulness, ecstasy.

Is it at all possible, since all three are shunned by modern psychology, that these three areas of human existence are interconnected? The

126

answer, an affirmative answer, is now emerging from a study of the brain itself, specifically of that part of it called the cerebellum. The cerebellum is the heavily wrinkled mass of tissue situated at the lower rear of the head, behind the spinal cord and under the rear end of the cerebellum. It looks a relatively small item, but its surface area (cortex) is *three-quarters* that of the apparently much larger cerebrum.

In the last twenty years Dr James Prescott, a high-ranking psychologist in the US Federal Department of Health, along with an increasing number of other psychologists (Professor W. T. Greenough, Dr A. J. Berman and others), have been rescuing the cerebellum from the oblivion to which mainstream psychology and physiology have consigned it. Oblivion? We can justify the use of this word, again by reference to academic text books. S. P. Grossman's current massive *A Textbook of Physiological Psychology,* a volume of nine hundred and thirty-two pages, gives just fourteen pages to the cerebellum.

In the 1960s H. F. Harlow conducted pioneering work on maternal and social deprivation in monkeys and other primates. He showed that infants reared in isolation from a mother figure and playmates grew into hopelessly disturbed adults. They were unable, as adults, to make any social overtures to other monkeys. They could not perform the sex act. On the contrary, other monkeys invariably drove them away. These isolation-reared monkeys also showed fits of ungoverned rage and severe general withdrawal. They indulged in bouts of compulsive rocking, of self-sucking, self-biting and self-mutilation. When such females were artifically inseminated, so that they themselves gave birth, they either simply dashed the offspring to the floor in rage, or ignored it till it died.

These behaviours are horrendous, and fully documented. But what James Prescott and others have now shown is that such deviant monkeys, examined after death, show severe structural damage to the cerebellum. The research continues. But already Prescott is convinced that the whole of our emotional/affectional relationship with the world is mediated through the cerebellum. He believes that an enormous range of human behaviours, running from sexual deviance and inadequacy to child battering, criminal behaviour and aggression, are the result of inadequate stimulation, and hence inadequate development of the cerebellum in the human being as infant. A recent suggestion is that dyslexia (word-blindness) and other such learning disabilities are also cerebellar defects. ('Of 115 consecutive dyslexic children selected and referred for psychiatric evaluation on the basis of their poor or refractory response to reading instruction, 112, or ninety-seven per cent, showed evidence of cerebellar-vestibular dysfunction.') The stimulation in question involves almost continuous rocking, touching, manipulation and play with the infant. This position on stimulation should be hardly surprising, when we consider that in wild monkeys and apes, as also in primitive communities of human beings, the baby is carried continually by the mother in everything she does. Moreover, modern human babies are born about a year premature, for otherwise the head/brain would be too large for birth. During that year the baby ought to be carried and rocked in an embracing womb.

The rocking, twirling, self-touching, self-mutilating, head-banging that we observe both in the disturbed human child and the socially deprived monkey seem to be attempts on the part of the organism to obtain for itself the stimulation it knows that it needs. Dr Prescott has shown, for example, that a violent outburst by an autistic child can be dealt with by twirling it for a while in a typist's chair.

The cerebellar straws have nevertheless been in the wind for some time, as has the close link between emotion-affection and the paranormal. (Spontaneous telepathy, for instance, occurs far more often between individuals with a close emotional bond – parent and child, brother and sister, analyst and patient, husband and wife, owner and pet – than ever it does between strangers.) But in respect of the cerebellum itself, no less a psychic than Swedenborg reported that his visionary powers resided in the cerebellum; while Jerome Cardan, a royal physician (to Edward VI) who could go into trance at will, also reported that his trance state began in the cerebellum. Kaspar Hauser, the strange visionary boy who was found wandering as a teenager in Germany in the nineteenth century, proved after death to have had an abnormally enlarged cerebellum. Then again, Neanderthal man, the inventor (so to speak) of religion and mysticism, had a far larger cerebellum than we ourselves.

The following report from one of his workers (Edgar Chase, a former physicist) is quoted by Maxwell Cade: 'I am using an Omega One Skin Resistance Meter applied to the left hand of the patient. A second instrument is connected to my own left hand, my right hand being the positive hand which channels the power. Remarkable results have been obtained. A patient is immediately responsive to the healing power *and when the healer's hand is held over the cerebellum an increase in arousal is shown*' (my italics).

But probably the most exciting reference to the cerebellum (for me anyway) is contained in Dr Anita Mühl's astonishing book *Automatic Writing*. This was published in 1930, and like Osty's *Supernormal Faculties in Man* (chapter 5) has been completely lost from sight for fifty years. Dr Mühl, an American, was formerly physician at St Elizabeth's psychiatric hospital in Washington, and subsequently became Head of the Division of Special Education in California. Her book is not about spiritualism or the occult. It is about the use of automatic writing (and automatic drawing, automatic speaking, and automatic music) as a diagnostic and therapeutic tool in the study of mental illness and schizophrenia. In automatic writing, one's hand writes of its own volition, without the subject paying any conscious attention to it. In automatic speech, it is the voice which speaks of its own volition, and so on.

Some of Dr Mühl's patients produced automatic writing with both hands simultaneously, expressing two different personalities, neither of which was the patient's conscious personality. Others produced automatic writing with one hand, and quite different automatic speech at the same time. The case we look at here was that of a young woman, brought to the psychiatric hospital after a suicide attempt by drowning. She had a long history of mental illness, coupled with extensive physical illness, at the end of which she developed the severe mental fragmentation known as multiple personality.

This patient demonstrated not only automatic writing and automatic speech, but automatic piano playing. Ordinarily she was a mediocre piano player, but in (self-imposed) trance played quite beautifully. She would sometimes play the piano with one hand, write automatically with the other, while simultaneously speaking automatically. In one such session, while the left hand was playing a turbulent set of 'church' chords, the right hand wrote: 'The heart of a lily may be pure but its feet are sometimes sucked in by mire.' But the interest for us is in what she simultaneously said: 'Eyes, eyes, I see a cerebellum, anatomically speaking, physiologically and psychologically a brain – or maybe it's food for worms. Maybe it's cultural – planted like seed – food for humanity. We're put here to propagate–just to feed worms. Some think I am this, you are this. We are this. We are just tiny bits of atoms with a cerebellum.'

I believe the patient is telling us here that the origin of the unconscious and creative mind – and specifically her own five distinct personalities – is in the cerebellum. She is, perhaps, using a form of psychological autoscopy (see chapter 5.)

Carl Sagan, meanwhile, reports on an extremely interesting fish. This is the Mormyrid, an African freshwater fish that often lives in murky water. In these conditions normal visual detection by eye of predators, prey and mates is often impossible, so the Mormyrid has developed a special organ which produces an electric field around it, which it uses to detect other creatures. That organ is the cerebellum. This fish possesses a cerebellum that covers the entire back of its brain, 'in a thick layer reminiscent of the neocortex of mammals'.

Might not a very highly evolved organism, like ourselves, possess a cerebellum that could monitor a whole planet?

Some further important points about the human cerebellum are these. In several respects it is the most complex organ ever evolved by life on this planet. The Purkinje cells of the cerebellum can form as many as 100,000 connections with other fibre-bodies, more than those of any cell in the central system (the cerebrum). In the cerebrum, a more typical figure is 1,000 connections. And there are more cells in the granular layer of the cerebellar cortex than in the whole of the rest of the brain put together. Incidentally, one aspect of the cerebellar damage shown by the monkeys reared in maternal and social isolation was a drastic reduction in the number of cerebellar interconnections. As a general rule, the more connections formed between all kinds of brain cells in early life, the more intelligent, active, creative and socially normal is the adult.

Women have larger cerebella than men, and more importantly still, have cerebella which function differently from those of men. The research on this last point is only just beginning, but a first report states: 'Significantly greater correlations between cerebellar/forebrain and cerebellar/midbrain areas were obtained for females.' What this finding may mean is that the cerebellum in women exercises a greater influence on other brain structures than it does in males. What the precise influence might be we do not yet know – officially.

Modern Asiatics have far larger cerebella than modern Europeans. And, as it happens, the East has been responsible for all the major paranormal systems we currently possess – acupuncture, the I Ching (see chapter 16), yoga, and so on.

In the previous chapter we saw that the cerebral cortex contains extensive 'projection areas' which receive input from all external senses. The projection areas are believed to be closely associated with consciousness. The cerebellar cortex also has extensive projection areas of its own, receiving input from all internal as well as external sensory organs. Must these areas not also be associated with a form of consciousness? And if not, is it not then up to orthodoxy to show why not?

Dr R. A. Spitz has this to say on the matters under discussion.

> It is my opinion, however, that a large proportion of the pathways involved belong to a system of 'sensing' basically different from the system of perception that operates at a later age, and with which we are familiar. I have called...the one present at birth the conesthetic organization. Here sensing is extensive, primarily visceral, centred in the autonomic nervous system, and manifests itself in the form of emotions....I prefer to speak of this form of 'perception'...as reception.
> In contrast to this stands the later development of what I have

called deacritic organization where perception takes place through peripheral [external] sense organs and is localized, circumscribed and intensive. Its centres are in the cortex, its manifestations are cognitive processes, among them the conscious thought processes.

Here, of course, is the perfect description of an internal, visceral-mind that is distinct from and quite other than externally-sensing muscle-mind. (Both of these are of course 'body-minds', although I myself have been using the term body-mind in this book only in respect of the internal visceral-glandular system.)

The muscle-body-mind has its headquarters and its consciousness, that is, its 'brain-mind', in the cerebrum. It looks very probable that the 'brain-mind' of the visceral-body-mind is centred in the cerebellum.

Apart from having its own consciousness and being, the brain-mind of the cerebellum also lives, in a sense parasitically, through the cerebrum. (After all, the cerebellum has no mouth of its own and no eyes of its own, having lost the latter when its own eyes, once placed on top of the head long ago in evolutionary time, sank down into the brain to form our own pineal gland. One wonders if it was those evolutionary eyes which Dr Mühl's patient saw.) It looks, then, as if all forms of trance – ranging from outright possession, states of hysterical paralysis, dreaming, hypnotism and mediumistic trance, through to states like being in love, being religious, being a woman, being a child – are cases of the cerebellar-brain-mind taking over from the cerebral-brain-mind. Cases of spirit or demonic possession, in particular, seem not to be the result of any discarnate or inhuman spirit taking over a human being, but of just one part of our own brain taking over another.

The belief in discarnate spirit possession seems to have been a serious error on the part of the ancients. Yet they were not wrong in the great respect they gave to the state of trance, nor in their belief in its magical and mystical powers.

The mind with a mind of its own

12 Love and Mayday

Human owners react to the death of their pets thousands of miles away. Pets similarly react to the distant death of their owners.

Pets also foretell the death of their owners. But they seem to do this only when they are in the immediate proximity of the human being concerned. At a distance they seem to react specifically just to the actual moment of death, or to the threat of death, but then only provided that the owner perceives himself to be under such threat. These precise circumstances enable us to preserve some kind of electromagnetic explanation for the events concerned. But when, for example, animals and humans foretell their own death in a situation which does not yet exist, the electromagnetic explanation seems no longer really to help us.

We start with the thinner end of the wedge – odd and apparently predictive behaviour by an animal of the death of a loved one in close proximity. The case of Tim and the police sergeant given in the Introduction was one of these, though that case had the very special feature of the animal developing its master's symptoms, and dying at the same moment as he.

A girl was playing with her young brother, two years old, along with the dog, in the living room of their house. The boy fell down, as such young children frequently do, cried, and was picked up and comforted. The tiny incident was forgotten. But that evening the family noticed that the child was using its left hand to eat with instead of its right. The youngster's right arm was massaged, but there seemed nothing wrong with it. Suddenly the dog approached the baby's chair and began howling in a very odd and distressed way. They put the dog in the next room, and when his howling continued, out into the garden. He took up his position under the boy's bedroom window and continued the noise all evening, despite repeated attempts to quieten him and drive him away from the house. The boy died at one o'clock next morning. Outside, the dog abruptly fell silent.

A woman's husband had been an invalid for some time, but on this particular day he seemed no different from usual. On that day the house dog suddenly squeezed itself under an armchair and began whining pitifully and continuously. 'What the devil's the matter with that dog,' remarked the husband. 'Anyone would think he was announcing my death.' The dog was put out into the garden. On the following day the man died.

An old farmer and his dog were inseparable companions. One morning when the son took up his father's breakfast, the old man announced he would not be getting up any more, and that he was dying. The son told the father he was talking nonsense. But the old man was adamant, and asked for his dog to be brought up so that he could say goodbye to him. The exasperated son brought the dog up. It jumped on the bed, nuzzled the old man affectionately, then abruptly retreated into a corner, showing the whites of its eyes and howling. It was taken downstairs to its kennel, petted and offered food, but it would not stop howling. The dog died at 9.30 pm that evening. The farmer died at 10 pm.

There are many such cases on record. And interestingly, the two base elements – the fear or dislike of death, and the 'suicide' of a pet unable to face life without the loved one – are each found in isolation.

A man and wife returned from India, having given their dog away to a friend. Twice in the next few days the dog made the ten mile journey to the empty bungalow, and twice his new owner brought him back. The dog had by now stopped eating. Immediately he was missing again. When the new owner went to fetch him back a third time, the dog was lying dead on the verandah of his old home.

As to the fear of death itself, in the absence of any affectional bond, a 'trivial' case was reported to me by a correspondent. The reporter, a girl, lives on a farm in Canada. Here there was a continuous 'war' between the farmyard cat and the farmyard hens. The cat was fed in the barn, and often left food in his dish for when he would feel hungry later. While prowling around, he would nevertheless make sudden trips back to the barn, in order to drive away the hens who were always ready to take advantage of his inattention or absence – and of his food. Now the cat became ill, and for three days lay inert in a corner of the barn, not eating at all, and in fact dying. During those three days no hen made any attempt to approach the food.

A much more detailed and complex account comes from the naturalist Mme Rosalie Abreu (reported by Professor Yerkes in his book *Almost Human*). On her estate in South America Mme Abreu kept a number of chimpanzees, monkeys and other animals. One of the chimps, Jimmy, reacted strangely every time a death occurred. Sometimes he was normally aware of the death, at other times it seems he sensed it from a distance, but his reaction was always the same. Mme Abreu writes: 'The first time it happened...was on the death of Cucusa (a female chimpanzee). A moment before she died she took my head in her two hands and kissed it, very long. She saw that death was coming and was saying goodbye. Then she jumped from me to her bed and died. Jimmy who was outside in the park began to scream. He continued to scream, looking about as though he saw something....His scream was different from other times. The next day he still kept watching, far away toward the mountains.' Jimmy behaved similarly on three other occasions when monkeys died, and again more violently still when another female chimp died. He 'screamed and screamed and screamed' in a way quite different from any normal manner, his lower lip hanging, and 'looking and looking'. In Mme Abreu's words, 'it made my flesh creep'.

This strangeness and oddness of the whining or screaming is something that is very frequently remarked upon, and we shall meet it again in the various stories which follow. The police sergeant's dog Tim, like Jimmy, also ran about 'staring at nothing'. These various physiological parallels are significant.

In death cases we can certainly think of some local electromagnetic disturbance of the human body-mind, subtle anatomy or ka, which sets up unpleasant repercussions in the subtle anatomy of the animal. But to any such mechanistic picture we certainly have to add also some kind of conscious realization by the animal that something is very wrong, that the situation is changing for always, and that something is coming to an end. This awareness is even clearer in the cases which follow. What also becomes clear is that the idea of a purely 'local' disturbance (let alone any normal one) due to close proximity with the dying person is totally inadequate. It is true that close proximity may be necessary when the animal 'foretells' its owner's death, but in this case it may be reacting to some gross abnormality of the subtle or normal body that it senses close up, and which is about to become obvious (in the normal physical body) to all. Yet, as said, the idea of a purely local disturbance is inadequate, for we find also many cases of sensing across vast distances which remind us forcibly both of cases of psi trailing, and perhaps even of long-distance dowsing.

A case from the early part of this century is reported by Baron Joseph de Kronhelm. One of the officers under his command was transferred to Manchuria, to take part in the war against the Japanese. The officer left behind his hunting dog in the care of a fellow officer. One morning, three months later, the dog began howling 'in a terrible fashion'. Nobody could calm the dog, and it kept up the totally odd behaviour for three days before it finally desisted. Some time later word was received that the transferred officer had been killed on the morning when the dog began howling.

A story from the First World War is given by Mme Esperanza Payker concerning her brother Richard, who was a member of the armed forces in France. At seven o'clock one evening Richard's dog was asleep at Mme Payker's feet. Suddenly the dog sprang up and ran towards the door, wagging his tail, and barking and leaping as if someone well known to him had arrived. Then, equally suddenly, the dog drew back in terror, and began whining and howling pitifully. He did not stop whining and trembling during the whole of the following night. The next day the dog went out, and was not seen again. Some time later came news that Richard had fallen seriously wounded around seven o'clock on the evening of the dog's strange behaviour. He died the next day, approximately at the time of the dog's departure. Perhaps the dog had gone on the psi trail of his master.

Spiritualists would naturally be inclined to argue that the spirit of the dying solidier had visited the house, but a more reasonable explanation is that the dog experienced a hallucination or vision of his master, which perhaps began in a dream. This explanation seems all the more probable in the light of the next case, where clearly the dog was involved only in an event transmitted by telepathy. This report concerns the death of a well-known actor, William Terriss, at the end of the last century. The case is rather older than most of those we have looked at (although we come right up to date again in a moment), but was very widely reported in the responsible press of the day, because of the status of the victim.

Mrs Terriss, the wife of the actor, was at home in the living room of her house at Bedford Park in London. Her two sons were playing chess. The family's fox-terrier, Davie, was asleep on her lap. At 7.20 pm abruptly and without warning, Davie leapt from Mrs Terriss's lap and began dashing frantically around the room, yelping and snapping, in a paroxysm of mixed rage and fear. He appeared to be staring at something, and the boys subsequently testified that the mother called out 'What does he see? What does he see?' This behaviour on the dog's part was so extraordinary, and so completely out of character, that the family was upset for the rest of the evening.

Just after seven o'clock on that December evening, William Terriss, actor-manager of the Adelphi Theatre in the Strand, was about to open the door of his private entrance at the back of the theatre, when a man called William Prince, an actor who believed that Terriss was standing in the way of his career, sprang out of the shadows and stabbed him twice with a dagger. The cries alerted passers-by, and Terriss was carried into the theatre. He died some twenty minutes later.

We must assume that the dog Davie hallucinated part or all of the episode, at the point of Terriss's death. Again, perhaps, the communication had begun in a dream. (Louisa Rhine, who has collected examples of spontaneous psychic phenomena for some twenty years, reports that, in human beings at least, sixty-five per cent of such experiences occur in the course of dreams.)

J. G. Pratt reports a case from 1964. The pet dog of an American family in New Jersey suddenly went under the house, and began a whining, continuous crying. He had never behaved in this way before. The family were unable to persuade the dog to come out, or to stop his whining and 'strange barking'. Later that day came news that the elder son of the family had been killed in a car accident on the way home from college. The time of his death coincided with the onset of the dog's strange behaviour.

It is significant how often the words 'sudden' and 'abrupt' occur in these accounts when reference is made to the onset (and sometimes the cessation) of the animal's behaviour. This repetitive factor, like the strangeness of the whining or barking, is also a strong piece of circumstantial evidence.

The final case of this type is reported by a vet in 1970. A dog had been quartered with the vet while the family were away on holiday. At 10 am one morning the dog began howling and barking in an alarming fashion. Then abruptly, after an hour or so, he stopped. It was the only time during the stay that he displayed this behaviour. The vet examined the dog carefully, but could find nothing wrong with him. When the family returned, the vet told them of the incident. They reported, in astonishment, that at ten o'clock on that morning they had been trapped in a flash flood on top of their car. They had been rescued an hour later, around eleven.

It is clear that at moments of death or great danger to an owner, a pet animal, no matter how many thousands of miles away, reacts to the situation. The reaction varies from distress to detailed hallucination. But the telepathic link is not just there at times of danger (unless perhaps 'being away' counts as danger in a pet's mind), as an enormous case file shows. There are, for instance, many cases of animals producing an unmistakable, joyous reaction at the precise moment when an owner absent long-term on work or a trip sets out to come home.

An American sergeant in Vietnam had a surprise leave and arrived home on Thursday, totally unexpectedly. But early on Wednesday his dog Nellie had frenziedly dashed upstairs, jumped all over his bed, brought down his slippers to the living room, and then taken up her post at the front door, refusing to budge till Sergeant Johnson 'unexpectedly' came through the door. There are literally hundreds of such stories. And writing in *New Scientist,* Dr W. J. Tarver, chairman of the Veterinarian's Union, commented: 'Not many people have experienced, as I have, the noise of kennelled dogs who have been settled for a week or two, become wildly excited around the exact time when their owners commence the journey back from holiday.'

So the telepathic contact would appear to be continuous, at some unconscious level, and only becomes conscious when the news is very good – or very bad.

The very large majority of accounts of this type involve dogs. Occasionally a cat is concerned – but most interestingly, cats come strongly to the fore when we look at converse cases of human owners reacting to the distant death, or danger, of their pets.

We give only a passing mention to the many stories of owners reacting to nearby pets in danger, since as a rule it could be argued that these people were responding to a normal sound signal, below the level of conscious awareness perhaps, but nevertheless normally perceived at some level. However, that objection is not always justified.

One woman in Houston, Texas, was awakened about two in the morning by what seemed like a horse neighing, yet her two horses were pastured out of town, five miles away. Her compulsive awareness of a horse needing help was, however, so strong that she now drove down to the farm. One of her mares was caught in a barbed wire fence into which she had jumped, standing quite still but neighing repeatedly. Another case which also seems to forestall objections of normality is reported by the author and broadcaster Thurlow Craig. The story is his own. He awoke suddenly one night at his farm, with the strong feeling that Patience, one of his horses, was in trouble and needed his help, even though she was safely quartered in a fifteen-acre field. Part of the field was rather swampy, near a brook, but this circumstance posed no threat to a horse. Craig got up and put on some clothes. Outside it was dark, with visibility down to about ten yards in fog. With a flashlight, Craig went down to the field, four hundred yards from the house. Here he found Patience walking about, but limping heavily. She had trapped her foot. What possibly rules out Craig having been alerted by any cries of originally struggled against the wire and dragged it free. The wire was now deep in the flesh. Left till morning, the horse would have lost its foot. What possibly rules out Craig having been alerted by any cries the horse is that his window was shut tight, and he is himself nowadays so deaf that he cannot follow television programmes without lipreading.

Now, however, we can move on to cases which wholly avoid normal objections.

A man went to live abroad, giving his pet Timmy to a friend of his, Fernand Méry, who happened to be a vet. A year passed, during which the friend made no contact at all with Méry. Then he wrote, apologizing for his long silence, and saying that he was only writing now because of a recurrent dream he had had three nights in a row. He had dreamed that his cat, Timmy, was trying to get in through the closed window, but could not; and that the cat's head was swathed in bandages. Méry wrote back to say that on those three nights Timmy had been dying of meningitis, with his head wrapped in bandages. Timmy, then, had succeeded in sending a last message to his owner, the owner who had 'shut him out' of his life.

A British inventor had gone to New York on business. He had left his cat with his housekeeper. The cat was partially paralysed from an accident as a youngster. One night the inventor awoke from a nightmare. He had seen his cat struggling in the hands of a man with a white coat and a goatee beard. The hotel room seemed to the inventor to smell of chloroform, and the smell haunted him for days afterwards. Meanwhile he telegraphed home, but received no reply. When he finally got back to London, the inventor learned that the cat had refused to eat in his absence. The sight of the paralysed cat starving to death had been too much for the housekeeper, and instead of contacting her employer, as she should have done, she called a vet and had the cat put to sleep. The vet had not been known to the inventor, but had a goatee beard. The cat had been put down at the approximate time of the inventor's nightmare.

Osbert Hewitt was visiting friends in London. His cat Mitzi was at home in Oxford. That night Hewitt dreamed that his cat, dressed as a volunteer in the Spanish Civil War, had come to him badly wounded, begging and pleading for his help. He tried to reassure the cat, promising to take her to hospital, but the cat continued screaming. Hewitt woke very disturbed, and checked the time. It was 4 am. He told his strange nightmare to his hostess next morning. After he had done so, the telephone rang. His housekeeper reported that Mitzi had been very badly injured in a fight. She had been found howling on Hewitt's pillow, at 4 am, after waking the whole household.

Reading through a great many cases of such distant telepathic contact between owner and pet, over the last hundred years, it is quite clear that the very large majority of instances of distant contact from owner to pet involve dogs, while the very large majority of distant contact from pet to owner involve cats. This is a very interesting piece of internal evidence – and, of course, of internal confirmation. For how could it be that thousands of people around the world during a period of a hundred years have agreed amongst themselves to make dogs the star-performers in one kind of story, and cats the star-performers in the other?

We necessarily have to begin to think here in terms of differences in brain structure between these two animals, and perhaps also in terms of significant differences in the respective evolutionary paths these two species of animal had followed. Here is a possible fruitful field of research for scientists.

As far as psi trailing is concerned (see chapter 10), the honours seem to be fairly evenly divided among dogs, cats and birds, with occasional other animals also represented. V. and M. Gaddis have collected instances involving turtles, mice and toads; and horses are likewise occasionally concerned. One horse, in Britain, found its way from Dunmow in Essex back to the Welsh border, only a distance of some hundred and forty miles as the crow flies, but nevertheless across the railways, motorways and housing estates of modern industrial England.

What is also clear is that there are far more cases at moments of death or great danger between animal and human than there are between human and human. Cases emphatically do exist of human beings becoming aware of and sometimes seeing significant details of the death of a friend or relative, usually in dreams and often at the precise time that death occurs. A typical incident concerned a mother who dreamt that her son was drowning, when she had no reason at all to think he was anywhere other than on dry land. An unlikely set of circumstances had taken him to sea, and then into an equally unlikely shipwreck. (And once again, the time of the dream and the time of the shipwreck coincided.) David Fitzgerald, an estate agent in Ireland, had a son in Australia. One night Fitzgerald was awakened by the howling of the spaniel, the favourite dog of the son, Freddy, in Australia. Fitzgerald woke his wife and said he felt sure something was wrong with Freddy. Later he woke her again shouting, 'I saw Freddy! I saw Freddy! He was at the bottom of the bed looking at me.' The next post brought a letter with news of Freddy's recent death. But in any case, among Australian Aborigines such human to human contact at or near the moment of death is a commonplace, as we saw – although, curiously enough, the message there often comes as a vision of the dying man or woman's personal totem animal. And members of a number of European families also have a tradition of seeing, for example, a vision of a black dog whenever a member of the immediate family is dying. (Perhaps, then, some very ancient evolutionary aspect of our personality is involved?)

Nonetheless, in western civilization spontaneous paranormal contact from human to animal and animal to human seems far more common, and is usually far more dramatic, than contact from human to human. In looking to explain why this should be the case, it may be that love between human and animal is far more unconditional than perhaps it can ever be between complicated human beings. And it is even possible that we physically touch our pets much more often than we touch each other. Normal physical touching, involving strong affect (that is, emotion), may be an (almost) indispensable precondition of the setting up of telepathic bonds. Clearly there is considerable scope for experimental investigation of this particular variable.

As noted in the previous chapter, if we are prepared to extend electromagnetic theory beyond anything that science is currently willing to accept, we can put some kind of a case for an electromagnetic explanation of these various distant-contact phenomena. But then we come to the question of foreseeing the future. In the light of such cases, we may reluctantly be forced to abandon any kind of electromagnetic basis of explanation. Or may we perhaps, with more thought, still hope for some sort of 'unified field theory' of all aspects of the paranomal and the normal too?

13 Breaking the laws of space and time

Probably the least controversial way of beginning this nevertheless controversial chapter is to cite the experimental work performed with animals. These experiments may possibly help the sceptical mind to approach the human data, even though the human data require no props and provide their own complete defence.

Mice were introduced singly to a box from which they could move to any of a number of adjoining boxes. Once in the new box they could not return. After a batch of mice had made their individual choices, each choice was randomly correlated, by computer, with the two judgments 'correct' and 'incorrect'. The mice that drew the judgment 'incorrect' were then painlessly put to death. As the experiment proceeded notes were kept of the sex, weight, size, colour, and other physical features of the mice who successfully avoided the random selection for death. When fresh mice were selected, and tested, on the basis of these characteristics, this group now avoided random death at a level well in excess of chance.

Rats become less active when threatened with danger. One experimenter observed a group of laboratory rats, and rated them on their activity level. Then a second experimenter, who had no contact with the first, activated a procedure which randomly decided that certain of the rats should be killed. Significant correlations with low activity were found with those rats which were subsequently put to death. Yet when the activity level was being rated, the random decisions about death had not even been taken.

A similar experiment involved goldfish. Unlike rats, goldfish become *more* active when threatened with danger. Three goldfish were given a long series of trials. During two thirty-second periods each goldfish was given an activity rating. Then a random process designated which one of the fish should be briefly lifted out of the water. For a goldfish this is a very disturbing experience. The series of experiments produced significant correlations between high activity and subsequent lifting out of the water.

A statistically ingenious experiment was as follows. It was, incidentally, totally automated, so that no experimenter had any idea what was happening until all results were in. Mice were kept in a cage completely uniform in all respects, except that it was divided into two equal parts by a partition, over which the mouse could easily climb. The floor of the cage was of copper. A random process passed a brief electric current through one or other side of the box from time to time. If the mouse happened to be on that side of the barrier it received a shock. Now, there is no normal way that this situation can be solved or dealt with. It does not matter how often or how irregularly you move from one side of the box to the other, or whether you stay permanently on one side. You will nevertheless be shocked, in the long run, *exactly* as often as chance demands, namely fifty per cent of the time.

When the results were in, the experimenters analysed them in this fashion. They considered only two kinds of event where the animal behaved 'oddly': (1) when the animal moved from a side on which it was *not* last shocked to the side where it would next be shocked; (2) when the animal moved on to the side where it would not in fact be shocked, even though its last shock *was* on the side – and not on the side which it now abandoned: in other words it went back to the point where it was last shocked. One would not expect a mouse either to leave a position where it was not presently being shocked, or to go to a place where its last experience was one of shock. But whatever the normal logistics or rationale of these actions in the mouse's mind, these two sets of events should nevertheless cancel each other out. For you *cannot* avoid the consequences of a random series of events, no matter what action you take or what strategy you adopt. But in these two compared series of results the mice succeeded in avoiding shock at a very high level of significance. In 612 trials they avoided shock on average 53 more times than they should have.

There are a number of such animal experiments on record – not a vast number, certainly, but the total is growing. They represent a very useful first case with which to confront scepticism.

There are on record also many experiments involving human beings. Most of these involve the subject guessing the order of cards in a shuffled pack of cards in advance of the pack being shuffled. J. B. Rhine of the Parapsychology Laboratory in America devised a special pack of cards expressly for such experiments, using basic symbols like a cross and a circle, known as Zener cards. Some human subjects have produced very highly significant precognitive scores in experiments of this kind. However, the experimental design is actually extremely boring, and the large majority of people, after initially high scores, soon drop to producing chance results only. Nevertheless, the initially high scoring runs remain.

The spontaneous precognition of real life events is a good deal more exciting. The most mundane and checkable form of this phenomenon involves 'seeing' or 'guessing' the winners of horse races prior to the race being run. An astoundingly evidential case involving an American television producer was cited in the Introduction to this book. Equally impressive is the case, in Britain, of Lord Kilbracken. As a young man Lord Kilbracken dreamt the winner of horse races on several occasions, but what is more told his dreams to others before the race in question. He and others placed bets on these winning horses. Thelma Moss has also reported in great detail on two other individuals, in America, who dreamt the winners of horse races over an extended period. These were most unlikely people to undergo such an experience, and themselves initally had no interest whatsoever in horse racing. One was a devout Catholic woman, who told her husband of her dreams in which she saw the final stages of races and the race numbers on the saddle of the horses. The husband was able to trace the races in question. After several 'successes' on which they did not bet, being opposed to gambling, this couple finally placed a bet in the name of a charity, by buying a forecast ticket on the tote, and won nine hundred and sixty-four dollars. Another woman, an educational psychologist, also confided to her husband her dreams about horse races. She dreamt winners three or four times a week for about four months. She would clearly hear the name of the winning horse in her dream over the loudspeaker system. The husband bet these horses methodically, gradually increasing his bets as his confidence grew, and finally made a considerable amount of money.

As a boy Lewis Thompson, the brother of the writer Morton Thompson, could tell the winners of horse races by looking the horses over in the paddock. He said that the horses 'talked' to him, told him their feelings about themselves, about each other, the state of the track, and so on. He heard their talk in his head. Quite apart from his very substantial successes in picking winners in this way, Thompson sometimes obtained other information. Once he told an owner that one of his horses, an outsider, would win, while the other, which was fancied, was lame. Both statements caused some amusement, particularly as the fancied horse was obviously sound. However, the 22.1 outsider won the race, and the other pulled up lame.

We need not consider that Lewis Thompson literally spoke to the horses, or they to him, except in a subjective sense. Subjectively, paranormal information is presented to us in all kinds of strange ways. To consider that the circumstances are objectively true leads to all kinds of outright silliness. Of course, there is no doubt that Lewis Thompson did objectively have a remarkable rapport with horses. He could calm a rearing horse just by touching it and meeting its eye. This particular gift of rapport with animals has been shared by many psychics down the ages. St Francis of Assisi is a well-known instance, and in cases such as his the gift extends also to wild animals. Currently, it is said that when Ramana Mohan Maharshi goes out walking near his home in southern India, not only do dogs and escaped domestic cattle follow him, but when he walks along the edge of the jungle, birds, snakes and other wild animals do so also.

If foreseeing the winners of horse races does not seem a weighty matter (though in fact it shatters the framework of normal space-time just as completely as any more 'serious' item), presumably foreseeing one's own death is. Eugen Osty reports several cases of this phenomenon, mainly collected by his fellow doctors.

A woman of thirty, a teacher in a girl's boarding school, went to visit her parents in the holidays. She was in good health, apart from feeling rather tired. At the end of the holidays, when she was saying goodbye to her parents, a deep sense of sadness came over her, and she said impulsively: 'I feel we shan't see each other again.' She was as surprised as her parents to hear herself say this, and afterwards reproached herself for having made them needlessly anxious. On 24 April the teacher arrived back at school, still feeling somewhat tired. On 2 May the doctor, who reported this case, was called to see her. He found her running the symptoms of a mild form of typhus. She had no functional disturbance, not even diarrhoea, and apart from a temperature and a very slight swelling of the stomach was in good general health. The doctor is on record as saying that he had never seen a typhus case which gave less cause for anxiety. Nevertheless, the woman developed a conviction of approaching death: 'Doctor, I shall not recover.' The physician was also now told of the circumstances of the parting with her parents. At this, be redoubled his care. But, as before, he could find very little sign of infection or other effects. On 11 May the patient had a sudden intestinal haemorrhage that literally drew all the blood from her body. The bed itself was saturated and the blood had passed through the mattress to form a pool on the floor beneath.

An elderly man of seventy-six, although in good health, announced to his family that he would be dead before winter. Thereafter he mentioned the matter almost every day. At first no one took any notice of his dark mutterings. However, he began to eat less and less, and grew thinner. He refused to be put under medical care, saying it was useless, but said he would see a doctor when he knew the last few days were approaching, to avoid any charge of negligence against the family.

Some ten days before his death, the man announced he would die at the very start of All Saints Day (1 November) and agreed to see a doctor. The doctor reports that he found the old man very thin, but active and alert and leading a normal life. There were no organic defects, no temperature, and the heart was sound. The doctor did confirm, however, the slight chronic bronchitis from which the old man regularly suffered every winter. This had never been serious enough even to warrant him taking to bed. The old gentleman was cheerfully looking forward to his death. On 29 October he announced again that he would die at the start of 1 November, exactly at midnight. He said that he would not suffer at all, and would talk right up to the last. He added that after the death one member of the family would become hysterical.

On the morning of the 31 October the man complained of a pain in his side and went to bed. The doctors returned and diagnosed pneumonia in the left lung. In the evening the family tried to deceive the old man about the time, telling him at 11.30 pm that it was already after midnight. He answered that it was not after midnight, because he would die at twelve. Precisely at midnight he closed his eyes and died. His grand-daughter, normally a composed young lady, then had a violent hysterical attack.

In both the instances we have just looked at, a case could be made out for autosuggestion. In earlier chapters we already saw ample evidence that the body-mind can produce, hysterically, any symptoms that may be required, if it feels motivated to do so. Nevertheless, to cause one's own actual death, especially at a precise moment, would seem to go beyond anything we have yet seen.

Other cases, however, rule out any possibility of autosuggestion, or any possible connivance at the fatal outcome by anyone concerned.

An Italian barrister was on holiday with his wife, daughter and grand-daughter. Towards the end of the holiday, the daughter and grand-daughter set off back to their own home. When taking leave of her grandmother the little girl kissed her, with the statement that she would not be seeing her again. Once they reached home, the mother was occupied in getting her daughter ready for bed, and putting on her nightclothes. The child remarked that her mother was putting her into her grave clothes. She repeated the comment, despite her mother's protests, before going to sleep. A few hours later a very severe earthquake occurred (at Messina) and the child was crushed to death in the damaged house.

Dr Elisabeth Kübler-Ross has recently reported, at the Second European Conference for Humanistic Psychology, on a number of children who appear to have had unconscious knowledge of their own untimely deaths, revealed in their school and play drawings. One girl drew several pictures of rainbow-coloured waves, with a hand waving above them. A common enough drawing for a child to make, perhaps. But a few weeks later she was dragged into the sea by a shark from a public beach. When her horrified mother and onlookers reached the spot, all they found was a floating hand.

The wife of a Russian senior government official was awakened by her husband shouting 'Help! Save me!' in his sleep, and thrashing about in his bed. He had been dreaming of a shipwreck, where two liners had collided. He had been a passenger on one of the liners that had foundered. He himself had been thrown into the sea by the collision and was drowning. He had been struggling for his life in the water, along with another passenger. The official was much affected by his dream. He told his wife that he now believed he would die at sea by drowning in the near future. So convinced was he of this that he now put his domestic affairs in order and made a will.

Two months later the official received instructions to transfer his department, and all his staff, to a new location on the Black Sea. Taking leave of his wife at St Petersburg station, Lukawski reminded her of the dream, and said gently he did not think he would ever see her again. His wife naturally remonstrated with him, but with signs of deep sadness he repeated that he knew his end was near, and that nothing could stop it. He said: 'I see the port, the ship and the moment of collision, the panic on board and my end....I can see it all now, clearly.' He paused and then added that after she received the telegram and went into mourning, would she please not wear the long veil he disliked so much.

These many details tell us how convinced Lukawski was of the event he foresaw. Two weeks later the anxious Mme Lukawski read in the newspapers of a collision between two ships in the Black Sea, the *Vladimir* and the *Sineus*. Her husband was a passenger on the *Vladimir*. A week later she received news of his actual death. A Mr Henicke had found himself in the water, with a lifebelt, next to Lukawski. Because he himself could swim, and Lukawski was shouting that he could not, Henicke gave Lukawski the lifebelt. But even that gesture failed to save him.

Cases like these are perhaps commoner than most people realize. National publicity tends to be given to them, however, only when they are attached to some 'newsworthy' event like the Aberfan Welsh mining disaster, or the crash of a major airliner. Only then do we hear from those who dreamt the disaster in advance, or who cancelled their flight plans because of some inexplicable sense of unease.

Objectors to the idea that the future can be foreseen are able to challenge such cases on the basis of both fair and unfair statistics. They want to know how many people cancel their flights on planes that do not crash, for instance. Rather than get involved in endless arguments of this kind, it is better to fall back on the simple, yet philosophically devastating laboratory experiments which show that mice and rats and goldfish can experience a sense of their impending fate, and on the cases of men and women who dream the winners of horse races. Sceptics can always be asked to pick winners on the basis of their own dreams, for example, just to see how far they get.

It is a fact of life of psychic phenomena that they are always intensely personal. In this respect they carry a degree of total conviction to the person involved that it is not always possible for another person to appreciate, and we have to make the real effort of putting ourselves into the experiencer's shoes (which is especially why one ought to seek experiences of one's own – see below). The personal nature of psychic events is, however, a fact of life and cannot be used as an objection. In a similar situation Freud was once criticized for bothering to study dreams, on the grounds that they were so indistinct. He replied that indistinctness was part of the nature of dreams, that one could not dictate to phenomena what characteristics they ought or ought not to have, nor choose to investigate items on the basis of their convenience or inconvenience. So it is with psychic phenomena.

One example of highly personal communication comes from the case-book of the medium Mrs Piper, and is a telepathic incident, not a precognitive one – but the point is the same. The medium said that she could 'see' the sitter's deceased dog. She correctly described the general appearance of the dog, and said its name was Rover. But then immediately she corrected the statement saying, 'No, it's Grover'. The dog in question, as the sitter now told, had originally been called Rover, but in commemoration of President Grover Cleveland's election had been renamed Grover. Can we not appreciate what a tremendous degree of conviction such an event would have carried with ourselves, had we been the sitter, talking to a medium we had never seen before, and who had never seen us before?

Other important aspects of psychic and paranormal mental events certainly form a part of the explanation of telepathic phenomena relating to the present and perhaps offer a toe-hold of an explanation on the currently unclimbable and baffling mystery of foreseeing the future. One such aspect is the fact that communicated material proves to have very strong and well-worn associative paths in our own personal minds. These often have a strong emotional basis in us also, but the connections may be simply puns or plays on words. Is it permissible to consider that such mental 'associative paths' may have something in common with the 'paths of low reluctance' and 'paths of low resistance' of electricity? If so, then we would have another possible link between electromagnetism and psychic phenomena – and even a link between electromagnetism and paranormal knowledge of the future.

An example both of emotional association (in this case friendship) and a purely punning association is as follows. I was idling around at home one afternoon in London, when it suddenly occurred to me to wonder whether Colin Wilson, who was then writing his book *Mysteries,* was going to include in it mention of Robert Temple's already published book *The Sirius Mystery.* It seemed very important to me that he should, and it also struck me how well Colin and Robert would get along together and that they ought to meet. I now sat down and wrote a letter to Colin (in Cornwall), enclosing Robert's address (in Warwickshire), urging that he contact Robert at once. Little did I know that Colin was at that moment sitting down at home in Cornwall, writing to Robert Temple, care of Robert's publisher in London. I am myself convinced that I had picked up Colin's thought or intention, and in my further opinion part of the total package that facilitated this telepathic link was the use of the word 'mystery' in the title of each book. I am suggesting that such word associations and other punning references are not simply fortuitous or coincidental, but are meaningfully involved in the total equation. They are then what paranormalists and parapsychologists call 'synchronistic' to the event.

Another great plus from this line of associative thinking is that we can then also tentatively involve the severe states of mental illness known as psychosis and schizophrenia. Also relevant is the well-known fact that neurotics are sensitive to words which resemble or bring to mind words associated with their repressed unconscious fears, just as liars are to words which recall crimes or misdeeds being lied about. Taking the last point first, a guilty person connected up to a lie-detector, or even a simple skin galvanometer, will respond with involuntary autonomic signals (a major one of which is a change in skin conductivity) when words associated with the crime are mentioned. Repressed and unconscious neurotic conflicts can be detected in the same way. A woman, say, who has a repressed memory of being sexually assaulted as a very young child by a man, might well react unconsciously to words like 'attack' or even just 'sex'. Depending on the precise circumstances of the assault, she might also respond to 'cinema' or 'sweets'.

One of the marks of schizophrenia and other psychotic states is the tendency to produce masses of associative 'schizophrenese' or 'word salad' (as it is known). The patient produces streams of 'mad' rambling comment. But as R. D. Laing and many others have demonstrated, this material is not truly incoherent or purposeless or meaningless. Its associations are meaningful and 'logical' in the context of the emotional problems of the patient. One or two snippets from a patient of Anita Muhl's are as follows: 'Life doesn't necessarily mean everything. What do you little people know? God knows and who knows God – I don't think he is much acquainted with the vast majority – do you? Christ died to save our soles – no, souls – poverty has to do with soles not souls.' And: 'Alley – cats – alley cans – alley bums – Kyrie Eleison.'

Kyrie Eleison is a part of the Catholic liturgy. Following up that association revealed that the patient's father had been very bitter against Catholics, and furiously forbade his daughter to have anything to do with them. But her Catholic friends told her that if she stopped seeing them she would go to hell. The emotional turmoil generated had kept her awake at night in terror. In the last sequence, incidentally, it will be noted that the first item 'alley cat' is a partial spoonerism of Kyrie Eleison (pronouned 'alley-son' by the patient). 'Alley cans' also has this reversal of the initial letters of 'Kyrie Alley-son'.

Associational elements in paranormal perceptions of the future are equally easy to come by. The television producer who dreamt about the winning horse saw the event in his dream as a television programme, in colour, and heard a commentary on the race. The woman who in her dream saw the number of the winning horse (and heard nothing at all) was an accountant. A friend of mine foresaw an incident which involved a man reading a copy of *The Guardian* newspaper. My friend is a journalist.

The associational-emotional paths on view in the neurotic, the guilty liar, in schizophrenia, dreams and paranormal communication may be directly comparable to the 'paths of low resistance' or 'paths of good conductance' of electromagnetism. This aspect of unconscious mental life may, in other words, be a direct evolutionary product of the electromagnetic environment of our planet. In that case we would, as noted, have a direct link between electromagnetism and the ability to foresee the future, unlikely as that connection seems at first glance.

But there is another way of looking at the matter. It may be that electromagnetism and 'energy X' are two quite different energies, yet it may be that electromagnetism drags energy X along with it, in very much the same way as electricity pulls in magnetism, and moving magnetism in turn generates electricity. On that basis energy X (paranormal energy) and electromagnetism are quite different, although they exercise some kind of mutual influence on each other. We know that a magnetic field forms – or, at any rate, exists – at right angles to the direction of an electric current. Can it be that energy X forms, or at any rate exists, at 'right angles' to both electricity and magnetism taken together? Mathematically, there are no problems at all to such a model. Mathematically we can legitimately envisage an endless series of energies, each succeeding one at right angles to all the preceding energies, which are in turn all at right angles to each other. We are not limited, mathematically, to the maximum of three right angles observed in the normal physical universe.

151

Treating that normal universe now as if it were a single plane (and embracing not just electromagnetism, but also nuclear force, gravity and radioactivity, along with all the other phenomena of the normal universe), we can consider energy X to be at right angles to it. Phenomena such as consciousness, subjective time, and life itself may all be part of energy X – or they may be other energies also lying at right angles to 'lesser' energies. For simplicity's sake here, let us have just one direction called energy X/life/time/consciousness, at right angles to the direction (i.e. the sum of directions) of the normal physical universe. Figure 8 shows this conception. The point of intersection of

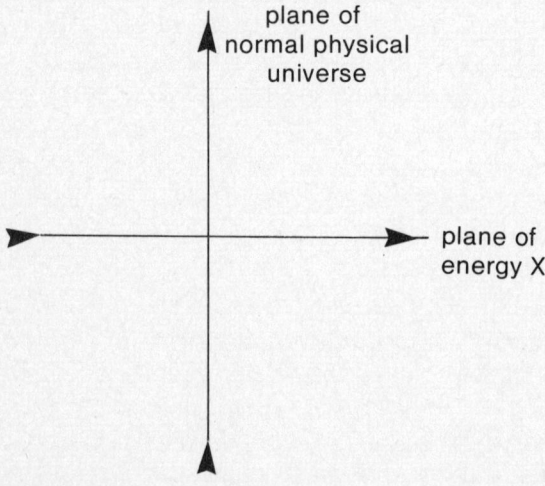

plane of
normal physical
universe

plane of
energy X

Figure 8 Energy X (paranormal energy) passing at right angles through the plane of the normal universe.

the two lines represents what we subjectively experience as 'now'. For us, of course, 'now' is a moving point not a static one, which poses difficulties for the model, as expressed. Yet we can still salvage the position by appeals to two other phenomena. One is the 'corkscrew' phenomenon shown in Figure 6 (chapter 10). As we saw, although, theoretically, magnetism forms as a static field precisely at right angles to any electric current, in practice the magnetic field creeps forward in a corkscrew movement in the direction of the current. Another observed phenomenon of our normal universe is that light, which theoretically always travels in a straight line, is caused to curve slightly in the neighbourhood of large bodies of matter (such as stars and galaxies). Perhaps therefore energy X, theoretically travelling in a straight line, is caused to curve slightly in the neighbourhood of a physical universe. Might it be that this is how we can catch glimpses, psychically and clairvoyantly, of a (not too distant) past which strictly no longer exists and a (not too distant) future that is yet to be?

These are all problems on which any definitive word must come from mathematicians and physicists, not from psychologists. But in at least a tentative way we have succeeded in suggesting a structure wherein the observed paradoxes of mental life (the ability to foresee the not yet existing future, for example) might be contained and resolved. What has been proposed is not exactly a 'unified field theory' of the normal and paranormal, but a model in which the two, even though quite different, might conceivably affect each other. The paranormal abilities displayed by numerous human beings and animals stretch normal models and explanations of the universe beyond their breaking point. It is precisely for this reason that so many orthodox scientists and thinkers so passionately deny the existence of the ability to see the future, even though the evidence for it far more than meets any reasonable demand for proof.

A number of scientists have admitted publicly that they would unhesitatingly accept the evidence offered in paranormal incidents as proof – in any other context except the paranormal. It is in fact difficult to see what else could be offered in the way of evidence. We can only keep on offering more of it. The best way forward, probably, is for every individual to obtain personally convincing evidence of the pre-existence of the future (some aspects of it, at any rate), as well as other paranormal experience. There are two readily available avenues even for those who, for whatever reason, draw back from developing their own secret gifts. One is a visit, or better visits, to a reputable psychic requesting a future scan and whatever (a Tarot reader or a psychometrist would be best). Another is to consult that remarkable book and oracle the *I Ching*, to which we come in chapter 16.

In the meantime, the revival and rediscovery of human secret life cannot wait for the conversion of every last sceptic. As Holmes was in the habit of telling Watson, when he shook him awake in the middle of the night, the game is already afoot.

14 The stellar aspects of astrology

We considered the planetary aspects of astrology in chapter 7. The reason for separating the stellar aspects of astrology from the planetary aspects is that while Gauquelin and others have produced hard scientific evidence in support of planetary influence, there is as yet none in respect of the stars. And probably among the biggest hurdles facing stellar astrology in its attempts to establish itself scientifically is the very enthusiasm of its supporters.

A French investigator offered free horoscopes in an advertisement in a French newspaper. Everyone who wrote in was sent the same fake horoscope. This contained statements like 'you have inner conflicts, life has many problems, you sometimes upset people' and much along similar lines. Comments were invited, and about two hundred people wrote back. The correspondents made remarks like 'what you say about my character is absolutely true, you can read my life like a book, I was sceptical about astrology but I am now convinced it is true'.

Michel Gauquelin substantially repeated the experiment. He also advertised a free horoscope. To more than five hundred respondents he sent a computer-generated horoscope (programmed by France's leading astrologer, André Barbault) based on the birth data of Dr Petiot, a notorious criminal who murdered several dozen people and disposed of their bodies by burning them in lime.

In respect of Dr Petiot himself the horoscope was a farce. It described a person of 'instinctive warmth...a worthy, right-minded middle-class citizen...bathed in a sea of sensitivity, total devotion to others...altruistic sacrifices...'. However, this was the horoscope which the respondents received. Of a sample of one hundred and fifty replies, ninety-four per cent found the fake horoscope strikingly accurate. And ninety per cent said this accuracy was confirmed by their families and friends.

Several other studies of this kind are reported by Geoffrey Dean in his book *Recent Advances in Natal Astrology*. They only too amply confirm the rather sad picture suggested by the example just described. The results of such studies have also been analysed to see what kind of factors in the horoscope (and the recipient) contribute towards its acceptance. Two findings are of special interest. One was that acceptance was significantly increased by the degree of mystery involved. It was also increased if the character description was favourable rather than unfavourable.

All in all, the lesson is that a large and ever-growing number of people desperately want astrology to be true. This is exactly what Jung found in respect of the phenomenon of UFOs (see chapter 3). The two areas actually have much in common – both involve influence from the sky and outer space, for instance – but that is not our concern here. More important is that both offer evidence of an enormous spiritual hunger, and an instinctive flight from the vacuum created by the death of conventional religion.

Reverting to the possibly genuine, objective and scientific content of astrology, however, surely this would be an easy matter for scientists to test, just as Michel Gauquelin tested, and confirmed, the planetary aspects of astrology? It is actually a very, very difficult matter to test, for more than one set of reasons.

For example, due to slight but cumulative differences in the solar year as compared to the sidereal (or star) year, the constellations always gradually slip out of the sun house to which they are assigned at any given time. About every three thousand years, the constellations of a given house will have slipped back entirely into the preceding house. In other words, the stars and constellations that three thousand years ago were the indicators or hall-marks of the sign Cancer are today those of the sign Gemini.

However, as far as the day-to-day practice of astrology is concerned, the names and dates of the twelve zodiac signs are fixed. Gemini always runs from 21 May to 21 June, Cancer always from 22 June to 22 July, and so on. Anyone born within the specified dates will, according to astrologers, necessarily exhibit the major psychological and fate propensities which tradition ascribes to the sign in question.

Now as it happens, people born at specific times of the year do have certain qualities in common. When large groups of people are examined statistically, certain broad patterns emerge which un-questionably relate to the yearly cycle of seasons – or whatever. But what exactly is the influence here? Is it some mystical or physical emanation from the stars, or is it rather that, for instance, pregnant mothers eating winter food take in smaller quantities of vitamins than mothers eating summer food? Although, on the other hand, a birth in spring may be less stressful than a birth in winter – it's a case of swings and roundabouts. In some countries religious abstinence severely limits conception during certain months of the year, and consequently produces fewer births nine months later. Very hot and very cold weather also affect the incidence of conception. Some workers migrate seasonally, leaving their wives behind, and so on. And during the present century birth control methods have increasingly allowed women and men to choose for themselves when they want a child conceived, so interfering with any natural rhythms of pregnancy. Still, these last items shouldn't stop a Gemini being a Gemini. But what of the yearly magnetic cycles of planet Earth, which seem to owe very little to the influence of the stars (though we cannot say that they owe nothing to them)?

At any rate, yearly analyses of birthdays and psychological characteristics certainly reveal some non-random groupings. For example, one large study has shown that the births of persons of high eminence or very high achievement conform more closely to a climatic cycle than do the births of ordinary mortals. As regards conception, hot weather is more unfavourable to the conception of a high achiever, and cold weather more favourable. The births of the eminent peak in months cooler than average. These results hold for groups as diverse as American presidents, achievers listed in *Who's Who*, and for doctors, engineers and clergymen.

We are left with the possibility that the ancients discovered numbers of such seasonal correlations, which they then assigned to the influence of the ruling or rising constellations of stars that happened to be in evidence at the time. They were not wrong in thinking that date of birth has some broad relationship with psychology, character and achievement. But perhaps they were wrong in assigning the causality to the stars.

In support of the possibility that the stars as such are irrelevant we can point to Gauquelin's successful studies of planetary influence. The stars seem to be totally without influence in respect of these studies.

So how could astrology work?

We are left with the fact that certain gifted astrologers, using the 'irrelevant' and 'outdated' tools and concepts of traditional astrology, nevertheless sometimes produce convincing results well above chance expectation.

Dr Norman Shealy ran an experiment using three clairvoyants, one palmist, one graphologist and one astrologer. They were each asked to diagnose what illness or illnesses a number of long-term chronic hospital patients were suffering from. For each of these patients detailed hospital records and reports existed. The clairvoyants were given a photograph of the patient, with name and date of birth. The palmist had a palm print, the astrologer the necessary birth data, and the graphologist a page of handwriting. As controls, a Professor of

Psychology was also given a photograph and name and birth date of each patient, while a computer was programmed to produce chance diagnoses.

All the various psychics scored well above chance level, while the Professor scored exactly at chance. So all these 'crazy' approaches actually do produce hard results. But while the palmist, the graphologist and the astrologer scored approximately equal marks, each of the three clairvoyants scored far higher. The clairvoyants, working on 'thin air', did much better than the astrologer, with all his charts and 'scientific' expertise.

The lesson in this experiment seems to be this. Stellar astrology, palmistry and graphology are not exact or objective sciences in the sense their exponents claim. They seem to be 'rituals' and 'incantations' which help the practitioner to focus and harness the unconscious, intuitive mind. They are 'aids to clairvoyance'. *But* at the same time, they may be a hindrance to clairvoyance. They may give the conscious mind too much to do, too much fuel, too much scope for interference. In this experiment, the free-floating clairvoyants, who had the courage to use pure clairvoyance with no props, easily beat this particular astrologer's score.

The position is possibly as follows. A gifted stellar astrologer using the techniques and procedures of traditional astrology may well be able to make meaningful, useful and accurate statements about the past and future life of a client, about his psychological make-up and so on. But these results do not, perhaps, arise from the influence of the stars, or from the workings of any objective principle. They may arise from paranormal perception, from clairvoyance.

The history of stellar astrology

Astrology has its roots far, far back in mankind's past. But the 'ancient' art of it practised today is only some three thousand years old at most. The evidence is that still further back the rules and the theoretical base were once very different.

Proof is steadily accumulating in all areas of religious and philosophical inquiry that where the number twelve, and the Sun, rules in historical times, the number thirteen and the Moon ruled before it. There were, for instance, originally thirteen tribes of Israel, not twelve; and an old English ballad vehemently challenges the then current orthodoxy; 'But how many monthes be in the yeare? There are thirteen I say; the midsummer moon is the merryest of all, next to the merry month of May.' In short, it looks very much as if the zodiac once had thirteen divisions, which were considered to be governed by the Moon.

The position is entirely logical, for there are thirteen moons in every year, and every lunar calendar has thirteen divisions.

James Vogh has performed some excellent detective work on this last issue in his book *The Thirteenth Zodiac*, following trails blazed by such eminent writers as Robert Graves (*The White Goddess*). James Vogh offers us evidence of a very solid kind. Gnostic Jews built a synagogue at Beth Alpha in the Jezreel valley in AD 520. Inlaid into the floor is a zodiac – at first glance a conventional twelve-division zodiac, shown in Figure 9. But at second look there are immediate inconsistencies. Even with the unaided eye, the twelve divisions can be seen to be unequal. Measurement confirms the impression. Virgo, for instance, is forty per cent larger than it should be. Furthermore, the four seasons around the outside of the circle are both irregularly and incorrectly placed in relation to the signs they govern.

Figure 9   Zodiac from Beth Alpha in the Jezreel valley.

As Vogh demonstrates, this zodiac can be made fully symmetrical by converting the twelve signs to thirteen. Six of the existing signs are already, in any case, one-thirteenth each of the full circle. It is clear that this zodiac was originally designed to be one of thirteen divisions. What is not quite clear is whether the original plan was abandoned in the course of construction, in response to some countermand, or whether the design was altered at some date subsequent to completion.

The central figure of the zodiac is also of great interest. It shows a goddess driving a very odd kind of chariot. The head-dress of this female figure has six panels divided by seven rays, a total of thirteen. To her left is the crescent moon. The four horses' heads are, presumably, again the four seasons (though Vogh thinks these heads were also added later). Then below these are eight – what? – wheels, legs or whatever.

James Vogh produces much evidence in his book to show that these eight objects represent the eight legs of a spider – and we come to that matter in a moment. But an interesting side question here is whether these objects also represent eight planets. The ancients are traditionally believed to have known of seven planets, and we ourselves only discovered the eighth planet (Neptune) in 1846. Subsequently, literally by accident, Pluto, the ninth planet, was discovered as recently as 1930.

In various museums around the world (including the British Museum) there are crude lenses ground from natural crystal which are agreed to be as much as four thousand years old. They, or others like them, may be far older – they are necessarily dated from the situation in which they are excavated, but the crystal itself is ageless and cannot be dated. If two of these crystal lenses are held up one in each hand and moved about till their focal lengths interact, they form a crude telescope. The improvement obtained by two aligned lenses is described as 'startling'. The question is, how many of these lenses could be aligned – by setting the edges of them in a length of wood, for instance – to increase magnification, before the crudeness of the lenses distorted the image beyond usefulness? How many degrees of magnification could be obtained? I have tried to get a straight answer – or even a cautious guess – to this question from scientific authorities, and have failed. Specifically I wanted to know whether these primitive telescopes could have detected Neptune. One of the problems is that the lenses are in different museums around the world. They cannot be brought together. So perhaps the ancients did at one stage know of the eighth planet. (But they could not have known of the ninth. Even our sophisticated techniques can only just detect it.) Maybe, then, the eight objects of this design are eight planets. But that they are in any case also the eight legs of a spider is not in doubt.

James Vogh's case is that the purged and hidden thirteenth sign of the old zodiac was Arachne the Spider Goddess, also synonymous with the Moon herself. She was likewise the overall ruler of the total zodiac, as well as of the universe and everything in it. Other ancient stone-carved thirteen-zodiacs have been found, incidentally, among the Australian Aborigines and the North American Indians. So there are plenty of links here with the material of chapters 1 and 2.

What James Vogh seems to have missed in his otherwise excellent investigation is the overwhelming psychological significance of the spider's web itself. It is a key that unlocks many further mysteries. The real spider makes its web by first establishing the straight lines radiating from a central point. Then from that central point it moves *in a spiral towards the outer edge*, laying down a widely-spaced cross-thread as it goes. But when it reaches the outer edge it turns, and now spirals inwards laying the narrow-spaced cross-thread of the finished web. As it goes it *gathers up the original outward moving spiral cord*, which was only a kind of structural sketch or guide.

Surely in these two acts of the spider we have the explanation of the ancient inward and outward spiral dance of the maze and the labyrinth? Sometimes the ancient dancers paid out and gathered up a thread – but there is a mass of confirmatory testimony in legend also. So when Theseus was condemned by King Minos to be shut in the labyrinth with the dreaded Minotaur, he was secretly given a ball of thread by Adriadne (the daughter of Minos, who had fallen in love with Theseus) so that he could find his way out again.

This ruse of the ball of thread had been suggested to Ariadne by Daedalus. Minos now wished to kill Daedalus, who fled. Minos believed that Daedalus was in hiding at the court of King Cocalus, so he went to Cocalus with a puzzle. Here is a snail shell and a thread, he said to Cocalus. How can the shell be threaded without breaking it? Minos knew that Cocalus would take the riddle to Daedalus, which he then did. Daedalus' solution was to tie the thread to an ant, which then followed the path of the spiral shell to the end and back again.

It was Daedalus also who procured the bull which made love to Pasiphaë, the wife of Minos, a union which produced the bull-headed monster the Minotaur. Pasiphaë is the Moon Goddess – and she is also the mother of Ariadne. Ariadne therefore also represents the Moon. In turn, some scholars consider that Ariadne and Arachne are one and the same. But that both of them are much involved with threads and labyrinths and weaving is in any case not in doubt.

What we have taken the briefest of looks at here is a mass of evidence which points again and again to conclusive but secret links between labyrinths, mazes, spirals, threads, spiders and moons.

But there is much more in these secrets than traditional scholars have realized. James Vogh has made the following interesting suggestion. The rightful place of Arachne, the Spider Goddess and the missing thirteenth sign of the zodiac, is between Taurus the Bull and Gemini the Twins on the conventional twelve-sign zodiac. (On Vogh's revised zodiac Arachne's house extends from 16 May to 13 June.) Vogh proposes that the word 'Minotaur' is a form of anagram between 'geMINi' and TAURus'. The fact that the order of the two houses on the zodiac are reversed in the anagram is no problem. Such reversals, plays on words, use of initials letters only of words in sentences to spell out meanings, and so on and so on, are absolute commonplaces in the writings and sayings of kabbalists, mystics and adepts down the ages. They were always trying to preserve and communicate the ancient truths for those who had eyes to see, while hiding them from the gaze of the stupid or uninitiated.

The central picture of the synagogue mosaic at Beth Alpha (Figure 9) is an excellent pictorial example of such a message with a hidden meaning. She has the crescent moon at her *left* side (and the crescent moon is the most powerful moon of all – see *Guardians of the Ancient Wisdom*). Her head-dress contains thirteen items. She rules the four seasons (or the four elements perhaps – earth, air, fire and water) and the eight planets (?) with reins or threads – and we have yet to consider the full implications of the thread. This is, in fact, Arachne the Spider Goddess, the ancient, true ruler of the universe.

As for the Minotaur, living at the centre of the labyrinth he therefore symbolizes the central mystery, and as the son of the Moon is also a disguised reference to her. I myself also think the Minotaur is a disguised reference to the cerebellum (the heavily folded and creased cerebellum is more of a labyrinth even than a walnut). So the Minotaur is the 'cerebellum-headed' human being. And since a birth in Arachne is *par excellence* the sign of the psychic individual (see below), the various interconnections are perfect.

But let us come back for the moment to the spider web itself, the most important symbol of all. I hope we have made it amply clear that all labyrinths and mazes are symbolic webs. The straight, radial lines of the spider's web are the straight lines of logical rational thought: and also at the same time the rays of the sun, the symbol of waking consciousness. The spiral line of the web is the symbol of intuitive, unconscious thought, the sideways oblique approach of the mystical mind – 'knight's move' thinking, as it has been called, in an image taken from chess. Such oblique, non-linear thought operates above all at night in dreams, and the Moon herself is likewise a symbol of unconscious thought. Scientific evidence is accumulating, by the way, that the phases of the Moon directly relate to amount and vividness of dreaming, an ancient belief in any case.

But matters do not end even here. When the spider is making its second and final spiral, it makes the thread sticky. But it would now itself stick to its own web. So the spider plucks its web, and the sticky substance arranges itself into droplets at the intervals dictated by the laws of harmonic vibration. Now the spider can run over the web, touching only the non-sticky parts.

Spiders communicate in a complex way with their mates and their young by twanging different harmonies on the web. The mother talks to her children in this way: 'stay in the nest, come and eat, remain motionless where you are on the web – there is danger' and so on. We need not seriously doubt that the ancient meditators observed and understood all this.

In antique Greece there was the belief that the planets were arranged in distance from the sun according to the laws of harmonics – and this is very nearly, if not quite true. The harmonies of the musical scale and the relative positions of the planets were thought to be expressions of the same basic laws of vibration in the universe – hence the phrase 'the music of the spheres'. These ideas are no doubt far older than the Greeks.

Now we can see how the ancients pieced everything together in their vision of the universe. (Let us not overlook here that the central motto was 'as above, so below'. What goes on in the heavens is the same as goes on below.)

The Sun is the centre of the web and his straight rays hold the planets in position. But the Moon, with her erratic path, is the spider, whom the web serves. And we, mankind, are the children of the spider – hence the umbilical cord of the new born baby. This is, again, the spider thread which connects the baby to the centre of the labyrinthine womb. (And trees were said to be the umbilical cord which joined the Earth to the sky.)

But many of the Moon's threads are invisible. The thread which draws up the tides is invisible – it is magnetism. The thread which draws the floating lodestone to the north is invisible – it is magnetism.

From here it is but one more short step to the 'web of fate' and the 'thread of life' which the Fates (or the Spinners as they are also called) cut when we die.

What a satisfactory picture this was (and is!). More or less everything has been accounted for. Here is an explanation which both clarifies and supports. The universe is not just a wild free-for-all. There are laws, and their workings can be discovered and identified. To some extent they can even be used and manipulated for our own ends.

Pushed for a one sentence explanation of events, the ancient priests might well have replied: 'It's all down to magnetism, really.' And perhaps it is.

Christ, King Arthur and the Moon Goddess

Once we have hit upon the central importance of the thirteen zodiac and the Moon, and all the symbolism logically associated with them, the mystery surrounding many of our central cultural puzzles falls away, as if by magic. Of course, the ancients always said that once the right key is found, all at once becomes clear.

The ancient Moon worshippers revered the Moon in the following respect: that in any one solar year the Moon shows either thirteen new moons or thirteen full moons, in rotation. There are not thirteen lunations in the year, however, that is, not thirteen complete cycles of the Moon from new to full. The thirteenth month is therefore a short, and in the sense 'weak' month. It is during this thirteenth 'weak' month that the Sun reaches its lowest point and 'dies'. So the thirteenth month is also an evil month. But in that same interval of time, the very next day in fact, the dead Sun is immediately resurrected and reborn, and begins his long climb back to his zenith. So the thirteenth month is also a good month. (Moon worshippers believed that it was the Moon who gave the Sun back its life – just as on Earth she made woman and the land fertile).

Many of the major legends of our own historical time, including the story of Christ himself, are disguised versions of this same story. Whatever the facts in the life of Christ, the life of King Arthur and so on, the fertility story of the thirteen-zodiac Moon was grafted on to them.

Note first that Christ led a band of twelve disciples, which with himself as leader makes a coven of thirteen. King Arthur likewise led a band of twelve knights. Several other covens of thirteen also managed to escape the general purging of that number in historical times – Robin Hood and his band, Odysseus and his crew, the judge and twelve jurors of our legal system.

The Christ story is briefly this. As just noted, his total group numbers thirteen. Christ the King is betrayed by a treacherous and weak member of the group, Judas, and meets his death. This death takes place on Friday evening. Christ then rises from the dead – traditionally on the third day. But the tomb is already empty first thing on Sunday morning. It was not inspected on the Saturday, because that was the Jewish sabbath. So perhaps Christ (like the Sun) was already resurrected on the day after his death.

In Scandinavian mythology a completely separate story tells of the death of Balder. Twelve of the gods – including Balder – have been invited to attend a banquet in Valhalla. Balder was the favourite of all the gods. He is the god of 'summer sunlight', the incarnation of the life principle, and also called 'the Good'. But while the feast is in progress, Loki, the spirit of Strife and Mischief, who has not been invited, nevertheless turns up. (So he is now the thirteenth 'weak' member.) He then kills Balder by giving the blind Hoder – already present, and who represents Darkness and Winter – an arrow of mistletoe, and getting him to fire it. In the Saxon version of this same story, Balder and Hoder slay each each other in a quarrel for the hand of the Virgin Moon. Both are subsequently resurrected and live together in the battle-hall of Odin. Their resurrection signals the Golden Age of Man.

The legend of Sleeping Beauty is, again, as follows. A great king invites twelve good fairies or wise women to attend the celebratory christening of his daughter. They arrive and each bestow a blessing on the child. But a thirteenth wicked fairy who has not been invited also appears, and curses the child with death if she shall ever prick herself. She does finally prick herself on a spindle. She then falls into a long sleep. But she is finally brought back to life (and happiness) by the kiss of a brave knight. It does not require too much imagination, does it, to consider that Sleeping Beauty is the land, which after the winter sleep is brought to life again by the kiss of the Sun.

King Arthur, King of Britain, has in his castle a round table at which sit with him his twelve most favoured knights, a total of thirteen. All the knights are loyal except one – Mordred. Mordred is always portrayed as rebellious and traitorous, and in one account it is said that wherever he went he ate everything in sight and left the land bare. He is therefore (like Hoder) a personification of winter. While Arthur is away fighting in Italy (i.e. 'while the Sun is low in the sky in the south') Mordred usurps the kingdom and marries Guinevere, the King's wife. When Arthur returns he and Mordred fight (like Balder and Hoder), both dealing each other mortal wounds.

Arthur is carried to Avalon (the Celtic Elysium). The report is that he is to be healed there by a queen and will then return. Other accounts say that Arthur is sleeping in a magic hillside and will wake again when his land is threatened. But an apparently older French source has a yet more useful ending to the story. A travelling groom stops at a castle in Italy (once again the south) and finds that Arthur is there, being treated for his wounds 'which break out every year afresh'. It is, of course, the Sun which is wounded and healed every year.

There are many other points we could linger on in these stories. The famous Round Table of King Arthur is, naturally, a zodiac – and a thirteen-zodiac at that. Apart from the Arthurian story, all the stories involve a feast. We can argue that 'feast' really means 'religious festival'. In particular the 'Last Supper' may well mean 'the last Festival of the Year'. In the Christ story, it is probably not too extravagant to consider that the Virgin Mary is the Virgin Moon. Christ himself is the Sun, which is why he is always associated with light, and has a nimbus or halo of light around his head.

The role of blood and bleeding in all these stories is extremely significant. The blood of Christ on the Cross, for example, which washes all our sins as white as snow, is captured in the Holy Grail by Joseph of Arimathea and brought to England.

Literally, this is the blood of the sacrifice of the most favoured male, elected King for a Year with every honour, by the High Priestess of the Moon at the ceremony of the Winter Solstice. As the Sun died 'above', so the king must die 'below'. The sacrificed male was probably castrated, to turn him into a menstruating woman, and the blood which flowed was no doubt caught in a bowl by the priestesses. As suggested in chapter 2, the act of male circumcision by Egyptians, Jews and Australian Aborigines alike seems to be a gesture of deference to the deposed Goddess of the Old Religion and her ceremonies.

Symbolically, the blood of the goddess is always the blood of the menstruating Moon. As we know from Australian legend and elsewhere, the magical and magnetic red ochre in the soil is literally the Moon Goddess's menstrual blood, which makes the Earth fertile to bear crops. (Fertility precedes impregnation and is a *sine qua non*, which is one reason why woman is more important than man.)

The resurrection of Christ (and of Balder, and of Arthur) which brings the 'Golden Age of Man' and the 'Gift of Eternal Life' is the resurrection of the Sun which brings another golden summer.

All these items and interpretations hang together very well indeed, and link equally well with the kinds of material we have been discussing throughout.

The thirteen zodiac

Scientists investigating the relationship alleged by astrology to exist between human personality and the twelve signs of the conventional zodiac have so far turned up nothing comparable with Gauquelin's discovery of planetary influence. However, in fairness to astrology, all the investigative work already performed ought to be repeated using the thirteen-division zodiac.

James Vogh draws attention to A. R. Ramsden's book *A Sign for Psi*? and some of the results it contains. Ramsden stumbled by chance across the thirteen zodiac. He heard that some North American Indian tribes spoke of a 'lost moon' or thirteenth sign. Accordingly Ramsden now divided up the year into thirteen equal parts, beginning at the vernal equinox. Ramsden had already tried to find some relationship between proven psychic ability and a particular sign or signs on the conventional zodiac. Actually his results here are by no means uninteresting. Using 127 psychics as his sample, he found a distinct clustering of birth dates in and around Gemini. Although Ramsden's psychic sample is not large, any statistician seeing the results would immediately have wanted to test further on a larger population. But Ramsden now went on to re-examine his 127 births in terms of the thirteen zodiac. Now he found that the greatest proportion of psychic births fell in the 'new' sign of Arachne, with some scattering on either side. The result was a highly significant one statistically.

Ramsden's work on Arachne and psychics urgently needs repeating and extending, and that task has already been taken up by Arthur Mather. Mather was, and is, Geoffrey Dean's chief collaborator on *Recent Advances in Natal Astrology*. However, *Recent Advances* is a permanent ongoing study, and the two, Dean and Mather (along with their fifty-two scientific collaborators around the world), are currently preparing the up-date of their work to the end of 1980. Mather already reports orally that a preliminary scan of the Arachne-psi connection looks promising, and an intensive large-scale investigation is now under way. This kind of item, if supported in the final analysis, will begin to give stellar astrology some of the scientific backing often claimed for it, but till now completely lacking.

I often get reproving letters from practising astrologers when I speak of stellar astrology as not being scientific. But if stellar astrology, as at present constituted, were a science, then everybody would be able to use it with the same accuracy as everybody else. Two astrologers given the same birth data would produce exactly the same report as each other. Neither of these statements is true, or anything like it. I once asked Liz Greene, the well-known astrologer (who also has a doctorate in psychology, incidentally), the following question. Suppose she were allowed to spend two months with a person, asking every possible question, barring that person's actual date of birth, could she then reliably tell me his or her sign? Without hesitation, Liz said no. That was a very honest and in the circumstances very brave answer. But what it emphatically means is that astrology is not a science (or is not yet a science). In science you can always argue from causes to effects and from effects back to causes with equal facility. Any astrologer, given a reasonable amount of data about a person, ought to be able to state that person's date and time of birth.

We are left with (a) astrology as an art and (b) astrology as an 'aid' to psychic-intuitive divination. In those two respects we ought to be

166

perfectly willing to endorse the practice of astrology. In those terms it has proved itself adequately.

However, to revert to the scientific aspect again, I cannot myself help being impressed by the 'fact' that I, as a Gemini, have several traditional Gemini characteristics, as my correspondents often point out to me. One of them is being a writer. Writing is probably the most universally agreed attribute of Gemini by all astrologers. I have been further shaken by some comments of James Vogh. He says that the Sun enters Arachne on 16 May and leaves it on 13 June. My own birthday happens to be 13 June. Anyone born on 13 June, says Vogh, ought to partake of some of the characteristics of both Arachne and Gemini. They should, he says, be both a writer and a psychic – and he quotes W. B. Yeats as an instance. 'A psychic writer' is altogether too accurate a description, for comfort, of myself also.

15 Satan wants you for a moonbeam?

A law-abiding, hard-working, christian man in his mid-thirties, the kind father of two little girls and a boy, one day at the dinner-table gives vent to a stream of obscenities. While he is doing this his body jerks and twitches violently. Meanwhile his eyes roll wildly in his head, and dart helplessly from side to side. The top half of his face is a picture of a man seized by a force he cannot control. Something is obviously going on against his will. But in the lower part of his face is the cruel, mocking mouth and its stream of verbal filth.

Suddenly all the tension and struggle goes out of the man. He leans brokenly forward on the table, holding his face in his hands, and begins quietly sobbing.

Now the children have been sent next door with a neighbour. The husband is in bed, resting, and awaiting the arrival of the doctor and the priest his wife has sent for. She sits next to him holding one of his hands in her two hands, and he tells her a little of what has been happening. He talks in whispers, glancing nervously about the room the whole time, as if expecting to see something. He tells her that he has commited a great sin, though he refuses to tell her exactly what it is. (Actually, he has been visiting a prostitute in the next town and engaging with her in all kinds of 'perversions'. He now has a small boil near his genitals, which he is sure is syphilis. He is equally sure that he has given this to his wife. But these facts come out only later.) Anyway, the man has sinned grievously. Because of the sin he has been unable to sleep. (His wife nods.) And a few nights ago, as he lay unsleeping, the devil appeared to him. The man begins sobbing again. His wife can scarcely understand what he is saying. But it appears that the devil has said that because the man chose sin of his own free will, the devil now owns his soul. He is the devil's plaything and servant, to be done with as the devil wishes.

The priest gets there first. In the middle of his visit the husband is again suddenly 'possessed'. He screams and shouts and curses, fragments of Latin, obscenities and whatever. His face is totally contorted. This is not the man's own face. It is not his own voice. With a maniacal laugh, the man, or the creature, evacuates his bowels. Then before anyone can stop him, he springs from the bed and runs off down the road.

168

The above is a fairly standard description of one kind of so-called diabolical 'possession'. It can be set in medieval times, or in a present-day city. The details haven't changed very much, except that the unfortunate man would once have been treated exclusively by the church authorities. Today in the west in the twentieth century the man will be treated by doctors and psychiatrists – as soon, at least, as they get to hear of it.

However, the idea of spirit possession is still a very common one even in the west, along with the more respectable beliefs that people have detachable souls which survive bodily death, and which can sometimes leave the body even during life (in astral travelling, for example, or during major surgical operations and accidents), or that there are such things as angels and other non-physical beings. Many people, by no means just Spiritualists, believe that the dead communicate with them, and that loved ones who have passed on watch over the living, and are constantly with them.

The belief in spirits and spirit life – and so therefore in principle in spirit possession – must be as old as consciousness itself. And at first appearances a very good case can be made out for the spirit hypothesis. To examine and show – at second appearance – all the actual weaknesses of the spirit hypothesis is an undertaking that would itself require a whole book. But here now are some of the considerations which lead to a very different view of the phenomenon of possession, and likewise of all the superstructure of both black and white magic which has been built upon it.

For instance, it is perfectly possible to see the 'ghost' or 'apparition' of someone who is very much not dead, nor even asleep. W. B. Yeats reports an incident from his youth. He had a message for a fellow student, which for personal reasons he was hesitating to send. Nevertheless, he thought very intently about sending the message at this particular point, and then shelved the problem. A couple of days later Yeats himself received a letter, from the other student, who was some hundreds of miles away. It seems that at the point when Yeats was so intently debating with himself about the intended message, he, Yeats, had suddenly appeared in a crowd of people in a hotel, looking very solid and as if in the flesh. Only the student friend had seen the visitation or vision, however, and he had mentally asked Yeats to come back when the others had gone. The friend saw Yeats as a vision again later that night.

The German poet Goethe was one day out for a walk in the country when he was startled to see in the road in front of him an old friend he had not seen or heard of for years. The vision vanished. When Goethe arrived home he found the friend waiting for him.

In these and other similar cases the person seen as a 'ghost' is fully conscious, wide awake and active, and in perfectly normal health. If some part of him has travelled many miles, then he himself has no knowledge of it, and no sense of being 'diminished', no sense of loss or detachment or whatever. So a more reasonable explanation of the event is that those involved (the sender and the percipient) were in telepathic communication with each other. The unconscious mind then signalled the contact or message received to the conscious mind of the percipient by producing a hallucination of the sender. Such a visual expression of a paranormal or other unconscious impulse or message is totally commonplace.

Now, if we can see an unconsciously generated vision of a person who is currently alive, conscious and well, why can't we also see an unconsciously generated vision of a person who happens to be dead? Why should we necessarily invoke the idea of the disembodied spirit of the dead person visiting us?

When we objectively analyse large numbers of reports of ghosts and spirit visitations – as Celia Green and others have done – many interesting facts emerge which argue for a straightforward use of our normal perceptual equipment, rather than for any paranormal presence. For example, around eighty-four per cent of ghostly experiences are visual, thirty-seven per cent are auditory, fifteen per cent are of touch and eight per cent of smell. These varying amounts of each sense impression happen to be very close to the degree of importance which each of those senses plays in our normal lives – and is catered for in the sensory cortex of our brains. Might one not have expected ghostly visitors to break some of the rules of normality, or even to make rules of their own?

It will be appreciated that the kinds of critical evidence and circumstances we are considering here are suggestive only. They do not in themselves constitute final proof one way or another. But on the other hand, there is a veritable mountain of such suggestive evidence, all of which seems to go rather gently but inexorably against the spirit hypothesis.

I had occasion to be involved in a television programme, when one of the other guests on the show was a comedian, the late Ted Ray. Mr Ray had some months before been involved in a very serious car accident, in which he had almost been killed. He told us of an incident which he experienced as he lay in deep coma, critically ill and between life and death. It seemed to him that he was in some kind of boat just off land. On the shore was a crowd of people, some of whom were former friends and relatives no longer alive. They were waving and calling and beckoning to him. And Ted Ray said that he somehow knew that if he went to join them, he would die. But he made the decision to turn away, and not to land.

Many similar cases are reported. Some poeple say that, while in critical coma, they find themselves in a tunnel with light at the far end, and perhaps a glimpse of a marvellous land. And they know that if they go forward out of the tunnel into the wonderful land, they will never wake up again on Earth. Sometimes in these experiences 'angelic' figures are met with and talked to. The subject is offered the choice of going with these figures, or of returning to Earth.

We need not dispute all aspects of these various visionary experiences. It is probably quite true that at some mental level the patient is faced with the decision to fight the illness, or to yield to it. But because these mental events are taking place in the unconscious mind the situation is dramatized into a play or a dream script. This is how the unconscious mind works. It does not think things through as the conscious, cognitive mind does. It *acts* them through.

So instead of denying the subjective reality and the subjective truth of these experiences as such, it seems reasonable to consider that they do indicate some life or death decision is being made, and we can put pressure on their allegedly objective values. It is very instructive to ask the patient about the clothes that the people of the 'other side' were wearing. How were these cut? Were they modern? Did they seem to be mass-produced or hand-sewn? Were they off-the-peg or made to measure? Were they apparently of natural or synthetic material? Would they have contained manufacturers' labels? If they were sewn, either by hand or machine, what does the patient think the needles might have been made of – metal, bone or what? And who is manufacturing the needles? And are they bought or given away, is the cloth given away, and who makes it...?

It is, I think, quite clear where this and other such lines of legitimate inquiry lead. They take us into a nonsense situation. The same point of reductio ad absurdum can be reached by asking, first, about the faces and hands of the angels. Were the men beared or clean-shaved? Were the beards trimmed? If so, what would they be trimmed with? Did the patient suppose that under the clothes the bodies of the angels had sexual organs, anuses, bladders, pubic hair? And if so, for what purpose? And so on.

If a subject cooperates with us in these questioning exercises – though most of them walk off angrily, which is sufficient comment in itself – one can soon obtain agreement that there was obviously a strong subjective element in the experience. And, finally, comes the admission that there is really no way of establishing what, if any, objective reality the experience contained.

171

We have not wandered off the subject of discarnate spirits. When talking to the spirit guides of mediums, it is possible, for example, if you do it gradually enough, to lead the alleged spirit of a seventeenth-century nun into considering whether on dates the girl ought to pay her share of the bill, and whether it is right to kiss on the first date (shades of Woody Allen). In so doing one is using words and concepts, like 'date', which the nun has no business knowing about. Or *ought* she to know about them? After all, she has presumably met and conversed with other more recently dead spirits. Sometimes a spirit guide will agree that that is indeed so. But on cross-examination, we find that the knowledge of the spirit guide, on any matter whatsoever, coincidentally nevertheless has exactly the same boundaries as that of the entranced medium – factual mistakes and all.

Certainly augmented powers *are* found in trance and we have seen much evidence of that already in this book. Artistic ability can be much improved, speed of working greatly increased, autonomic functions become accessible to consciousness, and so on. But what we are debating here is whether we need to invoke the existence of discarnate spirits to explain them.

Another variant on the spirit hypothesis concerns reincarnation. In recent years very considerable attention has been focussed on a large number of people who, under deep hypnosis, claim to be able to recall extensive detail of their own past lives.

At first inspection this material is impressive. The subject under hypnosis seems to be living out some very real experience, sometimes screaming in agony, perhaps speaking archaic English in a strange voice, and so on. Of course, precisely the same thing occurs with the Spiritualist medium, but there the 'explanation' is possession by a discarnate spirit.

But hypnotic regression, as it is called, also fails to stand up to detailed examination. If asked questions about motor-cars, television sets and the like, the subject in an eighteenth-century regression will ask in bewilderment what these things might be. Yet if we say to such a hypnotized subject, who is perhaps on the deck of a British man-o'-war of those days, 'check whether that ship on the horizon is French' or 'check whether the guns are made of iron or bronze', he will say 'yes, it is French' or 'yes, they are iron'. But in those days the word 'check' only meant to stop a horse or a moving vehicle. To check in the sense of examining something is a twentieth-century meaning.

Anyone well-informed on the history of language can find innumerable discrepancies of this kind.

Once in a while an entranced subject (sometimes even a more or less illiterate individual) *is* able to produce genuine fragments of medieval German, of Hebrew or whatever, without having had any formal training in these areas, or even any kind of conscious contact at all with such matters. This achievement seems a much more positive piece of evidence – at first. But in several cases investigation has revealed that the subject *has* had past contact with the material, perhaps in the form of visits as a boy to a professor's house where learned books were left open on desks. One woman proved to have been a cleaner in just such a house. Obviously her unconscious mind had retained fragments of that exposure experience, scarcely noticed by the conscious mind. Astonishing these events are – but evidence of a previous existence they are not.

Again, once in a very long while a hypnotized subject will mention a factual item which turns out on examination to be correct, although our current history books say otherwise. Joe Keeton, the Liverpool hypnotist, has a case on record where a woman in trance described a railway line several years before the line was known to have been built. But she insisted, and a subsequent search of public records showed that an experimental line had been built several years before the officially recorded date. We may be speaking in these rare cases either of paranormally acquired information, or a lucky guess. But let us say without argument that it is paranormal. On the other hand clairvoyants habitually obtain such paranormal information without any appeal to a past life. A psychometrist will psychometrize thousands of objects handed to him professionally. But there can really be no suggestion that the psychometrist has had thousands of past lives. And when that type of psychic psychometrizes the future, are we then going to speak of his or her *future* incarnations? Even if we make the very considerable step of accepting the idea of previous incarnations, this giant assumption then still leaves the large majority of paranormal (and psychiatric) phenomena unexplained. It is worth very little as an explanatory hypothesis, although it is obviously very exciting.

But the basic criticism of the regression hypothesis is even simpler. A normally hypnotized subject sees innumerable scenes and objects around him at the suggestion of the hypnotist. But no one would propose that what is seen by the hypnotized person is there in any objective sense. So why do we therefore need to think that the imagined past lives have, or ever had, any objective existence?

Throughout the ages and at the present time numerous people have claimed to see ghosts, spirits and demons. Specifically religious people are confronted with angels and deceased saints. Others variously see nature spirits, elementals, fairies and whatever. But people who drink heavily, who take drugs and who have nervous break-downs also see all these things and more. And we know, for all kinds of reasons, that in these cases the visions have no independent existence, but are part of the currently disordered mental life of the person concerned. When the drinking stops, the visions vanish. The devil who sits at the foot of your bed likewise vanishes when two things happen: your brain chemistry is regularized; and you learn at the psychological level to accept and integrate parts of your personality that you have hitherto rejected.

No one has yet shown that the 'hallucinations of the sane', as they have been called – the angels, the ghosts and so on – are basically any different from the hallucinations of the insane. No one has demonstrated that ghosts have an existence independent of people. On the contrary, it has been shown that poltergeists, at least, have an existence wholly dependent on people. It has also been frequently shown that new and 'genuine' ghosts can very easily be called into existence. A writer (Frank Smythe) deliberately put around a story that a particular locality was haunted by a ghost, which he described in detail. Very shortly after that reports began turning up of emphatic sightings of the ghost. A group of psychic researchers deliberately invented a spirit communicant, by committee decision. At their later seances this invented spirit duly manifested itself. Once a well-known, practising medium came to me in tears. She said that her spirit guide, whom she had been with all her life, had been stolen from her by a group of acquaintances.

So much, then, for differences between 'real' and 'imaginary' spirits. No matter which aspect we take of the spirit/possession hypothesis, it seems not to stand up.

What, though, of the psychics who in trance produce paintings or music, unmistakably, and in some cases brilliantly, reminiscent of the work of major artists and composers now dead? Luiz Gasperetto, working with astonishing rapidity and sometimes with both hands at once, produces a stream of remarkably impressive Picassos, Rembrandts, Modiglianis and whatever. Sometimes he even produces the painting upside down. These are new paintings, apparently done by the dead artist in question working from 'the other side'. Matthew Manning's Dürer drawings and etchings, produced in a similar way, are a positive joy. Rosemary Brown, a straightforward housewife, writes music in trance that has the unmistakable stamp of Beethoven, Mozart, Strauss or whomever.

There are a number of points. First, art experts claim they can distinguish fairly readily between a Gasperetto 'Picasso' and a genuine Picasso. The differences, they say, are slight and would not be perceived by a layman. Then again, none of the paintings or music produced by these psychics shows any development beyond that which

174

the artist was capable of in life. In real life artists do not remain in a given stage of their development, but are always evolving and progressing. These dead artists, despite what might be thought of as the freedom and opportunity of the after-life, can apparently only echo their former effects. In the case of Rosemary Brown in particular, experts and the general public seem to be agreed that the musical works produced are of a lower standard than that achieved by the artists concerned in life – though here of course we are dealing with opinions.

But quite aside from all these points, Anita Mühl's patients in trance also produced painting and music far in excess of their normal conscious ability to do so, yet these people were not possessed by spirits. They were simply suffering from fragmented personality and schizoid illnesses. Then again, the woman violinist hypnotized by L. Cooper was able, under hypnosis, to tap new sources of musical understanding and interpretation from her own mind. Surely this last case is the definitive one? There is not the slightest sign of the involvement of discarnate spirits, nor any call to postulate any such 'explanation'.

Obviously something very remarkable indeed is going on in all these cases – and moreover, we cannot discover what it is by reference to modern academic psychology.

It seems reasonable if we make the starting point of any investigation and the beginnings of any explanation of these phenomena in terms of the mentally ill. For if we turn to mediumship or hypnosis, there are literally no limits to what the compulsive sceptic will propose in the way of fraud and criminal conspiracy, and none to what the inventive supporter of those activities will offer in the way of extravagant hypotheses. But in the case of the severely mentally ill and hospitalized, both such extravagant opposition and support have to fall away.

Some of Anita Mühl's patients were suffering from that extreme form of the fragmented psyche known as multiple personality. One of them exhibited no less than eight distinct personalities. This is by no means a record – cases involving several dozen distinct and enduring personalities are known. Sometimes one of the personalities will be aware of the existence of some or all of the others, though sometimes again a particular personality has no knowledge of the others at all. In the first case personality A will complain of personality C or F: 'You can't do anything constructive when *she's* here'; or 'Look what D has done to my things – I wish you would get rid of her', and so on. During successful psychotherapy the warring personalities all disappear, sometimes one at a time, sometimes in batches, and at the same time another personality begins to emerge – which in the long run proves to be the integrated, real personality of this unhappy human being.

It is difficult not to compare the numerous personalities of the hospitalized psychotic with the personalities which speak through the entranced medium or the subject undergoing hypnotic regression.

Neither all of Dr Mühl's patients nor a majority of hospitalized psychotics show such clear-cut multiple personality. But we always note some tendency to fragmentation or splitting. Actions and remarks are readily 'forgotten' (that is, repressed). A patient with, say, a violent and ungovernable temper, when asked, describes himself as a mild-mannered, reasonable person – and everybody else as possessing a temper. And all Dr Mühl's patients, once introduced to the idea, showed a remarkable facility in producing automatic writing, automatic drawing and automatic music. We have, in this last respect, by no means yet fully described everything that happened.

Several of Mühl's patients wrote *backwards* at enormous speed. Sometimes the whole sentence was written backwards, reversing all letters. Sometimes each individual word was written backwards, although the letters were not reversed and the sense of the sentence read forward in the usual way. Sometimes the first line of text was written forwards in the normal way from left to right, then, without the pencil being lifted from the paper, the next line would be written backwards from right to left, reversing all individual letters.

Examples of the second and third kind are as follows:

> Won I ma a elzzup ot eht eye – ll'I yas I ma
> a elzzup. Rof eht hturt fo eht rettam si I ma a
> elzzup. Na eretsua nam emac ot eht esouh eh dais
> os.　　(Woman of 23)

> Oboman who
> eats little girls
> on the gate post
> lives up on the
> gate post all in the dark
> he jumps out at me
> (Woman of 24)

Dr Mühl reports that the speed at which the reversed material or mirror script was written was amazing. She decided to produce an objective measure of speed, and chose the woman who spelled words backwards (the first example above). Dr Mühl read a number of paragraphs of a story aloud to the patient. Then the patient was given something else to read aloud, while at the same time she was asked to let

176

her hand automatically write what she had just heard. The patient did as asked, and her hand quickly wrote out, backwards, the paragraphs she had just heard – she meanwhile reading aloud something quite different! – without any errors.

Now Dr Mühl asked the patient to copy out the test paragraphs consciously and deliberately, spelling all the words backwards. The patient did so, but with great effort, and numerous errors.

The automatic product was written eight times faster. What a striking parallel here to Cooper and Erickson's hypnotized subjects (see chapter 4) who, in trance, performed simple motor tasks such as copying out sentences up to three times faster than normal. But those subjects were not spelling words backwards, or writing reversed mirror script.

We must also not overlook the absolutely astonishing achievement of Dr Mühl's patient in recalling, word perfect, several paragraphs that she had heard only once, read aloud to her. (Try that for yourself with a friend, and see just how far you get. Try also writing out a couple of sentences from a book, reversing all the spelling. Then do the same thing with any phrase of a song or poem which you know by heart, listening to it in your head, and then writing it down spelled backwards. This is what the unconscious mind of the patient did – and it is far, far more difficult than the previous copying exercise.)

Again, in this example by the patient of instant, perfect recall we have another parallel with hypnotism. Under hypnosis people recall reams of material they thought they had long forgotten, or had never registered in the first place. To impress his new clients, Frank Bowyer the hypnotist uses the following device. Say his client has walked to the flat from the underground station a few streets away. Frank asks the client how many lamp-posts he passed. The bewildered client has 'no idea'. Then Frank suggests that the client, in light trance, mentally go back along the route and count them. To his own amazement, the client now does so, and gets the number right.

A psychologist read passages of Greek aloud in the presence of a fifteen-month old baby, repeating the same selection for a period, then introducing another selection. At the age of eight and a half the young boy, who had studied no Greek in the meantime, was asked to learn by heart several passages of Greek (which of course he did not understand). Among them were the pieces he had heard as a baby. He learned those thirty per cent quicker than the new passages. And that boy was not even hypnotized.

We cannot seriously doubt that part of the human mind records most, if not everything, that it ever hears or sees. But that part seems not to be an aspect of our conscious, waking mind, in which remembering is a laborious, time-consuming process, only achieved after much effort, practice and repetition. And if we do not continue the practice, the memory of what we have already consciously learned decays soon enough – everyone who has ever tried to learn anything knows this. But for the unconscious mind, it seems, learning is very easy.

If the ancients discovered that under hypnosis masses of 'forgotten' material could be recalled, as well as paranormal information acquired, might they not have postulated an 'Akashic record' – some 'place' where everything that people ever did or thought was permanently recorded?

There are yet other connections between the actions and the content of the actions of Dr Mühl's patients, and the behaviours of people allegedly 'possessed' by spirits.

Some of Anita Mühl's patients wrote with both hands at once. Luiz Gasperetto, the psychic painter, sometimes paints with both hands at once. Many of Mühl's patients wrote backwards. Gasperetto sometimes draws upside down. Reversals of all kinds are also a central feature of all magical thought and practice – so mystical dancers move 'widdershins', that is anticlockwise instead of clockwise, the Lord's Prayer is said backwards in the Black Mass, and congregants present their buttocks instead of their faces to the altar.

In magical practice the left hand is often used instead of the right. Reversed mirror-writing, moving from the right to left across the page, is much easier for a left-handed person – it is in fact their natural movement. You can easily test this for yourself. Sit so that your left and your right hand, with a pencil in each, are resting on two adjacent writing pads in a natural position for writing. Now write a normal sentence with your right hand, at the same time allowing your left hand to move at will (but from left to right), as if writing the same sentence. Then hold what your left hand has done up to a mirror.

Are normally left-handed people governed by their so called minor cerebral hemisphere? That is what left-handedness is commonly said to be. Or perhaps the more important point is that the cerebellum is left-handed. Whereas in the cerebrum sensory information from the body crosses over to reach the opposite cerebral hemisphere, sensory information to the cerebellum does not cross over. It stays on the same side of the body on which it originates.

Children and adults suffering from the disability known as dyslexia or word-blindness frequently reverse letters when they write. They will write a 'd' for a 'b' and a 'b' for a 'd' – 'I am a dab doy'. They also often reverse s (ƨ), z (ꙅ) and e (ɘ). And as it happens, dyslexic children appear also to be suffering from a malfunction of the cerebellum (see p. 127).

The cerebellum seems relentlessly involved in all these phenomena. As all text books agree, the cerebellum is also heavily concerned in all skilled movement of every kind – dancing, embroidery or whatever. Dr Mühl's patients drew better, played musical instruments better and wrote faster when in trance. Cooper and Erickson's hypnotized subjects produced much faster skilled movement under hypnosis than they were normally capable of. Luiz Gasperetto, Matthew Manning, and many other mediums of my acquaintance, draw far better in trance than they can normally. (And incidentally, it is not just skilled movement which is involved here. There is the allied matter of greatly increased creativity – a central question for a later chapter.)

The unifying statement that can be made about the unusual events of this chapter – including also many earlier such items as the kundalini experience – is that the people in these events have a much greater access than usual to the unconscious mind, to the unconscious body-mind. They are, in fact, rather swamped and engulfed by it. In these cases that mind has broken loose from its usual confines and taken over areas and functions as a rule governed by normal waking consciousness. But the only undesirable aspect is actually that the unconscious mind is out of control. There is nothing whatsoever wrong with allowing the unconscious mind into consciousness under licence.

While no one can be presumptuous enough to say with finality that there is no such thing as a conventional discarnate spirit or ghost, nevertheless the evidence for that particular hypothesis is far less impressive than that for the unconscious mind hypothesis. Yet, in turn, this statement is again not to say that no part of us survives physical death, or that there is no such thing as immortality. But we shall not arrive at an understanding of those matters through naivety, or by taking everything at face value.

In summary, it does not seem at all to be the case that we are haunted by discarnate spirits. It is, rather, that we are haunted by our own greatness.

16 Tao, immanence and Brahman

Two years ago I had a letter from a woman in Birmingham, England, in response to a broadcast I did there on local radio. I will come to the contents of the letter in a moment. It was a rambling letter, and not well punctuated, although the spelling was good. It is typical of many letters I receive from 'ordinary' people, telling of telepathic experiences, premonitions, and dreams which solve or resolve real, practical problems.

There is a ring of truth about these letters and what I can only describe as an embarrassed but defiant honesty, the voice of an honest person who does not expect to be believed – or at least, is ready not to be believed. I wish my psychological colleagues could read these letters without prejudice – an impossible attitude for most of them, since the majority have taken up the position not just that paranormal phenomena do not exist, but cannot exist. I know, however, that other writers, like Lyall Watson, also receive such letters, and that they are as impressed with them as I am.

These letters are evidence for me that the idea, or better, the sense of an all-encompassing 'magical' universe such as exists for the Australian Aborigine in 'the Dreamtime' also still exists as a reality for simple people throughout the world. And when I say 'simple' I do not mean stupid. I mean uncomplicated people not overburdened with cognitive constructs; of people who have not gained the world at the expense of their souls, that is, who have not gained a smattering of formal education and logic at the cost of their own inner world of magical dreams.

Jack Kerouac has described these individuals and what he calls 'this fellaheen feeling for life' throughout his books (perhaps especially in *Lonesome Traveller* and *The Dharma Bums*). He calls the place they live in the 'Pure Land', and speaks of the 'timelessness' of these people not involved in the 'great cultural and civilization issues'. Kerouac's contempt here for the western ideal of civilization, though one-sided, is from some points of view only too well deserved. What is this madness we are all involved in that is willing to sacrifice an entire half of our psychological birthright, in order to develop the other half to excess?

Even with many priests, clergymen and so-called mystics of both east and west, the living experience of the Dreamtime, of Tao, of Brahman and of Immanence has become a mere intellectual concept, an item to be mentioned from time to time in a solemn or slightly hushed voice in certain kinds of conversations or sermons. I would be prepared to swear that many of these people have never experienced the phenomenon they invoke.

However, as we recall from chapter 1, the concepts in question do refer to matters like 'the supreme reality which holds up the universe', the 'beingness of everything', the 'ultimate reality' and the 'celestial ether'. What all such items perhaps have in common is a sense of universality, of pervasiveness, and of enduring permanence amid the changes of the physical world. There is 'something', it seems, which overrides, or underpins, all local variants of culture and personality, all local and temporary manifestations of the phenomena of life and being.

Yet, after all, *are* these matters and items something detached from, superior to, other than human life? Or are they in fact hidden and currently not understood aspects of the human personality? Are they really some kind of generalized statement about the nature of our secret life?

One man of great intellectual gifts who certainly did experience the phenomenon we are discussing, and so necessarily became a great visionary, was Swedenborg. He has written of his experiences of 'the Pure Land' in several books, including his *Journal of Dreams:* 'Another vision is that between the time of sleep and the time of wakefulness...this is the sweetest of all, for heaven then operates into his rational mind in the utmost tranquillity'; and 'in ecstasy or trance the man holds his breath; at this time his thoughts are, in a manner of speaking, away...when that is represented which flows in from a higher source'.

Many 'ordinary' people experience fragmented and occasional entry into this altered state or states. But their visions, like those of Swedenborg, are equally dismissed by the western world. They are, nevertheless, a most important aspect of our secret life.

Mrs DPM's letter concerns a vision of a large country house. It is a waking vision, which has 'haunted' her most of her life, and is clearly seen in great detail and in colour. There is nothing too remarkable about the house itself, perhaps. It is the kind of description anyone who has seen costume films or read historical novels of any kind could easily put together. However, there are significant details – significant in the light of what follows. The house contains no furniture, for example, and one of the rooms which is oak-panelled also has an oak-panelled door.

Mrs M had never mentioned this vision to her family until one day (she does not say why) she did mention it to her daughter. To Mrs M's astonishment, the daughter admitted to having the same vision, which she precisely described. This was not the end of the affair. Mrs M's sister, it turns out, also has the vision, as does Mrs M's second daughter. But the eldest daughter does not have it.

Well, a curious business perhaps, but not something terribly evidential. After all, who remembers every conversation or chance remark? Perhaps the members of the family had unwittingly suggested the existence of this visionary house to each other over the years.

But now for the truly unusual. Mrs M was contacted by a woman with the same name as her own family name. This woman, quite unknown to Mrs M, was engaged in the currently fashionable game of tracing her ancestors. It appears, from this woman's research, that she and Mrs M are very distantly related, and have as a distant ancestor a former Governor of New South Wales. But the real surprise in all this was that the strange woman has also always had the vision of the house, precisely incorporating all significant detail.

Mrs M defensively ends her letter: 'No point in telling lies.' I do not think for one moment that she is. She wrote to me only to ask if I could explain this phenomenon. For sure, she will get no explanation from any of the established institutions of our society. From them she will get only contempt.

What exactly is happening, psychologically speaking, to these people who sense fragments of a universe not seen by the normal conscious mind? How is it that some people see fairy folk in every thicket, angels on every cloud, and God in every sunset? Where does it arise, this vision of a web of (radiant) beingness or otherness?

That sense and sensation appears to arise from the unconsious mind turned outwards, from a mind (that is, the normally unconscious part of our total mind) investing itself in the objective universe, and thereby animating it.

There is a kind of paradox here. What we normally call the external universe – the stars, the stones, the passage and interaction of light and other energies – is registered in our heads. It comes *into* us through our external senses. Even though the objective universe begins outside us in some independent way, its apprehension occurs inside us. But our own inner universe, that which originates *in* us, and which exists only when we exist, and ceases to be when we are absent or cease to exist, somehow *gets out* of us through the internal senses. And we perceive it finally not in us at all, but as if outside.

The objective universe consists of external events made into mind. The subjective universe consists of mind made into external events.

Neither of these processes is superior to the other. Equally, neither is inferior to the other. Both of those statements must be emphasized. But a major problem for us, existentially, is to know exactly when we are studying, or experiencing, universe made mind, or mind made universe.

A particular example of that general problem is the question of synchronicity. It looks as if this phenomenon has both a subjective and an objective component, and that both are inextricably entwined in the whole. In such close combination the two appear to yield a third class of phenomena which are neither subjective nor objective, but a type of event for which we do not really have a name. We could call them 'transcendental', except that this term has been heavily misused by religionists and mystics to describe events (like seeing visions of angels) which seem on investigation to be merely subjective, to be simply examples of 'mind become universe'.

The term 'synchronicity' refers to two or more events which occur, in some sense meaningfully, in each other's presence, but without the one in any sense *causing* the other. The one part of the whole incident has not caused any of the other parts to occur, and yet on the other hand the coming together or being together of these events is not due to chance. Many of the events of the normal universe and our normal lives *do* cause each other to happen. A car engine starts because I switch on the ignition. The one event causes the other. Other happenings are certainly due to chance. Many people, for example, have the same christian name as myself or yourself. That is a chance event, arising from the fact that there are an awful lot of people in the world, and relatively only a very few names to go round. But in the third class of events which we are discussing, and which are called synchronistic, it seems that happenings go together, or simply exist together, for reasons that we do not understand very well – but which are not causal, and yet again not chance. Sometimes we can see a personal meaning in synchronistic events, sometimes not. Perhaps there always is a personal meaning, but perhaps we cannot always see it.

An example of synchronicity. It had been firmly on my mind for a week or two to telephone two good friends of mine, who for reasons of geography, work, marriage and whatever I had not seen or spoken to for some time. In the meantime I received a copy of Robert Anton Wilson's book *The Cosmic Trigger: the Final Secret of the Illuminati* for review. I read the book and found much of it interesting, though I disagreed strongly with some of Wilson's interpretations. In the book Wilson makes a prolonged and often convincing statement of the way the number 23 has influenced his life (apparently synchronistically). But I thought he overdid his case, and by the end of the book I was thoroughly fed up with the number 23. I finished typing the review that evening, and decided finally to ring my friends. I checked their new numbers in my address book. They were (I have replaced the non-significant digits with zeros): 000 2300 and 230 2300.

I had obviously been on a collision course with the number 23 for some weeks. But I do not know what meaning this event had. Perhaps it was only to provide me with an instance of synchronicity.

It occurred to me several years ago that the objective component of synchronicity would be very easy to test. If it has any influence at all on or in the objective world, then that influence should show up in any random sample of objective events, for instance in a random number table. In fact, that ought to be the very best place – the most uncontaminated place – to look for it.

A random number table is a continuous (and in theory endless) list of numbers from 0 to 9 inclusive, in which the chances of any particular number occurring next are always equal. The fact that the previous digit was, say, a 9 in no way limits the chances of the next one being a 9 also – because the population of numbers drawn upon is infinite. That never gets used up or diminished in any way. The chances of any of the ten digits (0 to 9 inclusive) appearing next are *always* 9 to 1 ($9 + 1 = 10$). Random number tables can be produced by several means – including the random decay of atomic material. A more usual method today is by computer programme.

Statisticians have studied the nature of random numbers and they know very precisely what are the probabilities of particular sequences and omissions and interrelations occurring by chance. The conclusions of the statistician are available to us as a large number of mathematical formulae, which can be used to test whether any situation we are examining (like the incidence of an illness, or the behaviour of sun spots) is governed by chance or not, and if not, which other factor is operating. That 'other factor' is always assumed to be a form of causality. But in the test which now follows, the factor of causality has been deliberately, and completely, removed. If there is any other factor at work here, it might be synchronicity.

I took the first ten pairs of digits in the first six double columns of the random number table in the *Cambridge Elementary Statistical Tables,* a total of sixty pairs of digits. This is by definition a random sample, since all parts of the table are equally random. That is precisely the function of the table. But I now treated the digits as if they were sixty pairs of *scores.* Perhaps in each case, for instance, a sender had been trying to transmit the numbers he was looking at, telepathically, and a recipient a mile away had been writing down the numbers he thought the other was sending. In other words, the second column of figures was treated as if it was some kind of *result* from the first column. In actual fact it isn't and cannot be, because these are simply two columns of random numbers.

When, however, we suspect that any pair of numbers or scores which we have are not random, there are some simple statistical measures we can apply to test that belief. I have used the formula known as the Coefficient of Ranked Correlation. Within stated limits of probability, this test establishes whether or not there is any relationship between the pairs of numbers. A result in this test of 0 (zero) means no correlation, no relationship between the pairs of scores at all. Any result from + 0.1 to + 1 indicates a positive relationship between the scores, and any result from − 0.1 to − 1 indicates a negative relationship between the scores. In the positive case we know that some effect is making the scores more like each other than chance says they should be, in the negative case we know that something is making the scores more unlike each other than chance predits.

The table below shows the outcome of the test in full. The two columns x and y are the pairs of 'scores'. Column d is the difference between the two scores and column d^2 is that difference multiplied by itself (squared). The squaring operation removes the negative sign of the minus differences.

(The impressive-looking formula written below the columns cannot be simplified in words beyond this: the product moment correlation is one minus six times the total of all the differences between scores, squared, divided by the number of pairs multiplied by the number of pairs squared minus one.)

The result of the computation is a correlation of almost + 0.9, which is quite remarkably high. Any psychological experiment which produced such a result would be considered successful. It would be considered that a positive relationship between the two columns of scores had definitely been established. Yet we were using here simply two sets of random numbers.

Certainly, a sample of sixty pairs of digits from a table which, theoretically, stretches to infinity is not a large one. (But, for reasons we need not discuss, increasing the size of the sample would have no significant effect in the present case.) And the product moment correlation is only one of many tests which could be applied. Nonetheless, the result of this on the face of it fair little experiment does suggest that the products of any random system of events (such as a roulette wheel) may not be as totally or unconditionally random as the theoretical basis of statistics argues. Have we, possibly, demonstrated the existence of a 'synchronistic' sub-pattern in so-called random events?

One or two points need to be mentioned in passing. For instance, the distribution of the different numbers in a random number table is

An Apparent Case of Synchronicity in a Random Number Table?

x	y	d	d^2	contd.	x	y	d	d^2
2	0	2	4		2	8	–6	36
7	4	3	9		4	9	–5	25
9	4	5	25		3	1	2	4
2	2	0	0		1	5	–4	16
9	3	6	36		1	8	–7	49
4	5	–1	1		9	7	2	4
4	4	0	0		4	9	–5	25
1	6	–5	25		0	2	–2	4
0	4	–4	16		0	4	–4	16
3	2	1	1		7	2	5	25
1	7	–6	36		2	3	–1	1
4	9	–5	25		0	3	–3	9
7	0	7	49		3	8	–5	25
1	5	–4	16		6	9	–3	9
2	9	–7	49		2	7	–5	25
0	4	–4	16		3	6	–3	9
9	1	8	64		8	9	–1	1
2	3	–1	1		1	9	–8	64
5	0	5	25		6	5	1	1
7	0	7	49		0	3	–3	9
4	2	2	4		1	7	–6	36
0	4	–4	16		0	4	–4	16
4	9	–5	25		6	7	–1	1
7	8	–1	1		8	4	4	16
1	2	–1	1		3	0	3	9
7	7	0	0		1	4	–3	9
9	9	0	0		3	9	–6	36
9	1	8	64		9	6	3	9
6	5	1	1		6	5	1	1
1	7	–6	36		6	1	5	25

Total = 1110

coefficient of ranked correlation $= 1 - \dfrac{6\Sigma(d^2)}{N(N^2 - 1)} = 1 - \dfrac{6(1110)}{60\,(60^2 - 1)}$

$$= 1 - \frac{6660}{215940} = \text{(approx.) } 0.9$$

perfectly symmetrical about its mean and this and other features may well play into the hands of a simple correlation test. Any two sets of real scores – either those of two different people taking the same test, or the same person taking the same test on two different occasions – would certainly not be symmetrically distributed. But on the other hand, a standard test of telepathy *does* involve one person attempting to send a random list of numbers (or objects) to another person – who, if not responding telepathically, may just be writing down another list of random numbers....

These are highly specialist waters. Reverting to the general idea of synchronicity, this is probably best visualized as a pattern in both time and space, and one which is not confined to the three dimensions of our present universe, but which also extends both forward and backward in time. The notion of such a multidimensional pattern enables us at least to conceptualize a situation where we could, clairvoyantly, glimpse the future or the past. But we might also perhaps think of synchronicity as an irregular pulse, detected and detectable at any 'now' of our present universe, but actually pulsing along the energy X/life/time/consciousness continuum of Figure 8 (see p. 152).

These are ideas that we must face up to in our thought, not simply because of the provisional evidence of the small statistical exercise we performed, nor because of the approval given to the idea of synchronicity by outstanding individuals like Leibniz and C. G. Jung. We must face up to them by reason of the existence of the *I Ching,* the ancient Chinese oracle and Book of Changes.

The ancient designers of the *I Ching* – probably working simply intuitively – devised a successful method of sampling and evaluating the synchronistic influences present in any moment of time. Significantly, this method always involves one's own state of mind and consciousness as a central factor. Significantly also, the process of sampling involves a random selection and interaction of numbers, over which you have no conscious control.

The only sound way to understand and verify the working of the *I Ching* oracle is by using it oneself. The best available translation is that of Richard Wilhelm and Cary F. Baynes, which also contains a Foreword by Jung. Instructions for using the oracle are given in the book, as they are in all editions and translations. You may ask the *I Ching* any question concerning any present or forthcoming problem, or on any point or situation on which you require clarification. The same question can only be asked once (unless in the interim considerable further time has passed, or the situation has changed radically of itself) and the question should be one that matters to you. Used in this prescribed way, the *I Ching* will soon satisfy you concerning its powers and abilities. The explanation of the book's powers does not appear to lie within the province of orthodox western science – although Leibniz, among others, has extravagantly praised the mathematical principles which underpin its hexagrams.

The ability of the *I Ching* to reach outside normal time is the element which enables us to link the book, and synchronicity itself, with concepts like Tao and Brahman, particularly when they are defined as the 'pre-existent and post-existent beingness of everything', 'the supreme reality which underpins the universe', and so on.

These ideas are not just the fevered imaginings of priests or charlatans, dazed out of their senses by an intake of magic mushrooms or marijuana. They seem to be an intuitive and valid insight into an aspect of the universe that modern science has signally failed to register – and, in the full sense, is probably incapable of registering.

Into the future

17 Childhood's end:
(Beyond the physical)

There are a number of ways in which we have reached childhood's end on this planet. The positive ways concern our secret life.

In Arthur Clarke's novel of the same title as this chapter, *Childhood's End,* humanity's normal physical development ceases. Adults cease being able to have children and the existing children change psychically and psychologically. As if some long-lasting dam or barrier has collapsed, the children suddenly manifest powers of telepathy, self-healing and psychokinesis. They are all one with each other, and are split forever from the human race which produced them. A new and largely unforeseen stage in the development of life is about to take place. Finally the children abandon even their bodies and as a collective psychic energy leave to seek their destiny among the stars, destroying Earth and the solar system as they do.

There are aspects of this story which, in the light of the information in this book, do not seem all that far off the mark. What seems in any case quite clear is that conventional evolution has reached a point where it can only move forward by some kind of quantum leap, or come to a complete halt.

There are significant aspects of the evolutionary process which the scientific establishment chooses not to acknowledge, even though that establishment itself has gathered some of the information we are now going to look at. And then we have to add in – to the total evolutionary matrix, that is – also the secret powers which this book and others have demonstrated. Specifically we have to ask what is the role and the significance of the unconscious human body-mind and its sometimes incredible powers.

The last few decades of our history have seen the establishment of more than one new science. One of these earned for its founders (Karl von Frisch, Konrad Lorenz and Nikolaas Tinbergen) the Nobel prize for biology. That science is ethology. Ethology is the study of the relationship of organisms to their stimulus environment, and to each other, considered as sources of stimuli. What ethology in particular has demonstrated, experimentally and in the laboratory, is that in large areas of behaviour the ability to deal with a situation is present in organisms before the situation comes into existence.

191

This is such an important statement that we must make it again. The ability to deal with a situation predates the existence of the situation it deals with.

The grayling butterfly is an elaborately patterned and speckled butterfly, whose patterns are built up of a mixture of white, grey and black designs. As Darwin so brilliantly argued and as orthodox science teaches today, such complex patterns and shapes are, from one point of view, the outcome of thousands and in some cases millions of years of natural selection, whereby all the various items in the pattern have gradually been favoured over other variations. Just as we constantly plane, cut, drill and assemble rough lengths of wood to make the perfectly fitted shelves of an awkwardly shaped kitchen, so nature, Darwinists claim, planes and cuts and shapes the rough organism until it is a perfect fit for its environment – both the physical environment of the part of the planet in which it lives, and its social environment composed of sexual partners and offspring.

But this widely accepted view of evolution seems staggeringly wrong. The real situation seems to be not that the environment shapes the organism – *but that the organism shapes the environment.*

The hard, experimental evidence for this view comes from ethology itself. But once our attention is directed to it we can see further 'soft' (that is, non-experimental) evidence on every side. Ethology seems as yet to have missed the full implications of its own findings. Tinbergen himself, after puzzling over the findings, says only that their full significance is 'not yet clear'.

When the male grayling butterfly in the laboratory is given a choice among various paper models of females, he does not choose the 'most grayling' female. He does not choose, as Darwinian theory requires, the female which most closely resembles the typical female of the species, as found in nature. He chooses the darkest model available. And he chooses the largest model available. His maximum preference is for a completely black female. And his preference for larger size shows no upper limit.

The position here is quite unmistakable. If ever a chance mutation were to throw up a darker or larger female, that female would be more vigorously pursued and mated by the male butterflies than any other. The male butterfly himself will be the instrument that shapes the destiny of the female – and so the destiny of the offspring – and so the destiny of the whole species.

The philosophical implications of this statement are absolutely shattering in respect of conventional views of evolution.

In the course of the grayling's existence as a species darker and larger females must already occasionally have been born out of chance mutation (a process which occurs continuously in nature). Why then, has the projected design for the large, black female not been carried through? Here we have to understand the multiple pressures impinging on this organism, and give a definite nod in the direction of conventional evolutionary theory. Butterflies get eaten by predators, for instance. It is probable that dark or fully black graylings are more easily seen, so that they get eaten in preference to the speckled grayling. The speckling and patterning, and smaller size apparently act as a significantly good camouflage, which outweighs the purely breeding advantage enjoyed by the darker, larger female.

Back to conventional Darwinism, therefore? No, not at all. If we were to examine the feeding habits of the birds and reptiles which eat the grayling, we might well find that although these predators prefer to eat a black grayling over a speckled one, their real preference, given a choice in the laboratory, might be for a green grayling, or red grayling with yellow bars!

This is no far-fetched suggestion, no mere hypothesis. For an examination of some other responses of some other organisms (a small sample of responses only, from a small sample of organisms only, among the millions still waiting to be tested) shows that the psychological equipment, or mind, of the organism is literally seething with such unrequired and unfulfilled responses.

The young arctic tern is fed silver fish in its mother's red bill. But it wishes with all its heart that she would feed it red fish in a silver bill. For this is the model the tern chooses in the laboratory. The mother of the baby herring gull has an orange spot on her yellow bill, at which the chick pecks. (This pecking makes the mother regurgitate food.) But until the herring chick was 'interviewed' in the laboratory we did not realize that it would gladly swap its orange-spot mother for a red-spot mother, or how gladly it would swap the red-spot mother for a totally fantastic mother with an *all*-red bill.

The ringed plover tolerates its normal eggs, light brown with darker brown spots. But it is apparently longing for the day when it can get its hands (so to speak) on a clutch of white eggs with black spots. The oyster-catcher, like the grayling butterfly, is into giantism. It wants an egg as big as the world. Some flowers seem to us very complex. But none are as complex as the bee wishes them, when tested. Bees spend all their lives trying to encourage the flowers of the field to become yet more complex.

This last example brings us back very clearly to our earlier statement. Organisms are continuously engaged in shaping their environment. And they do this on the basis of appetites and needs *which have never once been satisfied* until the appropriate stimulus comes along. How very, very different is this picture of the active, shaping organism (and even the imagining, inventing organism, as we shall see) from the inert lump of organic Darwinian material, shaped and planed by the dead and senseless hand of environmental forces.

We can observe the inner, forming evolutionary push-from-within at every level also of human activity. At the basic level of sexuality, for instance, it is clear that most men want women to look otherwise than they presently do under strictly natural conditions. From a study of the fashion and cosmetic industries, from cartoon and pornographic drawings of women, from re-touched pin-up photographs, as well as from the extreme forms of fetishism (whose traces, however, are clearly observable throughout 'normal' society) it is clear that a majority of men want women to have thicker, fuller eyelashes, larger eyes, more abundant head hair, a turned-up nose exposing the nostrils, larger breasts, thinner arms, smaller hands and feet (with the diminution of toes almost to vanishing point), longer legs, rounder calves and thighs, thinner waist, a total absence of body hair leaving the skin both shiny and smooth (but see below), and so on. The large majority of women activity cater for these tastes, recognizing the deep, instinctive basis of them in the male – and a method, therefore, of influencing, controlling and manipulating the male.

The picture here is slightly complicated by the fact that we are a hybrid species with more than one set of instincts. The above comments apply rather well in a western European (or 'Cro-Magnon' society). But in societies and sub-cultures with a greater 'Neanderthal' mix the rules change somewhat. Whereas in the west generally, reduced pubic hair is favoured by males in a woman, elsewhere an entirely reversed tendency is noted. A large number of Australian Aborigine males, still living under their natural conditions, were asked to describe their ideal of beauty in a woman. 'There was throughout an emphasis on the requirement that the woman be fat and large in all respects, including a big *mons veneris*, and that there be a lot of hair on the *mons veneris*' (Geza Roheim). This last view is paralleled in a certain kind of pornography in the west, which may be considered to represent western man's shadow side. Here abundant pubic hair (though no other form of body hair, apart from head hair itself, which must be very abundant) is described, in great detail, and I quote from one such text: 'She braced her legs and drew up her skirt, exposing to his avid gaze a great pelt of black hair running all the way up to her navel.'

But quite apart from sexual matters, we see the driving influence of 'idealism' – the striving after an 'ideal' form more 'perfect' than any naturally occurring or so far available – at every level and in every kind of human activity. 'Idealist' and 'idealism' are words seldom far from our lips. The ideal result would be...Ideally, I would like...and so on.

This generalized, omnipresent and perpetual dissatisfaction with our lot, our opportunities and our achievements is the clear expression of the evolutionary force pushing onwards from within us. And as we have seen, a not dissimilar dissatisfaction exists throughout the animal and plant kingdoms, although there the means of acting on that dissatifaction are much less within the organism's grasp than these are within ours.

Back to the allied and quite specific point, from which this discussion started, that the ability or wish to respond predates the existence of that which will satisfy the response. Putting that idea into the technical jargon of academic psychology and biology, we can state that response always precedes, and predates, stimulus. The statement is a total reversal of the Darwinian position that stimulus creates or calls forth response – that environment makes demands on the organism, which it must either meet or perish. That aspect does certainly also exist, but it is a minor influence. The major influence in evolution appears to be the striving nature of the organism, into which creation constantly pours a stream of new appetites, new demands, new dissatisfactions.

It is not just ideas or psychological processes which are pre-formed. Actual physical structures are also pre-formed, ahead of their use and ahead even of the situation in which they can be used.

An acceptance of this view can actually be seen in a majority of recent books by biologists. It is a revolution in thought which seems to have gone unaccompanied by fanfares of trumpets and armies marching. Perhaps the full implications of the emergent position have as yet escaped realization, of this move away from the classical Darwinian position. But at any rate, biologists, like physicists, are showing a remarkable willingness to abandon entrenched positions, while psychologists, by contrast, remain hopelessly trapped in the prisons of nineteenth-century mechanism and determinism.

It is now commonplace to find in biology texts, for instance, the statement that 'organisms move into geographical and behavioural areas for which they are already pre-adapted'. Two examples of the process agreed by a majority of biologists are as follows. One, our ancestors learned to walk upright on two feet before they moved out of the trees and down on to the ground. They did move out of the trees and then as a result learn to walk upright – which is what Darwinism requires. Two, our ability to oppose thumb and forefinger in the classic human grip, which no other ape possesses, was achieved before we began making and using tools. The need for tools did not create the human grip. The grip evolved, and then went looking for tools. Once again, this is a total reversal of the position which Darwin describes.

Away from such specifics – which are terribly important nonetheless – there are still broader examples with still greater implications.

It looks, for example, as if the major part of our brains – specifically the neo-cortex of both the cerebellum and the cerebrum – evolved ahead of any conceivable use for them.

Neanderthal man actually had a larger brain than ourselves. That of Cro-Magnon was as large as our own. Now, it is true that we have no fossil brains to study, so that we cannot examine the microscopic structure of these Neanderthal and Cro-Magnon brains. What we can do, and do, is to take plaster casts of the inside of the fossil skulls. In this way we obtain a 'brain' outwardly identical to that which the dead man or woman once possessed. We detect no essential difference between those brains and our own, except in the relative sense that Neanderthal had a larger cerebellum than ourselves and relatively less frontal cerebrum, slightly larger temporal lobes and slightly smaller parietal lobes. As it happens, we cannot prove that the brains of Neanderthal and Cro-Magnon were microscopically the same as ours, but to assume that they were not is more of an assumption than to assume that they were.

The major point here is this. What were these cave men doing with a brain that could build a Concorde, devise differential calculus, compose symphonies, put a man on the Moon and a fully functional robot on Mars, invent materials which the universe had never seen before and build computers? All that was required of these men in the conditions in which they evolved and found themselves was the ability to catch game, to keep warm in winter and steer clear of predatory animals. What did they need a brain more complex than any modern computer for?

The answer must be that the brain was required not for then evolution, but for future evolution.

Our brains, too, have areas which seem to serve no function, the so-called 'silent areas'. Why do we have them? How can they be serving any Darwinian demand, when they are not, as far as we know, even used? Human babies, as we noted earlier, are born about a year premature. If that were not so, the head would be too large to permit birth at all. And this state of affairs existed a hundred thousand years ago (at least). To say it once more, what was the enormous brain *for* in those far-off times?

We are necessarily forced to consider a model very different from that envisaged by Darwin. We have to imagine some process in the universe which is concerned with – or, at least, results in – the production of ever more self-aware organisms. This process achieves its ends by 'working ahead of itself', in the sense that structures and capacities which will some day be used by an organism are supplied to the organism ahead of their use. The procedure is somewhat like that of an exploring party which first photographs a terrain from the air before moving into it, or a builder erecting a scaffold before starting work on the building itself. But these two images are inadequate. What nature provides its organism with is not a photograph or a scaffold; it is a finished product, ready for use – like an opposable finger and thumb, or the ability to walk upright.

Into this same category, on an altogether grand scale, comes our psychic endowment. It too seems to have been given to us in advance of its use.

To digress for a moment, it has often been asked why the ability to see the future, which has been demonstrated in both animals and man, has not been bred into any organism as a major capacity through the working of natural selection. Darwinism argues that any capacity which confers an advantage on an organism, however slight, will in the course of time be strengthened, through the benefits gained in competition with other organisms not possessing this faculty. It is a good question, but the answer is not what the questioner expects. The answer is that the conceptual basis of Darwinism is incorrect. It is not a case of natural selection gradually strengthening slight initial advantages at all. The advantage, or endowment, is given fully-fledged against the day of its use or possible use. We have to say 'possible use' because, as we saw earlier in this chapter, many organisms possess many response capacities which they are never likely to have any occasion to use. Every organism seems to be equipped, in advance and at every stage of its evolution, with a large battery of reserve responses – a kind of reservoir of contingency or emergency plans. Which, if any, of these ever get used will depend on how circumstances develop. The environment does throw continual challenges and opportunities at an organism, as Darwin argued. But the organism capitalizes on these opportunities thanks to its already existing reserve response capacities.

Thus the male bower bird no longer uses berries and leaves and coloured pebbles to build the very large 'bower and garden' with which he entices the female to be his mate. He uses the products of industrial society – fragments of coloured glass and formica, beads, bottle tops and what you will. The display is now much more dazzling than ever it was under natural conditions. And the female is delighted – because she always, secretly, wanted a more brilliant display than the male could naturally provide.

The circumstances have so far not been right for the wholesale use of our own psychic endowment. But we have to note how the whole unconscious-intuitive-psychic mind, or body-mind, has been steadily evolving over a period of hundreds of millions of years of evolution, against the day of its eventual use.

Let us just review some of the astonishing capacities which, as has been proved beyond any doubt whatsoever, the body-mind possesses.

A woman in the absolutely final stages of terminal, disseminated tuberculosis recovers fully in a matter of hours, and now shows no trace of the disease (p. 67). A fifteen-year old boy with a life-long genetic, structural disease recovers from it almost totally after a few mental treatments under hypnosis (p. 57). A woman suffering from terminal angina pectoris is totally cured after a session with a psychic healer lasting a few minutes (p. 55). People who are totally blind learn to see (p. 4). In trance and during sleep some individuals can spontaneously reproduce on and in their bodies wounds and injuries suffered in childhood. Others can spontaneously produce, to order, wounds and blisters never experienced by them. Under electromagnetic stimulation, rats regenerate appreciable amounts of amputated limbs, and children regnerate lost finger-tips. In trance some individuals can produce, in a matter of minutes, paintings and drawings after Rembrandt, Picasso, Dürer and other artists which only an expert can distinguish from the real thing. Under hypnosis, again, some individuals perform motor tasks, such as copying sentences, up to three times faster than normal but without any deterioration in standard. Some people are able to dream precise future events, sometimes over an extended continuous period. Others foresee in significant detail the circumstances of their own nevertheless fortuitous deaths. Yet others receive detailed reports telepathically of the death or injury of loved ones and animal pets. So the list continues.

But the point to emphasize here is that there is nothing tentative about these powers. There is no sense of Darwinian gradualism. Neither Marie Bailly nor her ancestors practised or rehearsed what she – what her body-mind – did with her tubercular condition, any more than did the boy with rhinoceros skin. These are fully-fledged, fully functional capacities.

The attribute of psi trailing (the ability shown by many animals to find their owners across thousands of miles of land and sea) is an excellent example of a capacity 'waiting to be used'. Only in the days of modern transportation could this extreme distance of separation between organisms that grew up together, between members of one family or 'family', ever have occurred. An animal in nature – aside from birds – could never be separated from its pack or family by more than a few miles. Granted, it would even then be useful for an animal to have a telepathic contact with the others, in respect of that short distance. But we see that nature has provided this capacity to a degree not required by any kind of normal separation, so anticipating a contingency and a situation that came into existence only a few hundred years ago – that of global separation. For all we know at present, an animal separated from its master might be able to psi trail him or her from one galaxy across the unthinkable distances to another, providing it could hitchhike a ride on a star freighter. By the same token, an owner on one of the planets of Alpha Centauri might register the death of a faithful cat on Earth.

One cannot, in short, escape the feeling that the whole paranormal apparatus, especially of mankind, has been prepared against the day of his becoming an interstellar species. More of this later.

It surprises even some scientists to learn that dreaming is a recent evolutionary phenomenon. Dreaming begins only after the reptiles, with the coming of mammals. (Birds also dream, but only in tiny fits.) Mammals are the latest creatures on Earth, and it is in them, in recent time, that dreaming has flowered. Dreaming is no throw-back, no leftover from some previous stage of development, as many otherwise informed people appear to think. It is a phenomenon of the evolutionary *present* – and, dare we say, of the evolutionary future. Even an arch-sceptic like Dr Carl Sagan has to admit the implications of the situation: 'The fact that mammals and birds both dream while their common ancestor, the reptiles, do not, is surely noteworthy. Major evolution beyond the reptiles has been accompanied by and perhaps requires dreams.'

Meeting the future half-way

One of the several forms of childishness which a petulant mankind must abandon if there is to *be* any future, of any kind at all, is the idea that science alone or religion alone can take us there. Apart from many other kinds of evidence which show that both these psychological endowments are necessary to our functioning, we have the purely physiological fact that we possess both a cerebrum and a cerebellum, each of which has never ceased to evolve, and each of which, from different points of view, can justly be described as the most complex organ ever evolved by life on this planet.

Here in the twentieth-century west it is currently science and the cerebrum which are being given almost total attention, to the detriment of all other functions and attributes. Undoubtedly we have gained from that one-sided concentration, but as of now the gains are becoming outweighed by the losses. Yet what we absolutely must not do is to abandon science in favour of any one-sided allegiance to religion, or intuition, or psychism, which, alas, is precisely what the large majority of new-age movements are advocating.

Scientific medicine is on the brink of a cure for leprosy. If – or rather when – the breakthrough comes, fifteen million sufferers will benefit. Recently, just a year or two ago, scientific medicine finally and completely eradicated smallpox from the world. Smallpox no longer exists. These are just two among the very many outstanding humanitarian achievements of science. They were accomplished by the unremitting work of brilliant men, dedicated to the scientific principle and the objective method. Deliberately I have chosen to mention two diseases, smallpox and leprosy, that have been with mankind throughout all history, a constant and relentless scourge. These are not the diseases of affluence or over-indulgence.

In no way are we going to throw away these many blessings of science, or the methods of investigating and describing phenomena that produce them. In no way are we going to abandon the cerebrum – which, after all, nature has gone to great pains to equip us with. And why should we possess the rational faculty in such great and complex measure, unless for an important reason?

What humanity has to do now is to add the intuitive dimension and the secret life to the rational. To the storehouse of science we have to add the so far neglected storehouse of the psychic and the paranormal, whose treasures also equal anything the former can offer.

We can well understand the fears of professional scientists that all their hard-won achievements are about to be thrown away. And it is up to the new-age revolutionaries to reassure scientists that this is not the case.

But still, a beginning must be made somewhere, with or without the cooperation and understanding of science, if the new age is ever to dawn. (Freud, for instance, was talked out of announcing his belief in telepathy by Ernest Jones – this is the kind of repressive situation the paranormal faces.) Two important steps appear to be possible and reasonable.

The first is that a medical centre or university be set up, offering all forms of alternative and paranormal healing. Representatives of any and every alternative approach would be invited to offer their treatments, though to avoid partisan jealousies the administration of the total complex would need to be in the hands of non-partisan independents. The crucial feature of this centre would be, however, that it would treat only cases that orthodox medicine had given up as incurable and hopeless. We would be treating here only those for whom orthodox medicine had done everything in its power, including people on the point of death.

Under these conditions, every cure – and we do not need to doubt that there would be many – would be a wholly deserved rebuke for orthodoxy, gall for the sceptic, and a marvellous propaganda exercise for the new age. Not least, some of the misery of the planet would have been further reduced, and some hope kindled in the many hearts that currently have none.

The second step is an educational one, and could be conducted under the auspices of one of the already existing systems of alternative education, such as Rudolf Steiner or Montessori, for the proposal which follows in no way violates the spirit of those institutions.

The proposal is for an education centre, a school in fact, which would take three types of children. Perhaps these might best be housed in three different buildings, even though the teaching methods in each would be the same. The three groups would be: (1) normal children of low intelligence, coupled with poor learning ability; (2) children officially classified as educationally subnormal, at the lower end of that range; and (3) autistic children. The children would themselves be taught simple methods of self-hypnosis (along with forms of meditation and allied matters) and also taught *in* that state. Most work – writing, painting, music, poetry – would be produced 'automatically', in the sense in which we have been using the term in this book.

First, this proposal is no wild flight of fancy. Peter Redgrove, in the opinion of many our finest living poet, and who is poet-in-residence at the Falmouth School of Art, already teaches his students poetry in this way. He, in fact, should be the headmaster of the proposed school.

Second, it is already proven beyond doubt that the trance state dramatically improves levels of creativity and retention. Rosemary Brown, Luiz Gasperetto and others we have already considered are from one point of view examples of enhanced creativity. But there are better examples. An untutored housewife, Mrs John Curran, began writing novels, using a ouija board. Later she turned to automatic writing. She published several successful historical novels under the name of Patience Worth (whom she believed to be the spirit that wrote through her). People in regression hypnosis show a similar degree of inventiveness quite absent from their normal lives. A man in Britain, who has appeared on British television, makes his living touring clubs singing as Caruso. He believes himself to be possessed by the spirit of the dead Caruso. The point here is not that he actually sings very like Caruso, but that in trance he sings far better than he normally can.

But let us come back once more to Anita Mühl's patients. Here again we find much evidence of hidden creativity released by automatic and trance techniques.

> A young woman, twenty-two years of age, who never had had
> any experience with automatic writing, asked me to try to develop
> it for her....She was ill in bed and was so weak that I hesitated

201

allowing her to do anything which might be an added effort. She was insistent however....

One morning she was permitted to try, and I placed a large pad of paper beside her on the bed and after she had become engrossed reading *aloud* to me an account of a current murder sensation (please remember she read audibly and continuously) I placed a pencil in her right hand, and much to my surprise she began to write at once in an unhesitating manner. The newspaper was placed so that she could not see the writing pad, and yet when she got to the end of the line her hand unerringly returned to the left hand margin and started off on a new line, correctly spacing the distance between. She wrote legibly in large characters, and her first production was a cunning little fairy tail in rhyme.

Voluntarily she could not rhyme, nor could she make up fairy stories; neither had she the friendly sense of humour exhibited in her writing. When the little fairy story was read to her she refused at first to believe that she had written it.

Most of the patients exhibited skills in poetry, stories and art-work of which they had before never been aware. A friend of Dr Mühl's, who was not a hospital patient, but who required psychotherapy, began writing music automatically. Some of the patients were highly intelligent, others were not. But all now exhibited the additional dimension of creativity.

Many professional writers, poets, composers and other creative artists are in close touch with their unconscious minds, more so probably than is the general public. There are numbers of them who readily admit to being literally and directly inspired by their own dreams and other trance states (R. L. Stevenson, Coleridge, Joan Grant, Peter Redgrove, Lindsay Kemp, de Quincey and many others). I once dreamt a complete science fiction story, which I wrote out next morning. It may well be that we can define a creative artist precisely as a person whose conscious and unconscious minds are in close and harmonious contact.

Reverting to the proposed school, the aim of that establishment would be to show what *can* be done with children of this retarded and disadvantaged kind, who are for the most part considered to be only minimally educable. And as far as conventional teaching methods are concerned, they probably are. The success of 'trance education' in these problem cases would hopefully permit this same approach to be introduced also into the general education system.

(When are dreams, for instance, *ever* mentioned in a conventional school programme?)

The schemes described would cost a good deal of money, but once launched they would certainly attract considerable public and private support. James McDonnell, the aircraft tycoon, has for example just made a gift of half a million dollars to Washington University to establish a Laboratory for Psychical Research.

The long-term function of the universe

Scientists shy away from any 'why' questions as to the function or purpose or goal of the universe. And yet it is quite clear that on this planet, and so presumably on many others, there has been in the course of its existence a dramatic increase in the sheer complexity in its physical materials (one single DNA molecule, for instance, can consist of five thousand million precisely placed other molecules), in the hierarchical organization of materials (into the miracle of the living creature), and most dramatically of all in the evolution of self-awareness. We cannot blink any of these facts. Unquestionably, some organizing and diversifying 'process' is taking place. Process is the most neutral word we can use. Any lesser word simply violates the readily observable facts of the situation.

A process is an event (or series of events) that goes through definable stages. In a sense every process in the world is a continuation of the first event (if there ever was a first one) that began the universe. But nevertheless we do speak, for instance, of the process of butter making, and we give that process a beginning and an end. We can say that butter begins as grass in a field, passes through a cow, emerges again as milk, and is then churned to produce butter.

What is the process of a planet?

This is a fair question, but at the same time there are planets and planets. The 'process' of Mars, for instance, may never have resulted, nor ever will, in the production of life. But planet Earth *has* produced life. This is part of *its* process.

Our concern, necessarily and reasonably enough, is with that part of the process on this planet Earth that comes next. What happens to life when it reaches the point we have reached? The basic structure of our planet, the purely physical part, is good for many millions of years yet. There is still plenty of time available to that part of its process which we call life.

So there is, still, plenty of time left for life. And yet, interestingly enough, we seem to be able to detect a speeding up of this category of events. Life certainly appeared on this planet as long as 3,000 million years ago (though some very recent evidence argues for still longer). It then took 2,700 million years to produce reptiles. But from then it took only a further 100 million years to produce mammals. The primates (monkeys, apes and so on) emerged only 40 million years after that. To reach man as a separate ancestral line took a mere further 28 million years. *Homo sapiens* himself is about half a million years old. Our own variety of *homo sapiens* is only twenty-five thousand years old.

But look what has been achieved in those twenty-five thousand years.

Or better, look at what has been achieved in the last one hundred.

Are these not good grounds for thinking that the speed of the life process has reached a critical point? Is the human species about to go nova, to become an exploding star?

There are a number of things we can say with absolute firmness about the present situation, and no scientist can challenge these. The first is that in respect of the mechanism of natural selection (although, as we have seen, natural selection is by no means the whole story) nature has run out of time. In respect of mankind, there is no time left to continue a process which cannot operate meaningfully in less than several dozen generations. But that point aside we have now reached the stage where we ourselves, literally, control the microscopic processes of the genes and chromosomes that produce all change of every kind. It is as if in a card game in a casino we had snatched the pack from the dealer and dealt ourself and our friends hands which the house cannot beat. We ourselves are no longer *dealt*. We have become the dealer.

One instance of the basic change which has now occurred. On a plantation in Malaysia hundreds of palm oil trees are now growing from one single cloned parent cell. In cloning, a series of female cells are fertilized by an identical cell from a male organism. The result is a series of absolutely identical offspring. These hundreds of palm trees are all *exactly* the same. Unilever's chairman, Sir David Orr, described the product at a press conference: 'I have seen them growing. They grow to identical height and all put out the same new sprig, at the same time, on the same day.'

The phrase rings in our mind: 'at the same time, on the same day'. With it the stories that science fiction magazines have been telling for the past fifty years cease to be stories. They are now reality. Nature's former slave has become its master.

And yet nature still clings, temporarily, to one last card of the pack we have now snatched from her. And it is the highest trump card of all. It is the card of death.

As we are all only too well aware, there is every chance that in the next few decades the very large majority of human beings on the planet will die in a nuclear war. Alternatively, it looks equally likely that hundreds upon hundreds of millions of people will die of starvation, or in the socio-political upheavals that are born just ahead of such a fate.

The simple, stark problem is that we have a rapidly expanding population on a finite planet. It does not matter how cleverly we cut the cake, the cake has its finite limits, and population, at present, has none. It is a permanent problem that could and can only be solved by a majority of people on the planet not having children at all, or from a strictly enforced limit of two children per couple.

Nature's solution to increasing population has always been an increase in the death rate. It is the only solution she understands. And it is no good anyone saying 'oh, yes, but'. There are no 'oh, yes, buts' in this particular equation.

It is also no good saying that humanity will escape the confines of the planet by escaping into outer space in any conventional sense. Several hundred thousand people would have to leave the planet every single day, for this is the rate at which world population is currently increasing. But in fact, when a highly developed country like Great Britain cannot afford even to replace its antiquated sewage system, is it likely that one single spaceship is ever going to be built? Where is the money to come from? The likelihood is that no space ships will be built in the foreseeable future, or perhaps in any future.

It is very questionable whether the human race (or any race) could psychologically bear the twin prisons of (1) no escape from the planet into outer space and (2) no escape into the current safety valve of producing children. I think at that point the species would necessarily die of hopelessness, even if it had miraculously survived all other disasters.

This brings us to the question of what has been happening on other planets like our own – planets in some cases many millions of years older than ours. What does evolved life habitually do, or at least sometimes do, when it reaches our stage? Does it inevitably perish, or perhaps fall continually back to square one, from civilization to barbarism, in its efforts to escape the planetary trap? Or is there some other outcome or conclusion to the process that we do not yet understand?

An alternative outcome

Humanity's psychological needs and attitudes would certainly undergo a radical change if it were possible for the individual to achieve any kind of personal escape from death, even the limited one of a lifespan of two or three hundred years. Such an altered factor in the total equation would transform the hopeless picture which currently confronts mankind, and each of us personally. A number of writers and thinkers today, ranging from Jan Merta to Richard Gardner (myself included), believe that a dramatically increased lifespan is well within our grasp, and perhaps even immortality itself. That state, which may be reached by more than one avenue, will involve developing our as yet almost wholly dormant paranormal abilities (which are probably located in the cerebellum), supported however by the techniques and understanding of conventional science.

First, in the light of the dramatic and fundamental recoveries of Marie Bailly and the rhinoceros skin boy, of the demonstrated faculty of autoscopy allied with self-manipulation, and the ability of many others to produce and remove fairly severe wounds at will, it is wholly plausible to imagine that we could personally take over and direct all the functions of our bodies. We could then routinely eradicate disease and malfunction from our lives. A normal lifespan entirely free of illness is then certainly ours. But the process need not stop there. Why could we not also take over the process of cell renewal? At present, the body has built-in limits concerning renewal – but these might well be overcome. At that point, barring sudden fatal accidents, the organism could live indefinitely.

Maxwell Cade's Mind Mirror, and the work of Robert Becker on limb renewal, are a definite and undeniable step towards this long-term aim from the scientific side. What we have here is the body's inborn ability to heal others and to self-renew *supported* by technology. The technology is not creating these abilities. There are two future possible developments. One is the further augmentation of those abilities by further technology. The second is that greater understanding of the processes involved – not intellectually, however, but experientially – will allow us individually to assume greater and greater personal and mental control over the abilities.

We should, already, be not just impressed but staggered that Dr Comar's patient M was able to give herself an internal 'operation' for appendicitis at her very first attempt. To say 'What a beginning!' would actually be a quite inappropriate remark. Because what we see here is a fully-fledged process, totally available at first attempt, and provided by nature for us against the day of its eventual use. There is nothing tentative here, no gradualism, no Darwinian reinforcement through natural selection.

A number of writers and thinkers in the paranormal field believe that paranormal events and abilities in the human arena will emerge as a kind of explosion if and when we can create the necessary climate of belief in the phenomena. Scepticism (informed or not, well meant or not) is the barrier which prevents the emergence of these faculties not just in oneself, but in others. How many times have I seen a gifted psychic reduced to helplessness in the presence of hostile and contemptuous scientists. When an actor, an athlete or a lecturer turns in a poor performance or no performance at all in the face of public hostility, we do not claim that the suffering individual concerned cannot act, run or put compelling sentences together. But having subjected the unfortunate psychic to the same treatment, the scientist and the educated public at large then claim that he or she has no psychic powers.

When we achieve a turn-around on this position, even on a local scale, the incidence of paranormal phenomena will increase dramatically. I and others have personally witnessed the sudden appearance of, for instance, a telepathic capacity in friends whom one has managed to influence gently over the years towards a positive attitude. Once one begins to have paranormal experiences of one's own, all the empty intellectual arguments against the possibility of their existence fall away.

There are still other sides to these matters.

It is true that for the moment we are physically trapped on a small, finite planet. But each of us has within us a universe that extends as far inwards as the physical universe extends outward. Nor is this statement simply a figure of speech or metaphor. It is the simple, literal truth.

There are no detectable limits to the inner universe, nor any apparent end to its diversity. Swedenborg visited and wrote about it constantly. He thought he had found heaven itself. De Quincy, Coleridge, Aldous Huxley and others caught appreciable glimpses of it through the use of drugs ('of caverns measureless to man, where Alph the sacred river runs'), but the drug road offers only a brief, superficial entry, followed as a rule by self-destruction. Other names applied to the experiential universe we are discussing are lucid dreaming, astral travelling and the Christos experience – yet these are actually all quite different expressions of it, and Swedenborg's 'continuous hypnapompic imagery' is yet a fourth variety.

There is really no point in trying to describe these experiences, for words are quite inadequate, although occasionally a gifted poet like Coleridge can give some faint inkling of their wonder and value. They are probably the source of the truly inspirational and magical aspects of fairy-tale and legend. Aladdin's cave, fairyland and paradise itself are metaphors and referents of the experience.

G. M. Glaskin has proposed that the Christos technique be taught to men and women in prison. But it should rather be taught to all the prisoners of this planet, the hopeless and the materialist. The Christos technique is actually a good starting point for most people. The method is described in Glaskin's books *Worlds Within* and *Windows of the Mind*.

However, the inner journey is not 'merely' a subjective experience. Evidence is increasing that, if desired, the inner journey can also take one (paradoxically) out into the physical universe. Ingo Swann and others have demonstrated, under laboratory conditions, their ability to go mentally to a given map location and describe precisely what is there. (This ability also strongly recalls the ability of some dowsers to dowse using a map only.) Attempts are now being made to see whether these psychics can describe features of other planets in the solar system. First results are promising, but obviously this is a difficult business to verify, since we do not as yet have too much knowledge of the local surface appearance of the planets against which to check the psychics' descriptions. However, if this ability to scan planets should be conclusively demonstrated, then there seems no reason why we should not also reach mentally beyond the solar system.

With such an ability we should finally have ceased to be prisoners of the planet, without a single spaceship being built.

There is yet one more extreme possibility. We know that the three dimensions of the conventional universe do not mark the boundaries of existence or of events (using the word events in the scientific sense). Because we can clairvoyantly glimpse both the future and the unknown past, we know that there must be other continua, other dimensions, where events are free to behave differently from the way they do in the normally observable universe. They may be free to run backwards. They may be free to last forever. There are no limits to the possibilities, and one near certainty is that most of them are beyond our power to imagine.

We can already enter this alternative universe, mentally, for short periods. We may one day be able to enter it, mentally, for extended periods. (Perhaps, too, a tiny part of us goes there after physical death, as the ancients continually claimed.) But maybe we shall one day, without dying, be literally able to enter the alternative universe as our total selves – and not just mentally, but in some sense physically.

Suppose that the case is this. Suppose the physical universe is some kind of eternal, self-renewing or cyclic event (such as envisaged in Itzhak Bentov's dynamic torus). And suppose the purpose of the universe is continually to produce highly evolved life forms, which then migrate out of this universe to another scenario altogether.

That idea could at least explain why our present universe is not peopled end to end with very, very highly evolved life forms, several million years ahead of us in development. Nor, incidentally, are sightings of UFOs and flying saucers any evidence that this is indeed the case. The allegedly real UFOs are subject to all the objections that we found for the discarnate spirit hypothesis in chapter 15, and still many others besides. They seem to be purely subjective phenomena, without any objective existence. Attention to such phenomena as literally true, as opposed to subjectively true, will certainly fade in the light of an increase in human-centred paranormal phenomena. As already said more than once, UFOs seem only to be symptomatic of humanity's deeply unsatisfied spiritual hunger.

We are in a better position than perhaps ever before to satisfy that longing in a genuine and meaningful way. Science and logic have brought us to our present stage of development, and that is no mean achievement by any standard. We can say unhesitatingly that science has given us the present. But now science has reached the limits of what it can achieve unaided. Only our secret life can give us the future.

Bibliography

Abbie, A. A., *The Original Australians,* Muller, London, 1969.

Alexander, H. B., *The Mythology of All Races* (12 vols), Cooper Square, New York, 1964.

Baker, Robin R., 'A Sense of Magnetism', *New Scientist,* 18 September 1980.

Barbanell, Sylvia, *When Your Animal Dies,* Spiritualist Press, London, 1969.

Bayless, Raymond, *The Other Side of Death,* University Books, New York, 1971.

Bayless, Raymond, *Animal Ghosts,* University Books, New York, 1970.

Bell, G. H., Davidson, J. N. and Emslie-Smith, D., *Textbook of Physiology and Biochemistry,* Churchill Livingstone, Edinburgh, 1972.

Bentov, Itzhak, *Stalking the Wild Pendulum,* Wildwood House, London, 1978.

Bestall, C. M., 'An Experiment in Precognition in the Laboratory Mouse', *Journal of Parapsychology, 26,* 1962.

Bettley, F. Ray, Letter, *British Medical Journal,* Part 2, 1952 (p. 996).

Bird, Christopher, *Divining,* Macdonald & Jane, London, 1980.

Bozzano, Ernesto, *Manifestations Metapsychiques et les Animaux,* Jean Meyer, Paris, 1926.

Brown, Beth, *ESP with Plants and Animals,* Simon & Schuster, New York, 1971.

Brown, Peter Lancaster, *Megaliths, Myths and Men,* Blandford Press, Poole, Dorset, 1976.

Burton, Maurice, *The Sixth Sense of Animals,* Dent, London, 1973.

Cade, C. Maxwell and Coxhead, Nona, *The Awakened Mind,* Wildwood House, London, 1979.

Capra, Fritjof, *The Tao of Physics,* Wildwood House, London, 1975.

Carlson, Rick, *The Frontiers of Science and Medicine,* Wildwood House, London, 1975.

Carrel, Alexis, *Man, the Unknown,* Penguin Books, Harmondsworth, 1948.

Clarke, Arthur C., *Childhood's End,* Pan, London, 1954.

Cooper, Irving S. *et al, The Cerebellum, Epilepsy and Behaviour,* Plenum, New York, 1972.

Cooper, L. and Erickson, M., *Time Distortion in Hypnosis: An Experimental and Clinical Investigation,* Williams & Wilkins, Baltimore, 1952.

Craig, Thurlow, *Animal Affinities with Man,* Country Life, London, 1966.

Dean, Geoffrey, *Recent Advances in Natal Astrology: A Critical Review 1900-1976,* The Astrological Association, Bromley, Kent, 1977.

Desmond, Adrian, *The Ape's Reflexion,* Blond & Briggs, London, 1979.

Donahoe, James, *Dream Reality,* Wildwood House, London, 1980.

Donahoe, James, *Enigma,* Wildwood House, London, 1980.

Douglas, Alfred, *Extra-Sensory Powers,* Gollancz, London, 1976.

Dow, R. S. and Moruzzi, G., *The Physiology and Pathology of the Cerebellum,* University of Minnesota Press, Minneapolis, 1958.

Droscher, V. B., *The Magic of the Senses,* W. H. Allen, London, 1969.

Duval, Pierre and Montredon, Evelyn, 'ESP Experiments with Mice', *Journal of Parapsychology, 32,* 1968.

Elen, Richard, *Radical Occultism,* Wildwood House, London, 1980.

Eliade, Mircea, *Australian Religions,* Cornell University Press, London, 1973.

Evans, Christopher, *Cults of Unreason,* Harrap, London, 1973.

Firsoff, V. A., 'Life and Quantum Physics', *Parapsychology Review,* Vol. 5, No. 6, 1974.

Freud, Sigmund, *The Interpretation of Dreams,* Allen & Unwin, London, 1954.

Freud, Sigmund, *Introductory Lectures on Psychoanalysis,* Allen & Unwin, London, 1952.

Gaddis, Vincent and Margaret, *The Strange World of Animals and Pets,* Cowles Book Company, New York, 1970.

Gauquelin, F. and M., and Eysenck S. G. B., 'Personality and Position of the Planets at Birth: An Empirical Study', *British Journal of Social and Clinical Psychology, 18,* 1979.

Gauquelin, Michel, *The Spheres of Destiny,* Dent, London, 1980.

Gauquelin, Michel, *Cosmic Influences on Human Behaviour,* Futura, London, 1976.

Gemme, R. and Wheeler, C. C., *Progress in Sexology,* Plenum, New York, 1977.

Glaskin, G. M., *Worlds Within,* Arrow Books, London, 1977.

Glaskin, G. M., *Windows of the Mind*, Arrow Books, London, 1975.

Goldsmith, I. E. and Moor-Jankowski, J., *Medical Primatology,* Karger, New York, 1971.

Gooch, Stan, *The Double Helix of the Mind,* Wildwood House, London, 1980.

Gooch, Stan, *Guardians of the Ancient Wisdom,* Wildwood House, London, 1979.

Gooch, Stan, *The Paranormal,* Wildwood House, London, 1978.

Gooch, Stan, *The Neanderthal Question,* Wildwood House, London, 1977.

Gooch, Stan, *Personality and Evolution*, Wildwood House, London, 1973.

Gooch, Stan, *Total Man*, Allen Lane, London, 1972.

Gooch, Stan and Evans, Chris, *Science Fiction as Religion,* Brans Head Press, Frome, Somerset, 1980.

Grad, Bernard 'Some Biological Effects of the "Laying on of Hands"', *Journal of the American Society for Psychical Research,* Vol. 59, 1965.

Grad, Bernard *et al.,* 'The Influence of an Unorthodox Method of Wound Healing in Mice' *International Journal of Parapsychology,* Vol. 3, No. 2, 1961.

Graves, Robert, *The White Goddess,* Faber, London, 1961.

Graves Tom, *Needles of Stone,* Turnstone Press, London, 1978.

Graves, Tom, *Dowsing: Techniques and Applications,* Turnstone Press, London, 1976.

Green, Celia and McCeery, Charles, *Apparitions,* Hamish Hamilton, London, 1975.

Greenway, John, *Down Among the Wild Men,* Little, Brown & Co., Boston, 1972.

Grimal, Pierre, *Larousse World Mythology,* Hamlyn, London, 1965.

Guirand, Felix, *New Larousse Encyclopedia of Mythology,* Hamlyn, London, 1969.

Haeckel, Ernst, *The Evolution of Man,* Watts, London, 1906.

Hardy, Alister, *The Biology of God,* Cape, London 1975.

Harlow, H. F., 'Love in Infant Monkeys', *Scientific American,* June, 1959.

Harrison, Michael, *Fire From Heaven,* Sidgwick & Jackson, London, 1976.

Harvey, David and Stemman, Roy, 'News Report', *Alpha,* No. 7, 1980.

Haynes, Renee, *The Hidden Springs,* Hollis & Carter, London, 1961.

Hitching, Francis, *The World Atlas of Mysteries,* Collins, London, 1978.

Hitching, Francis, *Pendulum: the Psi Connection,* Fontana, London, 1977.

I Ching (The Book of Changes), transl. Richard Wilhelm and Cary F. Baynes, Routledge, London, 1968.

Jastrzembska, Zofja S., *The Effects of Blindness and Other Impairments on Early Development,* The American Foundation for the Blind, New York, 1976.

213

Jung, C. G., *Synchronicity: An A-Causal Connecting Principle,* Routledge, London, 1972.

Jung, C. G., *Flying Saucers: A Modern Myth of Things Seen in the Sky,* Routledge, London, 1964.

Jung, C. G., *Modern Man in Search of a Soul,* Routledge, London, 1933.

Kingsland, Rosemary and Wright, John, *A Saint Among Savages,* Collins, London, 1980.

Krishna, Gopi, *Kundalini: the Evolutionary Energy in Man,* Watkins, London, 1970.

Lacey, Louise, *Lunaception,* Warner Books, New York, 1976.

Laing, R. D., *The Politics of Experience and the Bird of Paradise,* Penguin Books, Harmondsworth, 1967.

Liaros, Carol, 'Psi Faculties in the Blind', *Parapsychology Review,* Vol. 5, No. 6, 1974.

Manning, Matthew, *In the Minds of Millions,* W. H. Allen, London, 1977.

Mason, A. A., 'A Case of Congenital Ichthyosiform Erythrodermia Treated by Hypnosis', *British Medical Journal,* Part 2, 1952.

Merta, Jan, 'The Effects of Permanent Magnetic Fields on Avoidance Learning in Mice' (privately circulated research report).

Mery, Fernand, *Our Animal Friends,* Rider, London, 1954.

Moody, R. L., 'Bodily Changes During Abreaction', *Lancet,* No. 251, Part 2, 1946; and No. 254, Part 2, 1948.

Morris, Robert L., 'Some New Techniques in Animal Psi Research', *Journal of Parapsychology, 31,* 1967.

Moss, Peter, *Encounters with the Past,* Sidgwick & Jackson, London, 1979.

Moss, Thelma, 'Dreaming Winners at the Races', *Psychic,* Vol. 2, No. 4, 1971.

Mühl, Anita, *Automatic Writing,* Steinkopf, Dresden, 1930.

Onetto, B. and Elguin, Gita, 'Psychokinesis in Experimental Tumourogenesis', *Journal of Parapsychology,* Vol. 30, 1966.

Osty, Eugene, *Supernormal Faculties in Man,* Methuen, London, 1923.

Pratt, J. G., *Parapsychology: An Insider's View of ESP,* W. H. Allen, London, 1964.

Pratt, J. G. and Roll W. G., 'The Seaford Disturbances', *Journal of Parapsychology,* Vol. 22, 1958.

Prescott, J. W., 'Violence, Pleasure and Religion', *The Bulletin of the Atomic Scientists,* March, 1976.

Prescott, J. W., 'Body Pleasure and the Origin of Violence', *The Futurist,* Vol. IX, No. 2, 1975.

Prescott, J. W., 'Phylogenetic and Ontogenetic Aspects of Human Affectional Development' *see* Gemme, R. and Wheeler, C. C.

Prescott, J. W., 'Early Somatosensory Deprivation as an Ontogenetic Process in the Abnormal Development of the Brain and Behaviour' *see* Goldsmith, I. E. and Moor-Jankowski, J.

Prescott, J. W., 'Somatosensory Deprivation and its Relationship to the Blind' *see* Jastrzembska, Zofja S.

Prescott, J. W., 'The Effect of Cerebellar Lesions on Emotional Behaviour in the Rhesus Monkey' *see* Cooper, Irving S.

Purce, Jill, *The Mystic Spiral,* Thames & Hudson, 1974.

Randall, John L., *Parapsychology and the Nature of Life,* Souvenir Press, London, 1975.

Rhine, J. B. and Feather, Sara R., 'The Study of Cases of Psi Trailing in Animals', *Journal of Parapsychology, 26,* 1962.

Roheim, Geza, *Children of the Desert,* Basic Books, New York, 1974.

Rose, Ronald, *Living Magic,* Rand McNally, New York, 1956.

Sagan, Carl, *The Dragons of Eden,* Hutchinson, London, 1978.

Santillana, Giorgio de, *The Origins of Scientific Thought,* Weidenfeld & Nicholson, London, 1961.

Shuttle, Penelope and Redgrove, Peter, *The Wise Wound,* Gollancz, London, 1978.

Singer, Isaac Bashevis, *The Seance,* Cape, London, 1970.

Skeat, W. W., *An Etymological Dictionary of the English Language,* Oxford University Press, 1946.

Smith, Justa, 'Paranormal Effects on Enzyme Activity', *Journal of Parapsychology,* Vol. 32, 1968.

Spitz, R. A., *The First Year of Life,* International University Press, 1965.

Spontaneous Hallucinations of the Sane, Proceedings, Society for Psychical Research, Vol. 10, 1894.

Sulloway, Frank, *Freud, Biologist of the Mind,* Burnett Books, London, 1979.

Targ, Russell and Puthoff, Harold, *Mind-Reach,* Paladin, London, 1978.

Tarver, W. J., Letter, *New Scientist,* 24 October 1968.

Taylor, Gordon Rattray, *The Natural History of the Mind,* Secker & Warburg, London, 1979.

Temple, Robert, 'Olmec Magnetism and the Human Brain', *Second Look,* Vol. 2, No. 1, 1979.

Temple, Robert, 'Magnetism in the New World', *Second Look,* Vol. 1, No. 11, 1979.

Thompson, J. L. Cloudsley, *Biological Clocks,* Weidenfeld, London, 1980.

Tinbergen, Nikolaas, *The Study of Instinct,* Oxford University Press, 1969.

Tindale, N. B. and Lindsay, H. A., *Aboriginal Australians,* Angus & Robertson, London, 1963.

Tomas, Andrew, *We Are Not the First,* Sphere Books, London, 1972.

Tompkins, Peter and Bird, Christopher, *The Secret Life of Plants,* Allen Lane, London, 1974.

Underwood, Peter, *Haunted London,* Harrap, London, 1973.

Vogh, James, *The Thirteenth Zodiac,* Mayflower, London, 1979.

Walcott, Charles, Gould, James and Kirschvink, J. L., 'Pigeons Have Magnets', *Science,* Vol. 205, No. 7, 1979.

Warner, W. L., *Oceania,* Vol. 2, 1932.

Watson, Lyall, *Lifetide,* Hodder & Stoughton, London, 1979.

Watson, Lyall, *Gifts of Unknown Things,* Hodder & Stoughton, London, 1976.

Whelan, Elizabeth, *Preventing Cancer,* Sphere Books, London, 1980.

Willard, R. D., 'Breast Enlargement through Visual Imagery and Hypnosis', *American Journal of Clinical Hypnosis,* Vol. 19, No. 4, 1977.

Wilson, Colin, *Mysteries,* Hodder & Stoughton, London, 1978.

Wilson, Colin, *The Occult,* Hodder & Stoughton, London, 1971.

Wilson, Ian, *The Turin Shroud,* Penguin Books, Harmondsworth, 1979.

Yeats, W. B., *Essays and Introductions,* Macmillan, London, 1961.

Yerkes, Robert M., *Almost Human,* Cape, London, 1926.

Index

Index

Index

Index